MENTAL RETARDATION, CEREBRAL PALSY, AND EPILEPSY IN ALABAMA

MENTAL RETARDATION
CEREBRAL PALSY
AND EPILEPSY
IN ALABAMA

A SOCIOLOGICAL ANALYSIS

J. SELWYN HOLLINGSWORTH

WITH CONTRIBUTIONS BY
M. H. ALSIKAFI
AND
DAVID W. COOMBS

THE UNIVERSITY OF ALABAMA PRESS
UNIVERSITY, ALABAMA

Library of Congress Cataloging in Publication Data

Hollingsworth, James Selwyn, 1939–
  Mental retardation, cerebral palsy, and epilepsy in
Alabama.

    Bibliography: p.
    1. Developmentally disabled—Alabama.   2. Develop-
mentally disabled services—Alabama.   I. Alsikafi,
M. H., 1931–   joint author.   II. Coombs, David W.,
1939–   joint author.   III. Title. [DNLM: 1. Mental
retardation.   2. Cerebral palsy.   3. Epilepsy.
4. Health surveys—Alabama. WM300 H741m]
HV3006.A57H64   362.1'9'68   77-23418
ISBN 0-8173-2500-X

The funding for the research project reported in this volume was provided by the United States Department of Health, Education, and Welfare, through P.L. 91–517, the Developmental Disabilities Services and Facilities Construction Act of 1970. The grant was made on recommendation of the Governor's Planning and Advisory Council for the Developmental Disabilities in Alabama to the Mental Health Board of the Alabama Department of Mental Health, with which The University of Alabama served as cosponsor. The University's Department of Sociology was the unit conducting the research.

The University's College of Community Health Sciences kindly provided financial resources necessary for beginning manufacturing of this volume, which permitted a publication date much earlier than would have been possible otherwise.

CONTENTS

TABLES AND FIGURES

Tables

Figures

ACKNOWLEDGMENTS

Projects of the magnitude of that on which this book is based seldom depend upon the work of any one person or even one small group of persons. Countless people contributed to the completion of the present project, and the author takes this opportunity to express his gratitude to some of them. Of course, a complete listing of all the contributors is not feasible. Nevertheless, some of the persons who assisted in various ways will be singled out in the paragraphs that follow.

Irving L. Webber, Chairman of the Department of Sociology of The University of Alabama, gave counsel in the early stages of the project and was responsible for writing most of the grant proposal. He served as Assistant Director of the project and listened to my woes as project director, carefully and skillfully assessed the situation, and offered wise advice. He has long been a friend, colleague, mentor, and confidant. Without him and his level-headed counsel, many more hardships would have been encountered and perhaps not been met as successfully. He has long shaped my thinking, and I owe him a major debt of gratitude for his assistance on this project, for his friendship and support, and for his careful guidance over the years. He has read and criticized the manuscript of this volume. However, because I have not always followed his guidance, any errors or omissions must be my responsibility.

Majeed H. Alsikafi, a friend and colleague, has worked long and diligently on this project. His assistance has been invaluable: he served as assistant field director when I was absent and offered invaluable help and encouragement. Furthermore, he has been a contributor to this book, as has David W. Coombs.

Clifton "Tex" Oliver, a friend for many years, worked as a consultant and as a member of the interviewing team. His suggestions during the field stage of the project were invaluable; his good sense of humor and kindly recommendations helped all of us over many rough phases of the interviewing.

Dr. Roland Ficken, Assistant Professor jointly in the College of Community Health Services and the Department of Sociology of The University of Alabama, made various contributions during the planning phase of the project. He gave freely of his time and expertise without reimbursement, drawing upon his training as a medical sociologist.

The gathering of the data and its subsequent coding involved a very great number of persons. They are listed in this volume as "Project Personnel." Their work was indispensable.

Members of the staff of the Alabama Department of Mental Health and of the Governor's Planning and Advisory Council for the Developmentally Disabled in Alabama have likewise given valuable help. Specifically, I should like to mention the efforts of Taylor Hardin, Jerry Thrasher, Dale Scott, Donna Ceravolo, and Dorothy Fleetwood.

Patton B. Seals, Assistant Comptroller of Contracts and Grants of The University of Alabama, spent innumerable hours with the author in working out the tedious details of the budget and its several revisions. He has always been a pleasure to work with, and his encouragement has counted much.

Perhaps the greatest debt of gratitude goes to the many persons and agencies contributing to the data files of the project. For reasons of confidentiality (and because of the great numbers involved), they cannot be specified by name. Without their cooperation, the data essential to the writing of this report could not have been collected. May they rest assured that their assistance is already helping to improve the lives of developmentally disabled persons of Alabama.

Finally, a great deal of thanks goes to the secretaries who performed the necessary clerical tasks, often tedious and demanding, in an efficient and diligent manner. They are Dianne Hollingsworth, Sherry Englebert, and Diane Lawrence, of the Department of Sociology of The University of Alabama.

PROJECT PERSONNEL

Professional Staff

Dr. J. Selwyn Hollingsworth, Project Director
Dr. Irving L. Webber, Assistant Director

Dr. Majeed Alsikafi
Dr. Alfred Baumeister*
Dr. Jack Bruce
Dr. C. Hobson Bryan
Dr. H. Jeff Buttram
Dr. Yung-Teh Chow
Dr. David W. Coombs
Dr. Prithwis Das Gupta*

Dr. Roland Ficken*
Dr. Joe Gallagher*
Dr. Gerald Globetti
Dr. William Heller*
Mr. Clifton "Tex" Oliver, Jr.
Dr. Bob Palk
Dr. Dennis Runcie
Dr. Jack Tucker

Clerical Staff

Susan Atkins
Karen Baker
Sue Freeman*
Margie Goolsby
Dianne Hollingsworth
Donna Ceravolo*
Doris Jones*
Lola Lawson
Naomi Markham*
Susan Sumner
Kristie Unger*
Peggy Wade
Minyawn Ware
Susie Yerby*

Field Staff

Sandra Baker
Ernest Clement, Jr.
Kathy Fisher
Sandra Gill
Debra Godwin
W. S. Godwin
Travis Lynn Gordon
Judy Green
James Ingle
Robert Kennedy
Ted Lamb
Charles Langham
David Mintz
Charles Moorehead
Mary Murchison
Ricky Myers
Gerald McDonald
Alice Parker
Cynthia Ray
Jeff Risburg
Eugene "Chuck" Sellers
Mary Elaine Taylor

---

*These individuals donated their time and efforts to the project.

PREFACE

This book is designed to point up some of the problems—to "plug the gaps," so to speak—in services being offered to Alabama citizens who are the victims of the developmental disabilities: mental retardation, cerebral palsy, and epilepsy. Nevertheless, because of the careful, systematic manner in which the data were gathered, it will have applications much broader in scope than those usually associated with the confines of any geographical barrier.

Though the book deals with the developmentally disabled persons of Alabama as a whole, three rural counties (reflecting social, cultural, and economic differences among the various regions of the state) were chosen in which to conduct in-depth interviews. Additionally, a detailed search of medical records in one of the counties brought to light much new information about the prevalence of epilepsy and the personal characteristics and situations of individuals who are afflicted with this disability.

The book is written with the layman, not just the professional, in mind; its language is uncomplicated enough for nonprofessionals to read and understand. It provides information needed by all citizens and groups interested in planning and working for improved capabilities to ameliorate the problems of these disabled individuals in Alabama—and, by extension, in the nation.

Organization of the Book

In Part I of this work the author and contributors, Associate Professors of Sociology at The University of Alabama, deal with background information. Chapter One defines the developmental disabilities and states the nature of the problem in Alabama. The second chapter is concerned with some of the known causes of the individual developmental disabilities, as well as some of the other important factors associated with them. Chapter Two does not attempt to deal definitively with each disability, since other materials published elsewhere have covered the matter more completely, but it seeks rather to "set the stage" for what is to follow. Dr. Alsikafi contributed the introduction to the chapter and the section on mental retardation, while Dr. Coombs provided the information concerning cerebral palsy and epilepsy.

Part II includes detailed descriptions of the planning and mechanics involved in the field survey. In Chapter Three are explanations of the criteria involved in choosing each of the three counties in which the survey's in-depth interviews were conducted. Likewise, census data and historical information are utilized in order to give the reader a more complete understanding of the historical, social, demographic, and economic factors operating in the counties. Pseudonyms have been substituted for the names of the counties in which field data were collected. This procedure was adopted in order to prevent any possible invasion of the privacy of the families involved in the survey.

Chapter Four details the approach utilized in identifying the developmentally disabled, plus the results of the effort and a critique of the method. Furthermore, it traces the development of the questionnaire that was designed to elicit responses characterizing various aspects in the lives of the disabled and their effects on the family.

A discussion of the various aspects of the findings of the sample survey follows in Part III. In Chapter Five is a description of alternative approaches used in the past for the identification of the developmentally disabled. A discussion of the technique employed in the present investigation follows. Additionally, some of the problems encountered in applying this particular method are likewise recognized.

The concern of Chapter Six is with the prevalences of the developmental disabilities in Alabama and their relationship to rates of prevalence found in previous studies. This chapter reports the projections of the numbers of Alabamians who are directly affected by each of the disabilities.

The portion of the sample survey findings with specific reference to the prevalence of the developmental disabilities in the three Alabama sample counties is the subject of Chapter Seven. Comparisons are drawn between the numbers of the developmentally disabled who were located using the reputational method and the numbers predicted on the basis of estimates made in previous studies in other parts of the country. Furthermore, a detailed report is included on the search of more than 26,000 medical records in one of the counties. In this phase of the study, the researchers were seeking empirical verification of cases of mental retardation, cerebral palsy, and epilepsy. Finally, a discussion of the differences in the effectiveness of the three methods in estimating the prevalence of the developmental disabilities is presented.

Chapter Eight deals with some of the social factors involved in the occurrence and treatment of the developmental disabilities. The chapter relies on the data gathered in interviews with some 400 developmentally disabled persons (or with members of their families). Dr. William Dunlap, of The University of Alabama's Department of Special Education, analyzed specifically parts of the data dealing with problems of families with members who have mental retardation, cerebral palsy, and/or epilepsy and made the analysis available to us.

The specialized treatment of persons with developmental disabilities in Alabama is the subject of Chapter Nine. Dr. Alsikafi, author of this chapter, has been charged since the initiation of the survey with the responsibility of dealing with the facilities and agencies that offer services to the developmentally disabled. He describes the types of facilities serving the disabled persons directly, the staffing of these facilities, their patient capacities, the types of services offered, and the like.

Part IV of the book attempts to look at the future of the treatment of persons with mental retardation, cerebral palsy, epilepsy, or a combination of any or all three. Likewise, it seeks to draw some conclusions regarding the treatment of these people and to explore some of the implications. Chapter Ten discusses some of the plans for future assistance to Alabama's developmentally disabled population. In preparing this chapter, the author consulted with personnel of the Alabama Department of Mental Health regarding deinstitutionalization plans and served as a member of the Alabama Department of Mental Health's Advisory Committee for Deinstitutionalization. Furthermore, the State Plan for 1975 regarding services to be offered to developmentally disabled persons in the state was consulted. The State Plan was compiled jointly by the Alabama Department of Mental Health and by the Governor's Planning and Advisory Council on the Developmental Disabilities in Alabama, to which Dr. Hollingsworth also serves as a consultant.

Finally, Chapter Eleven includes a summary of the material presented and sets out some conclusions. Recommendations based on the data from the field survey and on the observations of the three major contributing authors are also detailed.

The field survey questionnaire and some tables that may add to the reader's understanding of the phenomena being discussed are offered as appendices. The bibliography will acquaint the readers with some of the materials published in the field, which will be of use to those who are interested in further readings.

The analyses and reports included in this volume have provided much information not previously available. However, by no means should the material reported in this book be regarded as providing final answers to the problems of our developmentally disabled population. It may be thought of, rather, as a constructive step upward on a long staircase toward the betterment of the lives of those who are affected. It is our fervent hope that the publication of this material will be a positive force in helping those who are destined to spend their lives affected by mental retardation, cerebral palsy, or epilepsy.

PART I BACKGROUND

CHAPTER ONE
INTRODUCTION

The desire most often expressed by expectant parents is that their baby be a sound, healthy one—a child who can run, play, receive and give affection, and do all the other things that most normally healthy children can do. Unfortunately, many children are confronted with disabling handicaps of various kinds and degrees. Parents of these children more often than not are unable to understand adequately the true nature of the disability, the struggles of the child in attempting to adapt his behavior to others of his age, and many of the accompanying uncertainties and perplexities that are associated with being a handicapped person in a society of people who, for the most part, were fortunate enough to be born without such conditions.

The volume that follows represents an exploration into some of the problems and concerns of those who are afflicted with one or more of three serious handicapping conditions—specifically mental retardation, cerebral palsy, and epilepsy. These three conditions, collectively, are referred to as the "developmental disabilities" as a result of federal legislation. The definition of developmental disabilities, as stated in P.L. 91-517, the Developmental Disabilities Services and Facilities Construction Act of 1970, is:

> . . . a disability which is (1) attributable to (i) mental retardation, cerebral palsy, epilepsy; or. . . (ii) other neurological conditions found by the Secretary (of the Department of Health, Education, and Welfare) to be closely related to mental retardation or to require treatment similar to that required for mentally retarded individuals; (2) originated before the individual attained age 18, which has continued or can be expected to continue indefinitely; and (3) constitutes a substantial handicap to this individual.

> *Substantial Handicap* is a critical term here. It is defined, for purposes of the Act, as: . . . a physical or mental disability . . . of such severity that alone or in connection with social, legal, or economic constraints, it requires the provision of specialized services over an extended period of time directed toward the individual's social, personal, physical, or economic habilitation or rehabilitation (Alabama Department of Mental Health, 1975:43).

While probably no one is totally unfamiliar with the terms mental retardation, cerebral palsy, and epilepsy, very few people fully understand them and their various implications unless they have been closely associated with a case of one or the other. Therefore, let us survey brief explanations of the developmental disabilities.

Mental retardation has been variously defined by a broad range of writers (see Mercer, 1973). Most current definitions, however, appear to hinge upon two basic criteria: (1) a below average intellectual function and (2) an impairment in a person's ability to meet the demands of the social world (see Mercer, 1973:140; Heber, 1961:64). Generally, the handicap becomes evident in childhood and may or may not extend into adulthood. Through the years, different levels of intellectual functioning have been utilized as criteria to delineate levels of mental retardation. The basic criterion utilized in this effort, IQ test scores, is not without criticism. Therefore, the second factor, level of societal functioning, has been added to standard IQ levels. How well a person is able to get along in his society is an important measure that has been introduced into the definition because of discussion in recent years of the term cultural retardation, meaning basically that some groups of people have not had the same educational opportunities as others. The usual tests of IQ more than likely will indicate that larger proportions of these disadvantaged groups will score below the specified levels of intelligence and thus be classified as retardates. Experience has taught that many of these people are not necessarily mentally retarded but have not had equal educational exposure.

Currently, approximately 5.5 million persons in the United States are victims of mental retardation (Conley, 1973:1). Conley (1973:239) further estimates the social costs of mental retardation in 1970 to have been more than $7 billion. The latter figure includes the loss of earnings, loss of unpaid work (household and family), and the excess cost of retardation services and research, construction, and training. In Alabama, recent estimates indicate that approximately 110,000 persons are victims of mental retardation (Hollingsworth, 1974). About 3 percent of Alabama's retarded population are institutionalized because of the severity of their handicaps; it is difficult, if not impossible, for most of these affected individuals to function in an adequate manner outside an institutional setting. Many others have assumed relatively responsible positions in their own communities and are not in need of any direct services from either state or community agencies or facilities. In the survey reported in this book, numerous noninstitutionalized persons (or members of their families) indicated that they were in need of various kinds of services and that they were not receiving any kind of assistance.

Cerebral palsy is a condition that usually becomes manifest in the first years of a person's life, depending on the nature and degree of involvement. "Cerebral" means brain-centered, and "palsy" is a term used to indicate lack of muscle control. The triggering factor is most often thought to be brain damage occurring either before or during birth. Cerebral palsy is not a single disorder, but a group of ailments having a wide variety of symptoms, all of which are brain-centered and affect muscular control. Different parts of the body are affected in varying degrees by the several forms of cerebral palsy; for example, some victims have spastic movements in various parts of their extremities, yet are fully capable of intellectual functioning on a normal or above-normal level. Others may exhibit less spasticity but be affected in other ways (U.S. Department of Health, Education, and Welfare, 1971).

Estimates by the United Cerebral Palsy Associations suggest that about 750,000 persons in the United States are presently afflicted with cerebral palsy (National Health Education Committee, Inc., 1971a). This writer was unable to find data reflecting the economic costs of the disorder. In Alabama, it is estimated that approximately 4,700 persons are cerebral palsied (Hollingsworth, 1974). Subsequent and more recent analysis has led the present author to believe that this number is far too low and may, in fact, be at least twice this estimate. Other studies of the prevalence of cerebral palsy have reported prevalence rates of between one per 1,000 persons to 3.5 cerebral-palsied individuals per thousand population.

Epilepsy comes from the Greek word, *epilepsia,* meaning seizure, and is regarded as a symptom of a disorder in the brain (National Health Education Committee, Inc., 1971b). An epileptic seizure occurs when a brain cell (or group of brain cells) discharges too much electrical (or nervous) energy. Differing degrees of the condition may be evidenced, ranging from only slight, mostly uneventful, episodes to total involvement of a person. The symptoms of the infirmity depend on the type of epilepsy that has gripped the individual. The disorder is marked by sudden and periodic lapses of consciousness and distinctive, usually measurable, disturbances in the electrical discharges within the brain. The seizure in its mildest form may consist merely of a blank stare or rapid blinking of the eyes, sometimes accompanied by small twitching movements, and may last from 5 to 25 seconds. In its more severe form, epilepsy is often associated with generalized convulsions, loss of consciousness, stiffening, muscle movements, and jerks of limbs and/or trunk, neck, eyes, and face. The attack itself is often described as a convulsion, seizure, spasm, fit, or spell.

The Epilepsy Foundation of America estimates that around 2 million Americans have epilepsy, while the National Institute of Neurological Diseases and Stroke estimates between 1 and 2 million; other authorities insist that both estimates are too low, that somewhere between 4 and 6 million is a more realistic figure. We have estimated that approximately 20,000 Alabamians suffer from the malady (Hollingsworth, 1974).

According to recent estimates of the Department of Health, Education, and Welfare (1965), more than $48 million are spent during the course of each year in direct public-assistance expenditures to epileptics. Additionally, more than $29 million are expended annually for insti-

tutional care of epileptics. Thus, more than $77 million, not including
payments made by voluntary agencies and local agencies not reporting
to the federal government, is the yearly direct cost for services to the
epileptic population. However, the statistical department of the Vocational Rehabilitation Service unofficially reported in March of 1967 that
the annual expenditures for epilepsy were in excess of $120 million. The
Epilepsy Foundation of America estimates that epilepsy costs the tax-
payer more than a billion dollars every year in state, local, and federal
welfare and medical payments (Epilepsy Foundation of America, n.d.).

The Problem in Alabama

In the state of Alabama alone, more than 133,000, or about 1 of every
25 Alabamians, are affected directly to some degree by the developmental disabilities (Hollingsworth, 1974). While past studies have revealed that some groups of people are affected to a greater degree than
others, the developmental disabilities are no respecters of money or of
social class—they hit people at all social and economic levels. The State
of Alabama allocates many scarce resources to the alleviation of problems resulting from these disorders. All 67 counties in the state have
special education facilities, employing 370 teachers to train and/or ed-
ucate some 21,000 developmentally disabled children; approximately
47,000 remain to be served (Alabama Department of Mental Health,
1973:54); some 1,500 mentally retarded persons were living at Partlow
State School at the time of this investigation; 22 comprehensive community mental health centers are in operation; additionally, 3 developmental centers, 10 community mental retardation programs and facilities, and a wide range of other programs serve this population, while
other facilities are in various stages of planning (see, for example,
Kulkarni, 1973).

The construction, maintenance, and staffing of these and numerous
other institutions to serve the state's developmentally disabled population require tremendous expenditures, yet the results of this investigation reveal that large numbers of persons are not receiving any kind of
services. In many cases, either the disabled themselves (in the case of
independent adults) or their parents are unaware of the services provided; others do not take advantage of the services offered by these
agencies and facilities because of other factors, such as lack of transportation, lack of information about their operations, fear, and super-
stition. Still others have assumed relatively satisfying roles and require
no direct services.

The Governor's Planning and Advisory Council on the Developmental Disabilities in Alabama has been assigned the awesome responsibility of making annually a state-wide plan for assistance to the pop-

ulation under discussion in an attempt to guide effectively and efficiently the heavy state expenditures to which reference has been made. In this task the Council has had to face several worrisome facts. Despite all past efforts, little is known about the effects of the developmental disabilities upon the lives of the people involved or upon their families. Members of the Council have often been in a quandary because of the great number of unknowns of the situation but nevertheless have been charged with the specific task of providing and revising each year a comprehensive state plan for the utilization of funds directed toward the alleviation of some of the many perplexing problems that beset the victims of the developmental disabilities and their families.

Questions to which answers were desperately needed included: How many persons are there with the various developmental disabilities in Alabama? How many of them are in need of special services? How many are in need of those services but are not receiving any of them? How are the agencies and facilities distributed about the state, and which services are offered where? Are such services readily available to all of the affected population, or are they poorly distributed? Are there parts of the developmentally disabled population who have no easy access to facilities that provide the services, or who may be unaware of them? What are the specific needs of the persons who suffer from mental retardation, cerebral palsy, and epilepsy? How are these needs presently being met, or are they met at all?

The survey team of the Department of Sociology of The University of Alabama, guided by the Council's needs, set out to "plug some of the gaps" in knowledge about the affected population as well as services needed and being provided in Alabama. Specifically, some of the major objectives of the study were to:

(1) Determine the numbers of persons in Alabama with mental retardation, cerebral palsy, epilepsy, or any combination of these conditions, and delineate their geographic distribution within the state.

(2) Conduct a survey of the services being offered by each agency or facility that provides direct services to the developmentally disabled.

(3) Relate the numbers of developmentally disabled who need assistance of some kind(s) to the services available for them.

(4) Explore the locations of the facilities with regard to where developmentally disabled persons live, in order to determine if such services as provided locally are reasonably accessible to those who require them.

(5) Conduct interviews with developmentally disabled persons in selected counties within the state in order to assess their recognition of their needs, determine how those needs are being met, discover what the affected population views as its greatest unmet needs, describe the effect of having a disabled member upon the rest of the household, etc.

(6) Make recommendations to the Department of Mental Health and

the Governor's Planning and Advisory Council on the Developmental Disabilities in Alabama as to what the most pressing needs are and where new services need to be provided.

The project was divided into two phases. In the first phase, an attempt was made to relate numbers of developmentally disabled persons to the services available and to point out some of the gaps in services. The report was a preliminary one, since the Governor's Council had to have the necessary data on relatively short notice for the formulation of the 1973 DDSA State Plan.

The second phase of the "Survey of the Developmentally Disabled in Alabama: Needs and Resources" (Hollingsworth, 1974) provided more complete data of the type collected in the first phase. In addition, an effort was made to locate all of the victims of mental retardation, cerebral palsy, and/or epilepsy in three selected counties by asking informed local people for the names and addresses of the persons who suffered from these conditions. A survey was made of a random sample of those nominated as having one or more of the developmental disabilities. Their homes were visited, and trained interviewers asked questions related to the major objectives of the survey.

Finally, investigation of more than 26,000 medical records was made in one of the counties, seeking information that would provide clinical verification of the disabilities. Epilepsy was the condition most often entered in these files. This step also provided a check on the method of asking local informants which of their neighbors had one or more of the disabling conditions, since this was one of the three counties previously studied using the community-informant method.

In attempting to evaluate the usefulness of the entire research effort of three years' duration, the author is indeed gratified that the data collected have already been put to use. It is often the case, especially in social science research, that data are gathered in a truly scientific manner, but no practical use is ever made of them. In past data-gathering efforts on aspects of human problems in the state, perhaps more often than not, the reports have only gathered dust on the shelves of a few people who receive them but have no practical applications in mind.

Various service and planning agencies scattered throughout virtually every section of Alabama already have utilized extensively the report of Phase II of the project in applying successfully for grants designed to offer better services and treatment to the state's developmentally disabled population. For example, the data concerning the prevalence of mental retardation, cerebral palsy, and epilepsy have been utilized as departure points for 13 community planning grants that covered 47 of the state's 67 counties. During each of the years 1974 and 1975, approximately $214,000 was obtained as a result of these planning grants. Therefore, in those two years alone, data published in Phase II have assisted in bringing almost a half million dollars into use for the developmentally disabled of Alabama. The data have been utilized to substantiate the need for locations of new centers, such as day care centers. They have also been used by the Department of Pensions and Security in making plans for compliance with Title XX.

The publication of this book, with materials that have been researched exhaustively since the release of the other reports, should provide additional findings that may be used, not just in this state, but perhaps throughout the nation, in our never-ending efforts of doing a better job than we have in the past in assisting our citizens who have mental retardation, cerebral palsy, and epilepsy. Data gathered in a sound manner may now be used to forge ahead in this endless responsibility.

References

Alabama Department of Mental Health
  1973   1973 State DDSA Plan. Montgomery, Alabama.
  1974   1974 State DDSA Plan. Montgomery, Alabama.
  1975   1975 State DDSA Plan. Montgomery, Alabama.
Conley, Ronald
  1973   The Economics of Mental Retardation. Baltimore, Md.: Johns Hopkins Press.
Epilepsy Foundation of America
  n.d.   Data Pak: Facts about Epilepsy and the Many Groups Concerned with its Medical and Social Management. Washington, D.C.
  1969   Epilepsy, Recognition, Causes, Diagnosis, Treatment: Current Information. New York.
  1972   Epilepsy. New York.
Heber, R. F.
  1961   "A manual on terminology and classification in mental retardation." American Journal of Mental Deficiency 64. Monograph Supplement (2nd ed.).
Hollingsworth, J. Selwyn (ed.)
  1974   Report of Phase II of "Survey of the Developmentally Disabled in Alabama: Needs and Resources." Montgomery: Alabama Department of Mental Health.
Kulkarni, Kamala D.
  1973   Directory of Alabama Resources for the Mentally Retarded. Tuscaloosa, Ala.: The University of Alabama, Mental Retardation Service Program.
Mercer, Jane R.
  1973   Labeling the Mentally Retarded: Clinical and Social System Perspectives on Mental Retardation. Berkeley: University of California Press.
National Health Education Committee, Inc.
  1971a   What Are the Facts about Cerebral Palsy? New York.
  1971b   What Are the Facts about Epilepsy? New York.

United Cerebral Palsy Foundation
    1973   Fact Sheet. New York.
United States Department of Health, Education, and Welfare
    1965   Epilepsy: A Review of Basic and Clinical Research. National Institute
            of Health Publication 73-415, Washington, D.C.
    1971   Cerebral Palsy: Hope through Research. Washington, D.C.: Public
            Health Service, National Institutes of Health. DHEW Publication No.
            (NIH) 72-159.
    1972   Epilepsy: Hope through Research (rev.). Washington, D.C.: Public
            Health Service, National Institute of Neurological Diseases and Stroke.
            DHEW Publication No. (NIH) 73-156.

CHAPTER TWO
THE ETIOLOGY OF
THE DEVELOPMENTAL
DISABILITIES

DAVID COOMBS AND M. H. ALSIKAFI

The objectives of this chapter are threefold: (1) to present definitions of each of the three disabilities, using the latest findings available in the literature; (2) to discuss the causation and classification of the disabilities, individually and in relationship to one another; (3) to delve, summarily, into selected research findings related to the causes and epidemiology of the three disabilities. The authors of this chapter do not intend to deal exhaustively with each disability, because entire books have been written on each. The aim is, rather, to provide some basic information for the nonprofessional who has an interest in one or more of the developmental disabilities.

Mental Retardation

Controversy over a proper definition of mental retardation has been raging for a relatively long time. Part of the difficulty stems from lack of precision of the concept of retardation itself. The question of what constitutes retardation, physiologically and behaviorally, is not completely resolved although the degree of agreement among researchers of the field is greater today than in the past few decades. The definition is further complicated by the tendency on the part of some specialists to use the concept of retardation interchangeably with mental deficiency (McCulloch, 1949:130–36). Still a third source of confusion results from the introduction of the term mental subnormality, which is sometimes used to cover both retardation and deficiency. It is commonly agreed today that retardation should be reserved to mean low performance in the educational sphere due to lack of intellectual development, whereas mental deficiency covers cases of mental arrest leading to social performance judged to be inadequate by the community, but which is amenable to improvement through learning (Conley, 1973:6).

The most widely used definition of retardation today is that of Heber, which emphasizes that retardation includes three basic conditions: (1) the functioning of the intellectual ability is subnormal; (2) the subnormality begins in early stages of development; and (3) a form of social incompetence ensues (Heber, 1954:3).

Conley maintains that it is the third condition of Heber's definition that has aroused most of the controversy surrounding the definition of retardation. Researchers who object to inclusion of this condition contend that verification of retardation must take place prior to the question of whether the person can adapt to social demands. To them the problem of retardation must be ascertained through measurement of level of intelligence in its "purest" possible form. The use of IQ tests is believed by many to be the proper procedure to verify the existence of retardation. The advantages of this procedure are that: (1) it minimizes the amount of confusion regarding what constitutes retardation since IQ tests usually measure a single variable (intelligence) about which most professionals have considerable agreement; and (2) it facilitates the process of identifying those retarded persons who are in dire need of special assistance. In other words, the use of intelligence tests as a sole criterion for determining the existence of retardation is more pragmatic for purposes of program planning and evaluation than any other available method (Conley, 1973).

In contrast to the foregoing approach, advocates of the importance of measuring social incompetence maintain that the "acid test" for retardation must by necessity be derived from a measure of functional performance of the person in a social setting. Intelligence does not exist in a vacuum. Rather, it matures in a social environment. It follows that only those persons who show a significant measure of incompetence are to be labeled as retardates. IQ tests are not designed to achieve this objective; they are not useful in "getting at" practical aspects of the person's daily life because of limitations built into the process of selecting items of measurement, and in administering the test itself (Mercer, 1973: 235–54).

Whatever definition is chosen, it must be stressed that researchers in this field do not equate retardation with illiteracy or mental illness. As Conley points out, "although some persons who are illiterate or mentally ill are retarded, many function at normal or even superior levels" (Conley, 1973:10). Also, persons who for one reason or another do not perform to the highest level of their potentials but score "adequately" on IQ tests must be excluded from the retardation category.

CAUSES OF MENTAL RETARDATION

According to Conley, the reported causes of mental retardation exceed 200. However, these causes can be grouped into three major categories: (1) poor genetic background; (2) physical damage or maldevelopment of the brain; and (3) environmental deprivation (Conley, 1973:11). In general most retardates exhibit conditions showing the effects of two or more of these causes.

Causation of mental retardation is approached through the development of systems of classification of levels of retardation. At least three such classifications are in evidence, depending on the criteria employed by the researcher. They are:

(1) Classifying mental retardation on the basis of level of intelligence, with the profoundly retarded having IQs ranging from 0 to 19; the severely retarded, 20 to 34; the moderately retarded, 35 to 49; and the mildly retarded, 50 to 69.

(2) Classifying mental retardation on the basis of level of learning. Thus, retardates are either *educable*, meaning they are able to learn basic reading, writing, spelling, and arithmetic skills, or *trainable*, meaning they are unable to learn these skills but can be trained to attend to most of their personal needs. Often, these definitions are based on IQ levels.

(3) Classifying mental retardation on the basis of level of dependency. Thus retardates are marginally dependent, semidependent, or dependent.

These classifications and the causative factors associated with them must be approached with a great deal of caution. Neither system of classification nor the cause of retardation can be assessed precisely. Specialists in the field maintain that only one-fourth of the population of retardates can be diagnosed with certainty (Conley, 1973:50).

Despite these difficulties the field of mental retardation has reached a significant degree of growth not only in terms of numbers of studies dealing with the problem of causation, but also in terms of level and accuracy of explanation achieved in these studies. The former has been manifested by an increasing number of epidemiological surveys of mental retardation, whereas the latter was achieved through examination of logic of proof used in these studies. Both aspects are highly interrelated because surveys of distribution of the disability (the field of epidemiology) involve the search for causative factors.

EPIDEMIOLOGICAL STUDIES

In the last few decades several important epidemiological studies have been conducted in different states and regions of the country, all having the objective of finding patterns of distribution of mental retardation in the different categories of the population. Although the findings of these studies show some significant differences, most of them reveal striking consistencies in the relationships between the likelihood of mental retardation and such factors as age, sex, race, social class, location of residence, and the like (see for instance, Lemkau, et al., 1942; Wishik, 1956; Levinson, 1962; Kennedy, et al., 1963; Jastak, et al., 1963; New York State Department of Mental Hygiene, 1965; Richardson, et al., 1965; Taylor, et al., 1965).

These studies reveal that the likelihood of discovering mental retardation in an individual "increased steadily with age until the middle teens after which it began to decline" (Conley, 1973:18). Regarding the sex of the surveyed population, these studies show that in general males are more prone to mental retardation than are females. However, the race factor reflected the highest differential in most of these studies, with blacks holding a striking disadvantage over whites.

The most systematic basis of viewing differential rates of mental retardation, according to studies cited above, is that of social class. Almost all indicate that the lower classes are more likely to have more mentally retarded persons, in some surveys as high as 13 times greater, than are the upper classes. Also rates of retardation tend to increase in urban ghettos and in isolated rural places, probably because of the low socioeconomic level of the surveyed population. Moreover, most retardation is self-perpetuatory since it is reinforced by continuous interaction with other retardates (Mercer, 1973:20–37).

Focusing on the severe level of mental retardation, it is noted that about one third of retarded children have an IQ of 25 or below, most of whom die within the first five years of life. Among severely retarded adults, the chances for longer life have recently increased, although they still range from one third to one half of the life expectancies of the general population. On the other hand, the majority of mild retardates are free of major physical handicaps and thus are more likely to approach normal life spans.

The prevalence of physical handicaps among retarded populations tends to be higher than among the general population. These disabilities include hearing loss, loss of sight, and related defects. By the same token, mental retardation is more likely to occur among persons with severe hearing defects and visual difficulties. The same principle holds for cerebral palsy, epilepsy, and psychiatric disorders. These disabilities tend to occur more often among mental retardates, especially among those who are more severely affected.

THE SEARCH FOR CAUSATION

The question of what specifically causes mental retardation has occupied specialists for a relatively long time. The search for causation has generally focused on two broad areas: the link between social class and retardation, and the incidence of brain damage in retarded populations. Some studies have related these two areas to one another in such a way that it is not easy for the researcher to ascertain the part played by each factor separately. Despite this difficulty, the literature is rich with systematic studies of causation that merit attention.

Malamud (1964) provided one such study that attempted to measure the effects of brain injury on mental retardation. He found that severe retardation was more likely to occur among babies born with brain damage or congenital malformations. The significance of brain damage as a cause of retardation increased among nonwhites and among the lower socioeconomic groups. Moreover, poor women are more likely to be younger when they deliver their first child and older when they have their last baby. Since both early childbirth and late childbirth are more risky than the in-between periods, it is evident that poor women are more likely to deliver proportionately more babies who are retarded.

Despite these convincing relationships, brain damage alone cannot explain all forms of mental retardation. Thus, researchers turned to the "classic" question of heredity versus environment: Is the cause of retardation connected in some way with genetic defects or with environmental deprivation?

To argue for the former—heredity—one has to accept three basic assumptions: (1) that biological differences exist in the genes determining levels of intelligence; (2) that parents with subnormal intellectual endowments tend to produce intellectually subnormal offspring; and (3) that the environmental forces have only a minimal effect on intelligence test performance.

The first assumption has been subjected to extensive testing in the work of the British psychologist, Cyril Burt. In his study of the question of the extent to which mental disability is inherited, Burt found that among children who had been reared in similar environments, "individual differences in intelligence . . . varied over an unusually wide range" (Burt, 1958:6). Harvard educator Arthur Jensen's study of the extent to which intelligence can be increased tends to support this finding (Jensen, 1969:9).

The second assumption—that subnormal characteristics are passed on to the next generation—is somewhat more complex than the preceding one. It involves understanding some basic genetic laws and the relationships between dominant and recessive genes. The assumption was tested by studies that attempted to compare differences between the intellectual levels of children with those of their parents. A study by Burt (1955) shows some significant relationships between the two, although such relationships must be viewed with caution. Jensen (1969) found similar results. The Reeds went even further and asserted that (1) the mentally retarded are more likely to reproduce mentally retarded children; (2) most retarded persons tend to have close relatives who are mentally retarded; and (3) mental retardation caused by social deprivation is very insignificant (Reed and Reed, 1965:206).

The third assumption proposes that environment has a small effect, if any, on intelligence. The obvious implication of this assumption is that differences in intelligence between social classes and racial groups are

cinctly that "a patient seldom has only one type of attack, of the same pattern, duration and severity" (U.S. Department of Health, Education, and Welfare, 1965:29). Thus a localized convulsion may, during the same attack, become generalized as other areas of the brain begin excessive neuronic discharges. Attacks of absence simple may, after some years, become generalized convulsions. Charlton and Yahr (1967), in a study of 275 children with absence simple, found that most began experiencing generalized convulsions by age 16.

Whatever the type of seizure, the aftereffects are usually as varied as the reactions themselves. They include confusion in thinking and behavior, paralysis, amnesia, fatigue, muscular aches, etc. Fortunately, these effects are transient, although some are known to last several days.

INCIDENCE

The rate of occurrence of a malady in a population in a given time period is incidence. Diagnosis in an individual is made from clinical histories of seizures and from evaluations of the degree and type of neuron discharge shown in the brain by an electroencephalogram (EEG). Estimates of epilepsy's prevalence, or the number of people who have epilepsy at a given time, are little better. The Epilepsy Foundation of America (1972) estimated that about 4 million epileptics were in the United States.

Precise estimates of the incidence of epilepsy in the United States or within different demographic subgroups have been impossible to determine because of difficulties in diagnosis and the reluctance of some doctors and patients to report it. There is evidence, however, that certain groups have a higher incidence of epilepsy than others. Males, for example, appear to be at a higher risk than females though some studies show little difference. Lower class people in general and racial groups such as blacks and Puerto Ricans, which are disproportionately "lower class," are reported to have a higher incidence of epilepsy than middle or upper status groups. Moreover, studies show that while death rates from epilepsy in general have declined since World War II, rates for nonwhites are, relative to whites, still much higher (see for example, Kurtzke, 1972:21–36). In a special study at the Jefferson Medical College of Philadelphia it was concluded that for *black* children, 10 years of age, epilepsy was the seventh most important cause of death in 1970. For 10-year-old white females epilepsy ranked fourteenth as a cause of death, and for white male children it was (apparently) insignificant enough in causing death as to be unranked (Kurtzke, 1972). Kurtzke (1972) reports that U.S. death rates for epilepsy in 1959–1961 for nonwhite males averaged 3.9 per 100,000 population versus a rate of 1.2 for white males. For nonwhite and white females, rates were 1.7 and

0.8, respectively. Overall, the rates indicate that epilepsy is rarely a primary cause of death. When epileptic seizures do cause death, they do so most often among infants and young children.

If these differentials are accepted as genuine, then the question arises as to why they exist. Although many brain defects that cause epileptic reactions are inherited, it is not likely that genetic factors are greatly responsible. Instead it appears that: (1) males and lower class individuals, of whatever race, because of their physical and social environment, are more subject to head injuries, which can produce brain damage, and (2) lower class children are more likely to experience poor prenatal care, premature birth, and postnatal malnutrition and disease, all of which can produce brain damage. A special study of black Americans conducted by the prestigious Brookings Institute concluded in 1960 that a gap of about forty years separated whites and blacks with regard to health levels (Fein, 1966). A perusal of national vital statistics for 1971 reveals that a major gap still exists. The neonatal mortality rate (number of deaths occurring among infants 0–28 days old per 1,000 born) for whites in 1971 was 13.1 (U.S. Department of Health, Education, and Welfare, 1974). The rate for maternal deaths resulting from pregnancies and complications during childbirth (maternal mortality rate) in 1971 for whites was 13.0 versus 45.3 for nonwhites. Differences between whites and nonwhites in death rates from influenza and pneumonia are almost one to two while nonwhite death rates from tuberculosis are six times greater than white tubercular death rates (U.S. Department of Health, Education, and Welfare, 1974).

These statistics indicate the relatively low levels of health care and healthfulness that nonwhites experience in the country as a whole. Unfortunately, recent statistics of this kind were, as of this writing, not available at the county or state levels, though it is known that in rural areas of the South levels are even lower. Thus, the influence of environmental factors in producing brain damage is likely to be greater in such places.

With respect to age groups there are also marked differences in the incidence of different types of epilepsy. Absence simple, for example, occurs most frequently in infancy and early childhood, decreasing as the brain matures, while focal convulsions concentrate at both ends of the age scale.

Despite increasing knowledge about these differentials, epilepsy remains, according to Robb (1972) and many others, a "major medical and social problem" whose true dimensions are hidden.

SPECIFIC CAUSAL FACTORS

All of the abnormal physical-chemical brain conditions that produce epileptic seizures are most directly a result of some tangible physical event. Thus, whatever the underlying causes, seizure-production abnormalities are assumed to be a result of one or more of the following tangible factors:

(1) Inheritance of chromosomal cellular defects that may directly produce seizures or a predisposition to seizures under certain precipitating conditions. In clear-cut cases of this type there is a 10 to 15 percent chance that the siblings of the victim will suffer from the same abnormality and experience at least one convulsion (Pryse-Phillips, 1969:82).

(2) Antenatal events harmful to the foetus, such as ingestion of a poisonous substance or drug, a blow to the abdomen, or deprivation of oxygen (anoxia).

(3) Perinatal events or birth traumas, which make childbirth difficult and result in brain damage to the infant through suffocation or a blow to the head. Naturally these kinds of circumstances more commonly occur during deliveries that are not attended by professionals. They frequently cause not only epilepsy but also cerebral palsy and mental retardation.

(4) Postnatal events that involve physical injury to the brain or nervous system and cause permanent damage. These are numerous, although the distribution of their occurrence is not random through all groups. Some are more likely to happen to small children than adults, while others more often affect lower class adults. Brain damage caused by excessive consumption of alcohol and other drugs is obviously more common among lower class adults than middle class children. Circulatory disorders causing brain damage and brain tumors are almost universally encountered in older adults. Head injuries and metabolic or nutritional deficiencies (especially a severe lack of protein) occur most commonly in the lower class. On the other hand, infectious diseases, such as virus encephalitis, and excessive heat or suffocation, which cause brain damage, appear to occur with the same frequency among all groups.

The above group differences in the occurrence of postnatal brain damage indicate that social factors determine both exposure and susceptibility. Thus, as Dwayne Reed (1972) cogently states, an individual's risk of becoming an epileptic depends not only on his genes or chance circumstances but also on his social class, age, race, sex, occupation, life style, etc. But because the incidence of epilepsy within populations or its variation among them has not been precisely determined, a complete etiology of epilepsy in general or of the various types is not precisely known. When all the factors that contribute to epilepsy, as well as their interactions, are described and explained, then perhaps epilepsy can be prevented as well as treated.

Two related phenomena bear mentioning. Because epilepsy is a symptom of brain abnormality, it is at times only one manifestation of the underlying problem. Associated behavioral disorders that may stem from the same cause include psychotic reactions of a schizoid or manic-depressive nature, cerebral palsy, mental retardation, and specific learning disabilities such as faulty memorization. The Epilepsy Foundation of America (1972) estimates that approximately 1.2 million epileptics in the United States are also mentally retarded while 200,000 epileptics also suffer from cerebral palsy. Another source estimates that between 21 and 37 percent of all epileptics are mentally retarded (Conley, 1973:13).

Certain other behavioral disorders such as paranoia, chronic irritability, and aggressiveness, leading to problems in interpersonal relations and social isolation, are associated with epilepsy but are likely derived from the epileptic reactions themselves and the social stigma attached to epilepsy rather than pathological brain abnormalities (see Geist, 1962). For many otherwise normal epileptics whose seizures have been controlled by drugs, real and/or imagined rejection is perhaps a bigger problem than the disability itself. Around twenty anticonvulsant drugs are now prescribed for epileptics, the most common being dilantin, mysoline, and phenobarbital. Drug therapy can be used to control seizures completely in over half of all epileptics while reducing their frequency in most of the rest.

Various environmental stimuli may act as catalytic agents by setting off the discharge of neurons in the affected area of the brain. These stimuli include such innocuous activities as hearing music, watching television, reading a book, or smelling a particular odor. More powerful events, such as being subjected to verbal abuse and/or generalized anxiety, can also precipitate a seizure. Chronic precipitating factors are usually avoided by epileptics. Parenthetically it seems that for some epileptics goal-oriented activity, including routine, satisfying work, can lower the frequency of epileptic reactions. This observation lends itself to the hypothesis that some kinds of epilepsy may be due more to learning than to brain abnormality.

Cerebral Palsy

Like epilepsy, the term cerebral palsy refers to a group of disabling physical symptoms that manifest brain abnormalities. Adler (1961), drawing from several sources, defines cerebral palsy as a condition characterized by a motor deficit or defect (paralysis, lack of coordinated movement, hyperkinesis) due to malfunctioning of the motor control areas of the brain. In other words, the cerebral palsied individual cannot, to a greater or lesser extent, effectively control the use of certain muscles. Bowley and Gardner (1969) emphasize that lack of control does not mean damage to or paralysis of the muscles or limbs, but is a consequence of brain malfunctioning.

In contrast to epilepsy, the lack of muscular control in cerebral palsy is chronic rather than intermittent so that both the nature of the disability and its effects are usually more serious for the victim and his or her family.

TYPES OF CEREBRAL PALSY

Cerebral palsy is a label for a variety of involuntary behavior disorders stemming from several brain abnormalities and thus there are, in a manner of speaking, a number of "cerebral palsies." All of them are grouped into the four basic categories or types below.

(1) *Spastic* cerebral palsy (which includes about 75 percent of all known victims) is generally characterized as involuntary rigidity of movement caused by an inability to relax certain muscles. Within this category, four subtypes can be found: (a) monoplegic, in which one arm or leg is affected; (b) hemiplegic, in which one side of the body is affected; (c) paraplegic, in which both legs are affected; and (d) quadriplegic, in which arms and legs are affected.

(2) *Athetoid* cerebral palsy involves chronic abnormal jerking and writhing movements. Drooling as well as hearing and speech defects are also common. Between 5 and 10 percent of known cerebral palsy victims have this type.

(3) *Ataxic* cerebral palsy is a type in which balanced body movement is difficult and hand/eye movement is uncoordinated.

(4) *Mixed* cerebral palsy is a category in which the victim has more than one of the above types or subtypes of affliction. Although the number of mixed cases is thought to be under 10 percent of the total, Mitchell (1962) believes that a much larger proportion of the cerebral palsied is in fact mixed, with one type of palsy being predominant enough to effect another categorization.

Naturally, the degree of disability varies from individual to individual irrespective of the palsy involved. However, a study by Klapper and Birch (1966) of 89 cases found that spastics were generally least affected and tended to have higher IQs, more education, and greater socioeconomic autonomy. Within the spastic group the monoplegics and hemiplegics fared the best in overall functional ability. Ingram (1964:520) and Bowley and Gardner (1969:254) found similar relationships in England and both generalize that children with the greatest physical handicaps tend to be less intelligent.

INCIDENCE

The frequency with which the various types of cerebral palsies occur in the United States or anywhere else is not precisely known. Various surveys conducted in specific communities, or in a few cases, states, (see Chapter Six of this volume) indicate that an approximately accurate estimate of incidence would be 5 per 1,000 population. Because very few people acquire the disability after birth and because many (perhaps 15 percent) cerebral palsy victims die in childhood, the prevalence rate after early childhood is somewhat lower—estimates range from 1.5 to 4.0 per 1,000 population.

Little variation in incidence is reported among different demographic or socioeconomic groups. Of the studies reviewed by the authors, only in Ingram's (1964) was such variation encountered. He found that acquired hemiplegia more often occurred among younger children of large, lower class families than any other group. Thus, he concluded that poor social conditions and poor child care in a lower class environment increase the risk of postnatal cerebral palsy. Otherwise, cerebral palsy due to prenatal and perinatal factors (estimated to be 90 percent) may occur with equal frequency among blacks and whites, lower class and middle class, etc. Given the demonstrable fact that infant and maternal mortality rates are much higher for nonwhites than whites in the United States, this supposition seems to be unlikely.

SPECIFIC CAUSAL FACTORS

Cerebral palsy is unquestionably a symptom of damage to the brain or of a developmental defect in it. Spasticity, for example, is usually a consequence of a wound on the cortex, athetosis of damage to the basal ganglia, and ataxia of a wound in the cerebellum. Events causing such wounds or injuries are numerous, and as yet, not entirely known. It is now believed that postnatal events such as head wounds, suffocation, or infectious diseases—e.g., meningitis, encephalitis, polio—account for no more than 10 percent of the known cases (Keats, 1965:75; Bowley and Gardner, 1969:254). Thus, most of the crucial, causal events take place during pregnancy or at birth.

During the 1950s and 1960s antenatal factors were the focus of much research. Intrauterine anoxia (deprivation of oxygen) was found to be the principal causal factor, although a study by Churchill (1970) of 1,364 premature palsied infants found that a significantly large number of those who were spastic had suffered from cerebral hemorrhage. Hereditary-genetic factors are thought to act rarely as causal agents. Adler (1961) notes that even the frequent occurrence of cerebral palsy in siblings of the same stock does not prove that endogene familial hereditary factors are directly important as causes. Adler (1961) examined 120 cerebral palsy victims and found that 16 had near relatives who were similarly afflicted. He also found that most of the 16 were especially difficult to rehabilitate. From these observations, Adler suggests that some genetic factor *may* be operating where there is an accumulation of cerebral palsies in a family through several generations.

So-called perinatal factors or damaging events at childbirth appear to be the most common causes of brain damage culminating in cerebral palsy. Mitchell (1962) learned that in most of his intensively studied sample of "mixed" cases there was a "recognizable event" during pregnancy or delivery that involved suffocation or trauma. In 10 of the 19 cases where the birth history was known, the labor or delivery itself was abnormal. He estimates that 50 percent of the mixed type of cerebral palsy is due to cerebral injury at birth. Ingram (1964:528) states that an abnormal birth history, usually involving suffocation, has been encountered in about 70 percent of hemiplegic cases. Most frequent abnormalities of childbirth encountered are prolonged labor, precipitate labor, forceps delivery, and breech extraction. Keats (1965) also mentions the injudicious use of analgesics and anesthetics as complicating factors.

Abnormal childbirth is somewhat more common among very young or relatively old mothers. We might also expect to find these problems more frequently among lower class mothers, especially those who are black and/or live in isolated rural areas.

As in the case of epilepsy, a number of other behavioral disabilities occur with cerebral palsy and stem from the same cause or causes. Neilsen (1971) states that mental retardation is the disorder most frequently associated with cerebral palsy. Estimates of the proportion of cerebral palsy victims who have an IQ classified as subnormal range from 40 to 80 percent. Ingram (1964) is more specific, citing a study in which 44 percent of the cerebral palsy victims had an IQ equal to or less than 69, 22 percent scored equal to or less than 55, while only 32 percent had IQ scores equal to or greater than 85. Of 57 palsied children whom Ingram categorized as being of *normal* intelligence, 17 had reading difficulties, 16 were hyperactive, 10 could not hear normally, 35 could not see normally, and 26 had epilepsy. In general, epilepsy is estimated to occur in 26 to 55 percent of all cerebral palsy cases.

Some specialists believe that the extraordinarily high correlation of mental retardation with cerebral palsy is only partially due to brain abnormalities but also occurs because the palsied child's opportunities for learning are limited by the palsy, as well as by parental attitudes toward it. Additionally, there is thought to be a bias in the IQ tests. Shere and Kastenbaum (1966) found that mothers of palsied children unwittingly restricted their children's intellectual development because of preoccupation with the handicap's physical aspects. With regard to the test factor, it is pointed out that most such tests are designed for normal children without impairments in motor control, vision, etc. The palsied child, whether of normal or subnormal intelligence, thus has much more difficulty in focusing his attention during a test. Moreover, many children develop emotional and physical barriers to testing and learning as defeat follows defeat. Yet, Neilsen (1971), along with other researchers, found that retesting cerebral palsy patients in various time periods produced no more variation in IQ scores over time than is found among normal children.

Little is known about the development of cerebral palsy victims in later years. Their overall integration into society is apparently very limited. Those with lower IQ scores (below 50) seldom achieve even a modicum of independence. Those scoring 90 or above have, in many cases, completed high school, acquired a job and some financial independence, although few married or were able to live alone. Those with intermediate IQ scores showed a wide range of adaptations, which were undoubtedly dependent upon other handicaps, amount of learning, motivation, etc.

Psychological disorders occur with above-average frequency among the cerebral palsied and seem to be largely a consequence of avoidance-rejection by others and the frustrations inherent in attempting to adapt with such a severe disability. They range from outright psychotic breaks to neurotic inabilities to maintain personal relationships. Generally speaking, the otherwise normal epileptic is highly autonomous and fortunate in comparison with the victim of cerebral palsy.

References

Adler, Emil
    1961   "Familial cerebral palsy." Cerebral Palsy Review 22 (February):4–6.
Bowley, Agatha A., and Leslie Gardner
    1969   The Young Handicapped Child: Educational Guidance for the Young
            Cerebral Palsied, Blind, and Autistic Child. London, England: E. S.
            Livingstone, Ltd.
Burks, B. S.
    1928   "The relative influence of nature and nurture upon mental devel-
            opment: a comparative study of parent-foster child resemblance and
            true parent-true child resemblance." Yearbook of the National Study
            for the Study of Education: 219–316.
Burt, B.
    1955   "The evidence for the concept of intelligence." British Journal of
            Educational Psychology (November):6.
Burt, Cyril
    1958   "The inheritance of mental ability." American Psychologist (Janu-
            ary):172–73.
Charlton, M. H., and M. D. Yahr
    1967   "Long-term follow-up of patients with petit mal." Archives of Neu-
            rology 16:595–98.
Churchill, John A.
    1970   "On the etiology of cerebral palsy in premature infants." American
            Academy of Neurology 20:405.

Conley, Ronald
    1973   The Economics of Mental Retardation. Baltimore, Md.: Johns Hop-
            kins Press.
Epilepsy Foundation of America
    1972   Epilepsy: Recognition, Onset, Diagnosis, Therapy. Washington, D.C.
Fein, Rashi
    1966   An Economic and Social Profile of the Negro American. Washing-
            ton, D.C.: Brookings Institution.
Geist, Harold
    1962   The Etiology of Idiopathic Epilepsy. New York: Exposition Press.
Heber, Richard
    1954   "A manual on terminology and classification in mental retardation."
            American Journal of Mental Deficiency.
Ingram, T. T. S.
    1964   Pediatric Aspects of Cerebral Palsy. Baltimore, Md.: Williams and
            Wilkins.
Jastak, J. F., H. McPhee, and M. Whiteman
    1963   Mental Retardation: Its Nature and Incidence. Newark, Del.: Uni-
            versity of Delaware Press.
Jensen, A. R.
    1969   "How much can we boost IQ and scholastic achievement?" Harvard
            Educational Review 39 (Winter):1–123.
Keats, Sidney
    1965   Cerebral Palsy. Springfield, Ill.: Charles C Thomas.
Kennedy, W. A., et al.
    1963   A Normative Sample of Intelligence and Achievement of Negro El-
            ementary School Children: The Southeastern United States. Yellow
            Springs, Ohio: Antioch Press.
Klapper, Z. S., and H. G. Birch
    1966   "Relation of childhood characteristics to outcome in young adults
            with cerebral palsy." Developmental Medicine and Child Neurology
            8:645–56.
Kurtzke, John F.
    1972   "Mortality and morbidity data on epilepsy." Pp. 21–36 in Milton
            Alter and W. Allen Hauser (eds.), The Epidemiology of Epilepsy: A
            Workshop. Washington, D.C.: U.S. Department of Health, Educa-
            tion, and Welfare, Public Health Service, National Institutes of Health,
            National Institute of Neurological Diseases and Stroke Monograph
            No. 14.
Leahy, A. M.
    1935   "Nature-nurture and intelligence." Genetic Psychology Monograph
            (June):241–305.
Lemkau, P., et al.
    1942   "Mental hygiene problems in an urban district." Mental Hygiene
            26:275–88.
Levinson, E. J.
    1962   Retarded children in Maine: a survey and analysis. University of

Maine Studies, Second Series, No. 77. Orono, Maine: University of Maine Press.

McCulloch, T. L.
1949 "Reformulation of the problem of mental deficiency." American Journal of Mental Deficiency (October):130–36.

Malamud, N.
1964 "Neuropathology." Pp. 431–49 in H.A. Stevens and R. Heber (eds.), Mental Retardation: A Review of Research. Chicago: University of Chicago Press.

Mercer, Jane R.
1973 Labeling The Mentally Retarded: Clinical and Social System Perspectives on Mental Retardation. Berkeley: University of California Press.

Mitchell, Ross G.
1962 "Mixed types of cerebral palsy." Cerebral Palsy Review 23:3–6, 13–15.

Neilsen, Helle H.
1971 "Psychological appraisal of children with cerebral palsy: a survey of 128 re-assessed cases." Developmental Medicine and Child Neurology 13 (December):707–20.

New York State Department of Mental Hygiene
1965 A Special Census of Suspected Referred Mental Retardation, Onondaga County, New York. Syracuse, N.Y.: University Press.

Pryse-Philips
1969 Epilepsy. Baltimore, Md.: Williams and Wilkins.

Reed, Dwayne
1972 "The epidemiological approach." Pp. 3–11 in Milton Alter and W. Allen Hauser (eds.), The Epidemiology of Epilepsy: A Workshop. Washington, D.C.: U.S. Department of Health, Education, and Welfare, Public Health Service, National Institutes of Health, National Institute of Neurological Diseases and Stroke Monograph No. 14.

Reed, E. W., and C. Reed
1965 Mental Retardation: A Family Study. Philadelphia: Saunders Co.

Richardson, W. P., A. C. Higgins, and R. G. Ames
1965 The Handicapped Children of Alamance County, North Carolina: A Medical and Sociological Study. Wilmington, Del.: Nemours Foundation.

Robb, J. Preston
1972 "A review of epidemiological concepts of epilepsy." Pp. 13–18 in Milton Alter and W. Allen Hauser (eds.), The Epidemiology of Epilepsy: A Workshop. Washington, D.C.: U.S. Department of Health, Education, and Welfare, Public Health Service, National Institutes of Health, National Institute of Neurological Diseases and Stroke Monograph No. 14.

Shadak, M., and H. M. Skeels
1949 "A final follow-up study of one hundred adopted children." Journal of Genetic Psychology: 91–114.

Shere, Eugenia, and Robert Kastenbaum
  1966   "Mother-child interactions in cerebral palsy: environmental and psy-
          chosocial obstacles to cognitive development." Genetic Psychology
          Monographs 73:255–335.
Shuey, M.
  1966   The Testing of Negro Intelligence. New York: Social Science Press.
Skeels, H. M.
  1966   Adult Status of Children with Contrasting Early Life Experiences.
          Chicago Society for Research in Child Development.
Speer, G. S.
  1940   "The intelligence of foster children." Journal of Genetic Psychology:
          49–55.
Taylor, J. L., et al.
  1965   Mental Retardation Prevalence in Oregon. Portland, Oreg.: State
          Board of Health.
United States Department of Health, Education, and Welfare
  1965   Epilepsy: A Review of Basic and Clinical Research. National Institute
          of Health Publication 73–415. Washington, D.C.
  1974   Vital Statistics of the United States—Mortality. Part A, Vol. II. Wash-
          ington, D.C.: U.S. Government Printing Office.
Wishik, S. M.
  1956   "Handicapped children in Georgia: a study of prevalence, disability,
          needs and resources." American Journal of Public Health 46:195–
          203.

PART II: PLANNING THE SURVEY

CHAPTER THREE
THE RESEARCH SETTING

DAVID W. COOMBS

The survey of the developmentally disabled reported in this book was conducted during the summer of 1973 in three predominantly rural Alabama counties. Rural counties were chosen because relatively little information is available on the prevalence and problems of the developmental disabilities among rural people. Previous research concentrated on urban settings, and almost all of the facilities and agencies dealing with cerebral palsy, epilepsy, and mental retardation are situated in such areas. Pseudonyms for the three counties in the survey are used in order to protect the privacy of developmentally disabled individuals and of organizations cooperating.

These particular counties, Highland, Piedmont, and Plantation, respectively, were chosen to represent the three most important agricultural regions of the state: the high and rugged Cumberland or Appalachian plateau that dominates northern and mid-central Alabama; the moderately hilly central pine belt and upper coastal plain that extends across the state in a northwesterly arc from south-central Georgia to northeast Mississippi, representing a transitional area between the Gulf coast plain and the Cumberland plateau; and the fertile, gently rolling Black Belt (so called because of its heavy, dark-colored soils) that also crosses the state in a southeasterly to northwesterly direction below the central pine belt. The Black Belt takes in most of the south-central portion of Alabama and historically was the center of plantation culture and large-scale cotton cultivation in Alabama.

The three counties are fairly typical of the regions they represent in terms of such basic criteria as race, income levels, and rurality. Hence, comparisons of the three should provide a relatively accurate picture of regional variations. Highland County, for example, like the Appalachian plateau in general, is almost exclusively inhabited by whites (98 percent), whereas Plantation County, in common with most other Black Belt counties, has a predominantly black population (almost 70 percent). Piedmont County is 86 percent white and, like the area it represents, intermediate in this respect. An additional reason for selecting the three counties is that each one is situated in a different mental health region of the state's Department of Mental Health.

Now, as in the past, the Black Belt contains the state's largest farms and the least amount of urban-industrial development. Cotton was dethroned in Plantation County and elsewhere in the state during the 1920s and 1930s, being replaced by more lucrative, easier-to-cultivate

items such as soybeans, hay, and cattle. Highland County farms are the
most diverse, producing corn, hay, cotton, vegetables, poultry, and eggs.
Partly because of its large size and partly because of intensive farming
methods, Highland County is one of the state's most productive counties
in the dollar value of its agricultural products (Lineback, 1973:65).

After the turn of the century the three counties, along with most of
rural America, experienced sharp population losses in spite of relatively
high birth rates, as many young and even middle-aged people sought
jobs and higher wages in distant cities.This trend was most marked in
the almost completely rural Black-Belt counties such as Plantation,
which showed population losses of over 30 percent between 1950 and
1970. This trend slowed during the 1960s and was slightly reversed in
Plantation and Highland counties since 1970, according to population
projections by The University of Alabama's Center for Business and
Economic Research. In view of the fact that crude birth rates in the three
counties have declined somewhat, the reversal of population loss is likely
because of a decrease in outmigration. This decrease is apparently the
result of an expansion in manufacturing and service jobs during the
1960s that has offset the continuing decline in the need for farm work
or workers. Between 1966 and 1973 the percentage of the labor force
engaged in nonagricultural employment in Highland County increased
from around 80 percent to almost 89 percent. In Piedmont and Plantation counties the proportions of nonagricultural workers rose from 85
to 90 percent and 71 to 81 percent respectively (University of Alabama,
Center for Business and Economic Research, 1973).

Interestingly, this incipient industrialization was not accompanied by
significant urbanization as of 1970. At that time Plantation County was
still completely rural, while the rural population in Highland and Piedmont counties had decreased by a mere 3 percent during the decade to
represent 80 and 70 percent of their respective totals (U.S. Bureau of
the Census, 1972b).

The growth of industry brought about badly needed increases in income levels in the counties, though all three remain far behind Alabama
and the nation in this respect. The U.S. Census for 1970 reports that
in 1969, 29, 24, and 46 percent of the families in Highland, Piedmont,
and Plantation counties, respectively, were living on incomes that placed
them below the "poverty" level. For the state as a whole the proportion
of families with below-poverty-level income in 1969 was 20.7 percent
(U.S. Bureau of the Census, 1972b).

The unusually high incidence of poverty found in the three counties
is the outcome of various historical and geographic factors that have
operated over much of the South. In a general sense rurality is closely
linked to poverty in the South, and all three counties are eminently rural. The particularly widespread impoverishment encountered in Plan-

tation County is due, of course, to the high concentration of land ownership and the quasifeudal relationship between white owners and black workers, stemming from the days of plantation slavery. Class differences are especially sharp in Plantation County because of simultaneous racial differences with their accompanying syndrome of prejudice and discrimination. More concretely, the U.S. Census Bureau (1972b) found that Plantation County's blacks had a per capita income in 1969 of just over $600 while Alabama blacks as a whole had a per capita income of $1,157. Yet, Plantation is but the poorest of the poor, and if the culture and life styles of poverty do increase the incidence of developmental disabilities (as previous writings suggest), one should expect serious problems with these handicaps in all three of the counties studied.

Historical Settlement

THE STATE

When white settlers began pushing into Alabama shortly after 1800, they found large portions of the state inhabited by two major Indian groups: the Muskogee (which included the Creek, Choctaw, and Chickasaw tribes) in the south and west and the more recently arrived Cherokee, who had been pushed out of Tennessee by white pioneers, in the north and northeast. A series of wars and skirmishes led the Muskogee tribes to cede and abandon their lands by 1818. In 1839 the remaining Cherokee lands in northeast Alabama were purchased by the U.S. Government under cloudy circumstances, and the Cherokees were sent West on the infamous "trail of tears."

The post-1800 settlement of Alabama was basically accomplished between 1810 and 1840 by two groups: frontiersmen and pioneers from the piedmont and mountainous areas of Virginia, Tennessee, the Carolinas, and Georgia, and moderately well-off planters with their slaves from the Tidewater areas of Virginia, the Carolinas, and Georgia. The frontiersmen settled the mountain and hill country in the northern half of the state and the sandy Wiregrass area in the extreme southeast. The planters established themselves in the Black Belt and to a lesser extent in the fertile Tennessee Valley of north Alabama. In 1810 the Alabama Territory counted 9,046 black and white inhabitants. By 1830 the population of the new state had reached 309,525, and by 1860 Alabama's population was 964,201, of whom 437,770 were slaves (Griffith, 1968:154). Statehood was conferred in 1819 on the heels of a frenzied land boom that had followed Indian removal.

Politically and economically the early years in Alabama belonged to the Black Belt planters whose fortunes soared with cotton. After 1890 the planters slowly began losing their political and economic control as

Birmingham and a few other cities began to develop. The twentieth century has belonged primarily to the urban areas of Alabama: Birmingham, Mobile, Gadsden, and more lately the cities of the Tennessee Valley, which developed with relatively inexpensive electrical power from the Tennessee Valley Authority. Between 1900 and 1970 the state's larger cities posted population increases of 200 to 400 percent, while losses of 48 to 64 percent were experienced in the Black Belt and Wiregrass counties (Lineback, 1973:29). During the years of World War II the rural-to-urban migration became so intense that 44 of Alabama's 67 counties suffered losses while Birmingham grew by 30 percent and Mobile by 95 percent (Lineback, 1973:29). In 1970 the population of Alabama was almost 60 percent urban and the great rural-to-urban migration within the state had slowed considerably. Between 1960 and 1970, Huntsville, site of the enormous NASA space research center, was the state's only major urban area that showed a significant population increase. More generally, many Alabamians leaving rural areas after World War II also left the state, so that Alabama has lagged behind most Southern states and the nation as a whole in population growth.

HIGHLAND COUNTY

The first significant intrusion by white men into what is now Highland County occurred in the late eighteenth century when British agent Alexander Campbell came to stir up the Cherokee Indians against white settlers to the north and east of Alabama. Following the Revolutionary War, frontiersmen and missionaries to the Indians began filtering in from Georgia, Tennessee, and the Carolinas.

During the 1830s the population grew more rapidly and white pioneers demanded that the federal government buy the Indian lands in the county and surrounding area and remove the Indians. The treaty of New Echota of December 29, 1839, opposed by most Cherokee, ceded all remaining Cherokee lands in Tennessee, Georgia, and Alabama for $5,000,000, and troops were sent to remove the remaining Indians west to Arkansas and Oklahoma.

By 1860 the county had almost 11,000 inhabitants, of whom less than 8 percent were black (Brewer, 1964:235). As the figures suggest, most of the settlers were small farmers. Roads were poor, and the average family was large and self-sufficient. Although most of the county's inhabitants opposed the secession of Alabama from the Union in 1861, many subsequently enrolled in the Confederate army. Fortunately for the county's residents, Union troops largely bypassed the area, and fighting was limited to a few skirmishes.

With the completion of a railroad through the area from Chattanooga, Tennessee, to Birmingham in 1870 the county became less isolated and a fitful process of development began. Since 1900 the county seat has grown modestly in industry and population, while the remainder of the county experienced a slow but steady decline in population until the 1960s. The 1970 census recorded a population of about 8,500 for the county seat, a figure 20 percent above its 1960 population (U.S. Bureau of the Census, 1971).

As late as 1941, when all-weather roads were just beginning to penetrate isolated rural areas, the mountaineers of Highland County were described as being self-sufficient and living like nineteenth-century pioneers in pine-pole cabins with homemade furniture. Their language was characterized as "Elizabethan" with the active use of such words as "swarve" for serve, "holp" for help, "wrop" for wrap, "handkercher" for handkerchief, and "sarmont" for sermon (WPA Writers Program, 1941:6). Such picturesque characteristics had largely disappeared by the 1970s with roads, higher incomes, television, and the feedback from relatives who had migrated to urban areas. Industry is and has been sought by county leaders with moderate success. With completion of an interstate highway through the county, efforts have been made to develop recreational facilities in the higher elevations for "flat-land" Alabamians. Still relatively poor and underdeveloped, Highland County is, nevertheless, struggling to catch up with urban Alabama and the nation.

PIEDMONT COUNTY

White settlers began establishing themselves on small and medium-sized farms in Piedmont County between 1805 and 1815. Many were frontiersmen from the mountains of Georgia, Tennessee, and the Carolinas like those who settled in Highland County. However, a sizable number were "yeomen" or the children of yeomen who owned and managed middle-sized farms in the piedmont areas of Virginia and the Carolinas. In effect, they composed an incipient middle class of family farmers who came with more resources and more agricultural skills than had the mountaineers. These men and their families emigrated in large kin and friendship groupings after settlement areas were scouted (sometimes entire communities in the Carolinas or Georgia moved together), occupied valley land in the county's public domain, and raised cotton. The mountain folk tended to settle in the hills to raise subsistence food crops.

The present county seat was incorporated in the early 1820s with the establishment of a county government. A road from the Tennessee Valley was opened in 1822, giving farmers an early outlet for cotton and other crops. This road and the booming cotton market seem to be responsible in large part for the evolution of some medium-sized farms into small plantations. This process is evidenced by the fact that the number of slaveowners in the county increased from 113 in 1830 to 327 in 1860. Though most of the county's slaveowners had 10 slaves or fewer in 1860, 63 reportedly owned from 11 to 26, while one had 63 slaves at his beck and call.

The county's total population during that period rose from about 3,000 white and 500 black residents in 1830 to more than 11,000 whites and almost 2,000 blacks in 1860. Blacks in the latter year constituted the same proportion of the county's population as they do today (Brewer, 1964:235). The increase in Piedmont County's population during those years is especially impressive in view of the fact that many of the county's immigrants or their children left to homestead in Texas between 1845 and 1860.

Piedmont Countians wholeheartedly supported the Confederacy during the Civil War, but the county saw no major battles or sacking. After the war and into the early twentieth century, Piedmont County grew more slowly in population and in economic development. Since the 1920s the county as a whole has lagged even further behind urban Alabama in both respects, losing population in spite of higher-than-average birth rates. The county seat, nevertheless, managed to acquire a number of small and medium-sized industries (plastic products, electrical equipment, and clothing) and consequently has grown, reaching almost 5,000 inhabitants in 1970 while the rest of the county lost population (U.S. Bureau of the Census, 1971). Recently projected deep-shaft coal mines in the southern part of the county are expected to give that eminently rural and poor district a boost. Further success in attracting industry will probably continue the recent slowdown in out-migration and the slow but accelerating rise in levels of living.

PLANTATION COUNTY

Plantation and other Black Belt counties were settled after 1814 when the Indians were effectively driven south and west. By 1820 around 1,600 whites and 1,400 blacks were living in the county, and a county government was established (Brewer, 1964:37). In 1830 the white population had reached 5,000 and the black was over 4,000 (Brewer, 1964:37). The tremendous increase in slave population during this antebellum epoch attests to the equally enormous rise in cotton production and wealth. Alabama cotton production rose from 20 million pounds in 1821 to 440.5 million in 1859 (Griffith, 1968:152).

Most of Plantation County's planter class originated as such in the Tidewater areas of Georgia, the Carolinas, and Virginia. Being relatively well educated, many left good, written descriptions of their migrations from the eastern seaboard by wagon or ship. Because of wagon breakdowns and other problems the overland trip usually took an excruciating five to six weeks and involved large-scale camping out by master and slaves alike. Land in the new state or territory was usually purchased and cleared in advance of arrival.

Dr. Frank L. Owsley (1949:185) sampled the land holdings of 2,351 landowners in the Black Belt counties and found that in 1850, 65 percent owned less than the 500 acres, which he believed was the lower limit for a true plantation. Another 20.5 percent held between 501 and 1,000 acres. Thus by his measure plantation owners were a minority of farm owners even in the heart of large-scale cotton cultivation, while most were middle class yeomanry somewhat akin to the American rural ideal of the middle class farm family. Yet many such "yeomen" owned 10 or more slaves and were primarily engaged in cotton growing. The planters dominated both the Black Belt counties (Alabama's most populous area until 1900) and the state as a whole during the antebellum era. A perusal of Alabama newspapers published in the 1830s and 1840s reveals a multitude of advertisements for plantation overseers and copious news stories about plantation life, leading one to conclude that the plantation was indeed the central focus of social organization in the Black Belt region.

Although the descendants of the nineteenth-century planters during this century lost their ironclad grip on Alabama politics, they continue to control their counties of residence both politically and economically and are still influential in state politics. Relationships with their black labor force remain formal, paternalistic, and very one-sided, facts which help explain the aforementioned persistence of grinding poverty (see for example, Adelman, 1972). Nevertheless, the fruits of the civil rights movement and federal voting laws began to reach the Black Belt in the late 1960s, and newly conscious, politicized black masses are developing and demanding changes in these traditional relationships through the ballot box and the courts.

The Counties and Their Regions: Contemporary Characteristics and Comparisons

In order to evaluate the representativeness of the three counties, the basic socioeconomic characteristics of each were compared with those of the region which they represent. Thus, for example, whereas Highland County grew by about 2 percent between 1960 and 1970, the seven other counties in that highland region grew, on the average, by 6 percent. Piedmont County's population increased almost 1 percent during the 1960s while the nine other counties of the region collectively grew by 3 percent. For Plantation County the decade brought a population decrease of 13 percent, which compares with an average decline of almost 12 percent in the twelve other Black Belt counties (U.S. Bureau of the

Census, 1971). Thus in terms of population change during the 1960s each of the counties may be considered somewhat typical of its context.

A comparison of county age structures is also relevant because a very large proportion of those labeled "mentally retarded" in the United States is so classified by school systems and many of these, after leaving school, lose this label if they can fill adult roles. Therefore, the known prevalence of mental retardation will, to some extent, vary in a given community with the percentage of the population under 18 years of age. In this respect all three counties were typical of their regions in 1970. Slightly more than 34 percent of Highland County's population were under 18, while about 33 percent in the other rural counties of Appalachian Alabama were in this age group. For Piedmont County and its region the corresponding figures were 33 percent and 34 percent, while in Plantation and other Black Belt counties the under-18 age group comprised 44 and 40 percent of their respective populations (U.S. Bureau of the Census, 1972a).

Race is, statistically speaking, related to the prevalence of mental retardation, although the disentangling of the true influence of race from those of poverty and culture has yet to be established. Nevertheless, knowledge of a population's racial composition does enable one to predict with more certainty the prevalence of mental retardation, and the study counties ought to resemble the areas they represent in this respect. With regard to race, however, there is some discrepancy, although the differential is not so large as to impair representativeness. In 1970 Highland County's population was approximately 2 percent black while in the other rural Appalachian counties the proportion of blacks was around 4 percent. Piedmont County's population was 14 percent black in 1970 while in her sister hill counties 12 percent of the inhabitants were black. In Plantation County the proportion of blacks in 1970 was slightly above 68 percent while in the other Black Belt counties the proportion was about 60 percent (U.S. Bureau of the Census, 1972a).

Poverty is perhaps the most crucial contributing factor to many kinds of mental retardation both directly through its effect on health care, life style, and socialization, and indirectly through its association with low levels of formal education. Poverty also has indirect influence on the incidence of cerebral palsy and possibly epilepsy. Therefore, it is important that the study counties closely match other counties of their region in the prevalence of poverty if they are to be considered representative. Census data for 1970 reveal a fair to good approximation on several key poverty indicators. For example, median family income for 1969 in Highland County was a bit more than $5,300 while in the other Appalachian counties it averaged out at $5,400. Approximate income figures for the other two study counties and their regions were: Piedmont County—$5,500, the region—$5,900; Plantation County—$3,900, the Black Belt—$4,500 (U.S. Bureau of the Census, 1972b).

Median adult educational levels in the counties and regions were in line with the predominant kind of employment found. For the nation's adult population (those 25 years of age and over) the median years of school completed in 1970 was 12.1. In Alabama the corresponding figure was 10.8, while in Highland and Piedmont counties the medians of years completed were slightly above 9, and in Plantation County it was just below that figure. Black adults in Plantation County, however, had completed in 1970 a median of two school years less than black adults in the other two counties or the state (U.S. Bureau of the Census, 1972b). These figures indicate that the minority white population of Plantation County was better educated than the white populations of the other two counties, while Plantation County's blacks were the most severely disadvantaged group in any of the three counties studied and, therefore, the probable locus of the highest rates of disability.

Compared with their elders, younger people in the study counties and the regions they typify are obtaining much more formal education. As of 1970, 87 percent of the population 14 to 17 years of age in Highland County was still in school while 86 percent of the same group was attending school in other rural Appalachian counties. In Piedmont County 80 percent of the 14-to-17-year-olds were in school in comparison with 84 percent in the rest of that region. Strikingly, the highest percentage of school attendance for youngsters in the 14-to-17 age bracket was in Plantation County where 88 percent were enrolled as were 90 percent of that group in other Black Belt counties (U.S. Bureau of the Census, 1972b).

All told, these statistical comparisons show that: (1) Generally the three counties selected for the investigation are indeed representative of the three agricultural areas for which comprehensive information on developmental disabilities is lacking and (2) levels of living are well below the national or even the state average in rural Alabama. It is likely that levels of living in rural Alabama are on a par, however, with those found in rural areas of other Deep South states. Relatively speaking, the magnitude of prevalence, incidence, and problems for mental retardation, epilepsy, and cerebral palsy found in the three rural Alabama counties studied should be very similar to that existing in other rural areas of the Deep South. Given the high correlations between the frequency of these disabilities and low levels of living, it is likely that these handicaps have more impact in the rural South than anywhere else in the United States.

References

Adelman, Bob
    1972   Down Home. New York: McGraw-Hill.
Brewer, Willis
    1964   Alabama: Her History, Resources, War Record, and Public Men. Tuscaloosa, Ala.: Willo Publishing Co.

Griffith, Lucille
    1968   Alabama: A Documentary History to 1900. University, Ala.: The
            University of Alabama Press.
Lineback, Neal G., and Charles T. Traylor
    1973   Atlas of Alabama. University, Ala.: The University of Alabama Press.
Owsley, Frank L.
    1949   Plain Folk of the Old South. Baton Rouge, La.: Louisiana State Uni-
            versity Press.
United States Bureau of the Census
    1971   Census of Population: 1970. Number of Inhabitants, Final Report
            PC[1]-A2: Alabama. Washington, D.C.: U.S. Government Printing
            Office.
    1972a   Census of Population: 1970. General Population Characteristics. Fi-
            nal Report PC[1]-B2: Alabama. Washington, D.C.: U.S. Government
            Printing Office.
    1972b   Census of Population: 1970. General Social and Economic Charac-
            teristics. Final Report PC[1]-C2: Alabama. Washington, D.C.: U.S.
            Government Printing Office.
University of Alabama, Center for Business and Economic Research
    1973   Alabama Business. University, Ala.: Center for Business and Eco-
            nomic Research.
WPA Writers Program
    1941   Alabama, A Guide to the Deep South. New York: R. R. Smith.

CHAPTER FOUR
METHODOLOGY OF THE SAMPLE SURVEY OF THE DEVELOPMENTALLY DISABLED

M. H. ALSIKAFI

Among the main objectives of the survey of the developmentally disabled in Alabama were the following: (1) to identify the developmentally disabled and (2) to draw samples of these disabled persons to be interviewed. This procedure was followed in three counties that represented as much as possible the different sociodemographic dimensions of the population of the state. The subsequent interviews were essential so that a comprehensive analysis of the characteristics and needs of the disabled population could be undertaken. Specifically, the research team wanted to examine in detail the nature and extent of the disabilities, how these disabilities had affected the relationships between the disabled person and his family, what patterns of adjustment the disabled person had been able to achieve and, finally, what pressing needs were shaping the life of the disabled and his future improvement.

The sampling task in any study, however, must be preceded by a careful delineation of the total population that possesses the characteristics the researcher has found to be relevant and important. In the present case the task was to identify, through a variety of methods, all those developmentally disabled persons who resided in the counties selected for the study (see Chapter Three). Both tasks (the sampling and the population delineation) required formalized methodologies in each of the different research stages.

The methodological procedures followed in the sample survey of the developmentally disabled were divided into two sections. The first stage consisted mainly of defining the approximate total disabled population in the three counties. In the second phase the objective was to select representative samples of the population, which had been delineated in the first one, so that a comprehensive examination of the physical, psychological, and socioeconomic characteristics of the disabled and their families could be undertaken. The two stages of this research project were so very interrelated that it may not be realistic to set one apart from the other. Work on the planning and implementation of the two stages went on simultaneously so that time saving could be achieved. However, for the purpose of this discussion, the division between the two stages is made.

Methodological Procedures Used in
Defining the Disabled Population

Methodological procedures utilized in the first stages of this study, although varying somewhat from one community to another, share the common characteristic of being dominated by what social scientists have come to refer to as the reputational method. It involved selecting the largest possible number of knowledgeable informants in every community from whom names of the developmentally disabled and their addresses or directions to their homes were obtained. Using a somewhat similar system of classification to the one used by Mercer (1973), informants in the different communities may be divided into the following classifications:

(1) *Professional Informants*. These informants were mainly technically trained persons who come into contact with the disabled persons through technical services provided to them. Mercer (1973:67–82) labels them as clinicians. They included physicians, dentists, pharmacists, private clinics, nurses, county health officials, and other health workers.

(2) *School Systems*. Informants connected with the different school systems of the three counties consisted of school superintendents, principals, special education teachers, school psychometrists, and other teachers.

(3) *Governmental and Semigovernmental Agencies*. These are state, county, and local agencies. They included the Vocational Rehabilitation Service, county departments of health, mental health officials, county agricultural and home demonstration agents, county commissioners, county and probate judges, city chiefs of police, postmasters, and rural mail carriers.

(4) *Civic Organizations and Community Leaders*. This category included disabled parents' associations, ministers, local community leaders, store owners, owners of large landholdings, local black leaders, and people who had lived in the communities a long period of time and were therefore likely to know most of the people residing there.

(5) *Referrals from the Informants Themselves*. Finally, each informant was asked to nominate other potential informants who resided in other sections of the community or in adjacent communities. In addition, families of disabled persons (in the subsequent interviews) and their neighbors served as informants for other disabled persons whom they knew. Nominations from these sources were obtained in the early stage of delineating the disabled population and during interviews with parents and guardians of the disabled.

Nominations by professionals were secured by visits with health workers in public or private clinics or, as in a number of small communities, in their private homes. Proportionately the number of cases defined as developmentally disabled by professionals ranged from 5 percent in Plantation County to about 18 percent in Piedmont County, with Highland County occupying a middle point (15 percent). This variation probably resulted from a number of factors, among which were the numbers of the professional personnel in the county and the degree of cooperation received from them. Nominations by this category of informants were of special significance because they were medically or psychologically verified, being drawn mainly from clinical case registers. Verification of the disability, in other words, was established by medical or psychological authority.

The role played by school systems in delineating the disabled population was very crucial in the survey. Nominations given by school officials were proportionately the highest. In Plantation County these nominees accounted for 40 percent of the total names obtained by the research team (35 percent in Highland County and 34 percent in Piedmont County).

The methodological procedure involved in obtaining names of nominees from schools consisted of requesting school systems' superintendents, principals, and special education teachers to give the research team names of all students in special education classes. Except for a few cases in Plantation County, all students who were part of the school registers had been given IQ tests previously, and other psychometric measurements had been utilized additionally to verify the existence of the disability.

Turning to the remaining three types of informants presented earlier, it should be noted that, except for nominations provided by public health medical workers and departments of pensions and security, almost all of the remaining names of disabled persons were secured through the reputational method. In other words, the majority of nominees provided by governmental and semigovernmental agencies plus all the disabled names given to the research team by civic organizations, community leaders, families, and neighbors were nominated on the basis of the reputation of the disabled. As Table IV-1 shows, some 40–50 percent of the names were obtained through this approach.

The reputational method, a recent methodological technique, was transplanted by the researchers of this study from the field of community studies. Students of community structure have advanced a number of techniques mainly to help them identify community leaders and in so doing have created a methodological tradition from which investigators in other fields draw a great deal.

The roots of the reputational method lie in the different community studies that became known in the 1940s as the "Yankee City" Series, and the "Jonesville" studies. W. Lloyd Warner and his associates started a number of studies of community social life, including what sociologists

Table IV–1.
Distribution of Nominees, by Type of Informant, in the Three
Study Counties

Type of Informant	County					
	Piedmont		Highland		Plantation	
	No.	%	No.	%	No.	%
Professionals	98	18.0	176	15.0	28	5.0
Schools	185	34.0	410	35.0	220	40.0
Governmental and Semigovernmental Agencies	98	18.0	234	20.0	122	22.0
Civic Organizations	136	25.0	293	25.0	138	25.0
Families and Neighbors	27	5.0	59	5.0	44	8.0
Totals	544	100.0	1,172	100.0	552	100.0

call the social stratification of the community. They attempted to study
how members of the community related themselves to one another, and
how they perceived other members' social status in the community, their
prestige, and their reputation. (Among the most influential books in
these two series are: Warner and Lunt, 1941; Warner and Lunt, 1942;
Warner and Strole, 1945; Warner and Low, 1947; Warner, 1959; Warner, Meeker, and Eels, 1960; and Hollingshead, 1949.)

Following its initial development, the reputational method was employed by a number of disciplines and specialized areas such as studies
of political structure, community elite groups, and industrial leadership,
all leading to varying degrees of success in furthering research objectives. (The list of books that describe, utilize, or evaluate the effectiveness of the reputational method in these areas of investigation is extremely long. A few of the most relevant to the study's objectives are
Belknap and Smuckler, 1956:73–81; Blankship, 1964:207–16;
D'Antonio and Erickson, 1962:362–76; Dahl, 1958:463–69; Fox, 1969:
94–103; Freeman, 1963:791–98; Gamson, 1966:121–31; Kaufman and
Jones, 1954:205–12; Miller, 1958:9–15; Polsby, 1959b:796–803; Preston, 1969:556–62; Schulze and Blumberg, 1957:290–96; and Wolfinger, 1960:636–44.)

The reputational method reached its peak of popularity in Floyd
Hunter's study of community power structure. In this study, Hunter
used the reputational method to identify "men of power" in the Re-

gional City (Atlanta) by locating persons in prominent positions in four groups: business, government, civic, and society.

> From recognized, or nominal leaders of the groups mentioned, lists of persons presumed to have power in the community affairs were obtained. Through a process of selection utilizing a cross section of "judges" in determining leadership ranks ... a rather long list of possible leadership candidates was cut down to manageable size ... (Hunter, 1953, 11–12. See also Hunter, Schaffer, and Sheps, 1956).

Since then the reputational method has often taken at least one of the following variations: (1) The panel-of-experts form. Here the researcher assumes that in every community certain key positions may be characterized as "observational posts." Community members who occupy these positions tend to exhibit leadership qualities and can provide the researcher with information about community affairs. (2) The community sample form. In this technique the researcher selects a sample of the community's household heads who are then asked to identify the best persons to contact in the community if one needs information on certain aspects of life in that community. (3) The "snowball" form. Using this technique the researcher asks various persons in the community to name the leaders whom they think are well known. Persons who appear more frequently in the different "nominations" are then contacted for information about affairs of the community. It should be noted that a variant of the "snowball" form was utilized by the researchers in various stages of the study, especially in the early stages of identifying the leaders of the various communities and during the process of delineating the disabled population. (4) The "issues" or event form. The focus in this technique is on issues or events that are of relevance to a community. The researcher must identify those persons who contribute to the decisions aiming at proposing and implementing solutions to these issues. For more detailed description of these techniques consult Sollie (1966:301–09). Each one of these techniques has been criticized by researchers. Much of their criticism is not relevant to the objectives of this study. Suffice it to say that the criticism revolves around the role played by the informant and his competence, the establishment of an arbitrary number of leaders, and the issue of the "hidden" leaders who are not likely to be identified by the issues technique. A more comprehensive discussion of the criticism of the reputation method in general will be presented in Chapter Five of this book.

The process of applying the reputational method to achieve the research objective of identifying the approximate numbers of the developmentally disabled population required a number of modifications. First, informants were identified in practically the same manner in the three counties used in the study. The informants were chosen on the basis of their knowledge of the community or segments of it. Many of them were included in the study because of positions of authority they occupied at the time the field work was undertaken. In other words, certain key positions in the community were used as observation posts from which researchers reached to identify a significant number of disabled. Second, no formal screening of leaders was performed. Actually, every available informant was requested to nominate any other experts in community affairs or leaders they knew of, whether in their own communities or in adjacent ones.

When nominating the disabled, the interviewers implicitly used at least two basic techniques that aided informants in recalling and placing each individual in the disabled category. W. L. Warner and his associates discuss them in their methodology of measurement of social status in great detail (Warner, Meeker, and Eells, 1960). These techniques were:

(1) Trait symbolism. The informant was familiar with a trait exhibited by the disabled that provided the necessary clue to the informant to place the nominee in the disabled category. The danger in utilizing this technique is that the informant may nominate as developmentally disabled those persons who exhibit similar attributes but may have been disabled by other causes. Of course, measures were taken to minimize the probability of the occurrence of this particular problem.

(2) Status reputation. The informant was asked to ponder a range of behavior patterns engaged in by the person he was considering for nomination and evaluating him as either normal or pathological. Also, he was evaluating the moral, aesthetic, intellectual, and educational capabilities of the nominee before he decided on mentioning him as disabled. The logic of the status reputation, resting as it does on familiarity of the informant with both the behavioral manifestation of the disability and standards of acceptable behavior, is similar to the Vineland Social Maturity Scale, which was developed in the 1930s to measure the degree of mental deficiency. The scale consists of guided interviews with a person who is familiar with the behavior of the individual being evaluated. Items focus on eating, dressing, locomotion, communication, and occupation (Mercer, 1973:145).

(3) Status comparison. Here the focus is on what went on in the mind of the informant when he was nominating a person to the list of the disabled. Social psychologists stress the fact that the informant consciously or unconsciously compares the assumed disabled with a hypothetical person. He visualizes a person as possessing certain levels of physiological, intellectual, and social characteristics that make him function "adequately." The informant then uses the person as a criterion against which he "sizes up" the nominee. But the most dominant aspect of this process is the degree to which the nominee can function ade-

quately in the larger society. To cite an example based on the author's field research notes, the following description is provided:

> I asked a rural mailcarrier in a small community if he knew of any persons who were mentally retarded, cerebral palsied, or epileptic. He replied, "yes, a boy called . . . seems to act differently every time I deliver mail to the folks in his neighborhood. I don't remember seeing him playing with other kids or doing anything. He always hangs around the house. I don't think he goes to school at all. He is big but clumsy. He is slow and everybody says he is retarded."

The presence of a minor physical distortion of the face or the body of the individual being nominated by the informant may influence the informant's decision whereby he would label a person as severely disabled or even attributing more than one disability to the nominee. Mercer found that even clinicians tended to diagnose a physically disabled individual with relatively high intellectual ability as a mental retardate (Mercer, 1973:71).

Verification of Disability and the Reputational Method

The problem of verification of a supposed disability occupies a central issue in the reputational approach. The literature contains a vast amount of criticism with a great deal of emphasis being placed on the reliability and the validity of the information obtained from informants. Closely related to that criticism is the contention that the reputational method is subjective, that it lacks the technical tools necessary for diagnosing the attributes to be analyzed, and that it is "little more than a methodological variant of other procedures of asking insiders . . . for a quick rundown on the local big shots in order to identify potentially useful interviewees" (Wolfinger, 1960:637).

In this study researchers attempted to remedy these problems by using a number of verification techniques. These techniques were either deliberately applied or made use of because of the availability of such community assets as private clinics, close relationships with the community leaders, the influence and the name of the university with which the researchers were affiliated, and even the size of the communities chosen for conducting the survey. Specifically these verification techniques are summarized as follows:

First, as has already been stated, the proportion of nominations obtained from physicians, dentists, pharmacists, nurses, private clinics, and other similar facilities ranged from 5 percent to 18 percent (see Table IV-1). These disabilities have been diagnosed by specialists, and as such their cases have been clinically verified.

Second, names secured from school authorities accounted for the largest proportion of the total developmentally disabled population (30–40 percent). Except for a few cases in the Plantation County school system, students in all special education classes in the three counties had been given IQ tests by the systems' psychometrists. These tests, though not necessarily fully sufficient for the establishment of the presence of the disability, are common grounds for academic classification and placement.

Third, many of the nominees' names were suggested by two or more informants (from 9 to 14 percent, depending on the type of disability and the county included in the study). Some of the nominees were suggested by informants who belonged to different categories, such as professional and civic, or schools and neighbors.

Fourth, a rather substantial proportion of the names was suggested to the researchers by a number of governmental and semigovernmental agencies that provided either financial support or vital services to the disabled. As Table IV-1 shows, those suggested to our research team by these agencies ranged from 18 percent in Piedmont County to 22 percent in both Highland and Plantation counties. These agencies tend to verify their cases with batteries of physical and mental tests performed by physicians and psychometrists in the respective communities.

Fifth, the fact that the study was conducted in small communities is in itself a source of verification, because inhabitants of small population centers tend to know one another informally and usually are familiar with the physical and social attributes of others. In other words, the informants were acquainted with the nominees and had known their physical and social characteristics for a long time in many instances.

Sixth, finally those disabled who became members of the sample of the survey were further verified as being disabled through an extensive set of questions asked by the interviewers. The questionnaire schedule (see Appendix I) included a rather detailed inquiry about the disabled's physical, psychological, and social conditions. Those who were found lacking a true developmental disability were eliminated from the disabled samples and subsequently were not included in the final stage of analysis. They accounted for only about 8 percent of the total members of the sample.

The elimination process resulted from two considerations: (1) A rather large proportion of them (about 40 percent) denied the existence of the disability. The denial, of course, was expressed by either the parents or the companion of the disabled who responded to the questioning performed by the research interviewers. (2) Incomplete interviews due mainly to either poor circumstances surrounding the question-and-answer process or lack of understanding of the intention of the questioning on the part of the responding person.

Methodologies of the Sample Survey of the Developmentally Disabled

The methodological techniques in this stage centered around the following objectives: (1) drawing representative samples for the different disabilities and for the three counties included in the study; (2) construction of an interview schedule (an instrument) for surveying the physical, psychological, and social conditions of the samples; (3) pretesting the instrument; and (4) conducting the survey.

SAMPLING DESIGNS

The study employed several sampling techniques, each being utilized to meet a specific research objective. As was pointed out in Chapter Three, "The Research Setting," the first sampling process took place when the researchers selected three counties to represent the sociodemographic and economic conditions in the rural parts of the state and to give the researchers sufficient empirical bases for making their recommendations to mental health authorities. Each county was chosen to serve a specific objective of the study. For instance, Piedmont County was chosen for its pretest qualities, but sufficient encouragement was given so that the data from Piedmont County were included in the total pool of information. Highland County was chosen as demographically and geographically representative of a northern Alabama rural county with a large proportion of whites. Plantation County, on the other hand, was chosen as demographically and geographically representative of a southern Alabama rural county with a large percentage of blacks in the populace. A major emphasis was placed on rural population, the principal reason being the relative lack of information about these disabilities in rural areas, and the attendant problems of providing care and service for citizens of Alabama who live in such areas.

The next sampling decision was determining the number of cases to be included in the survey sample. As shown in Table IV-1 the total number of nominees obtained from informants in the three counties was 2,268. It was estimated that, given the number of interviewers and the time available, approximately 600 interviews of the above total could be undertaken.

Within each county the nominees were organized into four disability categories reflecting the goals of the survey. These categories were mental retardation, cerebral palsy, epilepsy, and multiple disability. Persons classified as multiply disabled had more than one of the disabilities mentioned above. For example, when a nominee showed a combination of mental retardation and cerebral palsy, then he was listed as multiply disabled. (It should be noted that members of the research team were assessing only the three major developmental disabilities, and that per-

haps some of the developmentally disabled persons who were listed as
being only in the categories of mental retardation, cerebral palsy, and
epilepsy had other disabilities, such as blindness, deafness, etc. Nevertheless, for the purposes of this study, such persons were not listed as
being multiply disabled.) When the first stage of the survey was completed in all the three counties the total number of nominees in each
disability was distributed as in Table IV-2.

In a limited number of cases there was confusion on the part of either
a single informant or two or more informants concerning the type of
disability and whether the nominee had more than one disability. In
these cases the more authoritative source (such as a physician, public
health nurse, or a school psychometrist as compared with a store owner
or a community leader) was used as a basis for categorization. In some
instances, entire families would be nominated as a unit. In these situations each member was assigned a number and treated as a discrete portion of the proper disability category.

It was then necessary to determine how to divide the 600 nominees
mentioned earlier among the three counties. The decision was made
that the number of interviews to be conducted in a given county would
depend on that county's proportion of the 2,268 nominees. Therefore,
since 24.0 percent of the 2,268 cases nominated came from Piedmont
County, then 24.0 percent, or 144, of the 600 household interviews were
to be conducted there. On this basis, the allocation of interviews by
county was: Piedmont, 144 (24%); Highland, 310 (52%); Plantation, 146
(24%).

The next sampling process involved choosing those nominees within
each category to be interviewed in each county. The proportions of
nominees in each disability category were calculated from the list of all

Table IV–2.
Distribution of Nominees, by Type of Disability, in
the Three Study Counties

	County					
	Piedmont		Highland		Plantation	
Disability	No.	%	No.	%	No.	%
Mental Retardation	364	66.9	896	76.4	347	62.9
Cerebral Palsy	87	16.0	111	9.5	79	14.3
Epilepsy	71	13.0	104	8.9	77	13.9
Multiple Disability	22	4.1	61	5.2	49	8.9
TOTALS	544	100.0	1,172	100.0	552	100.0
PERCENT OF TOTAL		24.0		52.0		24.0

nominees from each county. These proportions were then applied to the total number of interviews allocated to each county so that the contribution of each disability category to those totals was as shown in Table IV-3. Thus, in Piedmont County for example, a total of 544 disabled persons were nominated. Of these, 364, or 67 percent, were said to be mentally retarded. Therefore, from the total sample of 144 household interviews to be conducted in Piedmont County, 67 percent, or 96, were to deal with the mentally retarded.

The actual cases for interviewing had to be chosen from the various pools of nominees. For instance, 96 mentally retarded cases had to be chosen randomly for interviewing in Piedmont County from the 364 persons in that county who were nominated by informants as being mentally retarded. The same choice had to be made for every other disability category in each of the three counties. This task was accomplished by first assigning a number to each case nominated. Then numbers that corresponded to those assigned to the cases were picked at random from a table of random numbers until the required number of interviews for each category in each county had been drawn. For example, with respect to the 364 cases in Piedmont County nominated as mentally retarded, 96 numbers between 1 and 364 were drawn at random. Leftover numbers were placed in a pool to be used as replacements in case any of the 96 cases originally drawn could not be interviewed. This need for replacements, in fact, occurred not infrequently for a variety of reasons, such as the inability of the interviewer to locate the residence of the case chosen, especially in isolated rural areas.

INTERVIEW SCHEDULE (THE INSTRUMENT)

Developed to help guide the interviewers in their survey of the physical, social, and economic conditions of the disabled who were included in the sample, the interview schedule (see Appendix I) was uniformly used throughout the survey and in all communities. A single schedule

Table IV–3.

Distribution of Interview Cases, by Type of Disability, in the Three Study Counties

Disability	County			TOTAL
	Piedmont	Highland	Plantation	
Mental Retardation	96	237	92	425
Cerebral Palsy	23	29	21	73
Epilepsy	19	28	20	67
Multiple Disability	6	16	13	35
Totals	144	310	146	600

was used for each disabled person. Interviewers had instructions to seek
the parents of the disabled, or a guardian, or in case of the absence of
either one, to interview the person in charge of the disabled person's
safety and well-being.

The instrument contained four sections. In the initial part the interview schedule asked for information about the personal identity of the
disabled: sex, age, racial background, and the marital status of the parents. It then moved on to inquire about specifying the type of disability
and the medical diagnosis, and concluded by dealing with the functional
performance of the disabled in everyday activities.

In the second part the instrument focused on the economic activities
of the disabled person and his marital status. It elicited information regarding the job history, the type of employment, and the difficulty encountered in continuing the job performance. In the marital status section the instrument attempted to discover the length of marital
relationship and the status of any offspring of those respondents who
were married.

The third section of the instrument focused on the relationship between the disabled and social welfare agencies. The objective was to reveal the extent of dependency on these agencies, and the number of
agencies providing aid to the disabled.

The problem of institutionalization was covered in the fourth part of
the interview schedule. Here the instrument searched for information
regarding the reasons behind placing the disabled in an institution and
the extent to which institutionalization had affected the relationship between the disabled and the parents. Despite the fact that the number of
institutionalized disabled constituted a negligible proportion of the total
number of disabled, it was felt that some information about the family
of the institutionalized person and the type of relationship maintained
with him while residing in a mental institution was vital to the objectives
of the study.

The parents or the guardian of the disabled constituted the center of
attention in the next section. The emphasis was placed on the sociodemographic aspects of the parents, their level of education, and their economic well-being.

The instrument then inquired about types of assistance the parents
received when having sickness or being temporarily incapacitated. It also
attempted to discover the perception of the parents of the best possible
source of help when they found themselves in dire need.

In the next part the interview schedule contained a scale designed to
measure the effect of having a disabled member on the family's function
and solidarity. The scale had seven items dealing with such matters as
the effect on plans for trips and vacations, going to religious and en-
tertainment functions, the degree of success of the parents' marriage,

their perceived degree of happiness, location of family residence, the job of the household head, and the need and probability of the mother's employment in a position outside the household.

The final section of the instrument attempted to measure the degree of tolerance of others of the disabled person and of the difficulties encountered in understanding and accepting the reality of the disabled. Here again the objective was to reveal types of relationships between siblings and the degree of adjustment to the disability on the part of parents and other immediate members of the family.

PRETESTING THE INSTRUMENT

Two types of pretests were performed in this study. The first pretest was conducted to perfect the present method of defining and locating the disabled population. As was pointed out earlier in this chapter, Piedmont County was used at the outset of the field work as a pretest county where the effectiveness of the use of the informant system was tested. It was also pointed out that the success of the method led the research team to include the county in the actual data gathering stage so that the county was no longer merely a pretesting ground.

The second pretest was related to the interview instrument itself. For reasons of familiarity and access, Tuscaloosa County was used in order to determine whether the language and the content of the interview schedule were of sufficient clarity and effectiveness to the target population. The total number of interviews conducted in the pretest stage was 23. The individuals on whom the interview instrument was pretested represented a range of age, sex, race, and socioeconomic backgrounds. No epileptics were included in the pretest stage because of the nature of the pretesting sample (volunteers were scheduled for the interview by a local voluntary organization).

The main outcome of the pretest was comprehensive revision of the interview schedules. The revision focused primarily on the language of the questions in an attempt to simplify the structure of sentences and to make them more direct and easy to follow. It also took into consideration problems of the feelings and the emotional reaction of the respondent so that questions were phrased in such a way as to avoid any stigmatizing effect that might develop in the course of the interview.

CONDUCTING THE INTERVIEW

The methodology of this stage was guided by two objectives. First, information was sought about the family characteristics of the disabled population, and secondly, attempts were made to elicit the thoughts and feelings of this population with respect to those things that they thought would be most helpful to them. The interview schedule attempted to achieve these two objectives by providing a series of questions that were used uniformly by a field research team specifically trained for that purpose.

The field researchers were teamed up in groups of two so that one member would state the questions to the parents or the guardian of the disabled while the other would record the response on the interview schedule. Because of the nature of the subject of the interview and the level of education of the respondents, no sound recording was used.

It must be noted that most respondents in this study were characterized by low socioeconomic levels, which were clearly manifested in the type of occupations reported. The amount of income earned and the level of education achieved by them were relatively low. The interview schedule was designed with these factors in mind, also considering that most respondents lived in rural areas. The language of the questions was rather simple and direct, and almost void of technical terms.

The element of time was also a significant consideration in conducting the interview. The time factor was important in two considerations. First, the fact that many of the respondents lived in scattered areas, somewhat remote from town centers, and sometimes off the main routes of travel, accounted for a rather long time needed to complete a single interview. The second consideration was that the subject matter of the interview was potentially depressing, since it might remind the respondent of some painful memories. Such being the case, the interviewers were careful in avoiding overt approval or disapproval behavior.

While conducting the interview, the two members of the team attempted to use their impressions of the physical surroundings, the type of relationships among members of the family, and other aspects of the household as significant sources of verifying responses given to them by the parents or the guardians. They also attempted to observe the disabled, especially if he were mentally retarded, cerebral palsied, or multiply disabled to assess the degree of disability. Although such observations lacked uniformity and a standardized procedure, they were necessary for the continuity of the interview since some parents or guardians tended to deny the existence of the disability.

References

Belknap, G., and R. Smuckler
    1956   "Political power relations in a mid-west city." Public Opinion Quarterly 20 (Spring):73–81.
Blankship, L. V.
    1964   "Community power and decision making: a comparative evaluation of measurement techniques." Social Forces 43 (December):207–16.

Dahle, R. A.
  1958   "A critique of the ruling elite model." American Political Science Re-
          view 52 (June):463–69.

D'Antonio, W., and E. C. Erickson
  1962   "The reputational techniques as a measure of community power: an
          evaluation based on comparative and longitudinal studies." Ameri-
          can Sociological Review 26 (June):362–76.

Fox, D. M.
  1969   "The identification of community leaders by the reputational and de-
          cisional methods: three case studies and an empirical analysis of the
          literature." Sociology and Social Research 54 (October):94–103.

Freeman, L.
  1963   "Locating leaders in local communities: a comparison of some alter-
          native approaches." American Sociological Review 28 (October):
          791–98.

Gamson, W. A.
  1966   "Reputation and resources in community politics." American Journal
          of Sociology 72 (September):121–31.

Hollingshead, A. B.
  1949   Elmtown's Youth. New York: Wiley.

Hunter, F.
  1953   Community Power Structure: A Study of Decision Makers. Chapel
          Hill: University of North Carolina Press.

Hunter, F., R. C. Schaffer, and C. G. Sheps
  1956   Community Organization: Action and Inaction. Chapel Hill: Univer-
          sity of North Carolina Press.

Kaufman, H., and V. Jones
  1954   "The mystery of power." Public Administration Review 14
          (March):205–12.

Mercer, Jane R.
  1973   Labeling the Mentally Retarded: Clinical and Social System Perspec-
          tives on Mental Retardation. Berkeley: University of California Press.

Miller, D. C.
  1958   "Industry and community power structures: a comparative study of
          an American and an English city." American Sociological Review 23
          (February):9–15.

Polsby, N. W.
  1959a   "The sociology of community power: a reassessment." Social Forces
          37 (March):232–36.
  1959b   "Three problems in the analysis of community power." American So-
          ciological Review 24 (December):796–803.

Preston, J. D.
  1969   "A comparative methodology for identifying community leaders."
          Rural Sociology 34 (December):556–62.

Schulze, Robert O., and L. U. Blumberg
  1957   "The determination of local power elites." American Journal of So-
          ciology 63 (November):290–96.

Sollie, C. R.
    1966   "A comparison of reputational techniques for identifying community leaders." Rural Sociology 31 (September):301–09.
Warner, W. L.
    1959   The Living and the Dead. New Haven: Yale University Press.
Warner, W. L., and J. O. Low
    1947   The Social System of the Modern Factory. New Haven: Yale University Press.
Warner, W. L., and P. S. Lunt
    1941   The Social Life of Modern Community. New Haven: Yale University Press.
    1942   The Status System of Modern Community. New Haven: Yale University Press.
Warner, W. L., M. Meeker, and K. Eells
    1960   Social Class in America. New York: Harper & Row, Publishers.
Warner, W. L., and L. Srole
    1945   The Social Systems of American Ethnic Groups. New Haven: Yale University Press.
Wolfinger, R. W.
    1960   "Reputation and reality in the study of community power." American Sociological Review 24 (October):636–44.

PART III: FINDINGS OF THE SURVEY

CHAPTER FIVE
PROBLEMS ASSOCIATED WITH IDENTIFYING THE DEVELOPMENTALLY DISABLED

J. SELWYN HOLLINGSWORTH AND M. H. ALSIKAFI

A principal objective of P.L. 91-517, the Developmental Disabilities Facilities and Construction Act, is to "plug the gaps," so to speak, in the services that currently are being offered to persons who are developmentally disabled. A major problem in implementing the provisions of the Act is the location and identification of such persons. As will be evidenced in Chapter Nine of this volume, various agencies and facilities in Alabama offer services to persons suffering from mental retardation, cerebral palsy, and epilepsy. However, the fact that no *one* agency has been designated as having responsibility for serving *all* the developmentally disabled persons in a given area makes the task of identifying them an almost impossible one. Bits and pieces of this necessary information are available from some agencies, but largely unavailable from others.

If the greatest amount of benefits available to each potential client is to be provided, and if each facility is to be supported so as to be operated in the most efficient manner, then the identification of the target population becomes a factor of paramount importance. A relatively accurate knowledge of the numbers of persons to be benefited by a particular piece of legislation is often a prerequisite to its passage and funding. (It is recognized readily, however, that not every individual who is classified as being developmentally disabled necessarily wants or needs the services available to him.)

In this survey, almost every respondent who was interviewed indicated a need of some kind that was not presently being met satisfactorily, in his opinion (see Chapter Eight). Therefore, the lack of knowledge about assistance agencies and the subsequent lack of knowledge of service center personnel concerning some of the population in need of their services constitute a serious problem. There are several reasons for the occurrence of this phenomenon.

In many instances, the developmentally disabled person or his family was not aware that certain services were available. In some situations, the needed services were not offered at a readily accessible local center. In still others, agencies offering the necessary advantages were so distant that access to them was of considerable inconvenience.

Oftentimes, parents of disabled children experience difficulty in accepting the fact that their child is not completely "normal." In some cases, this problem results from a sense of guilt feelings in the case of the parents, though often these emotions are unfounded. Likewise, some parents consider the social stigma of having a disabled child too great a strain on them, but most often do not wish to see the child characterized as being somehow "different" from other children. Still other parents with a disabled child face the challenge and regard him as "special."

In the case of epilepsy, many states have laws that prohibit epileptics from having a driver's license. Since many cases of epilepsy may be controlled completely through the use of such drugs as dilantin, phenobarbitol, and mysoline, people tend not to report the disability, because it poses no immediate problems to them, and its reporting would create problems that, in their minds, would outweigh the potential benefits.

Therefore, these and many other difficulties occur in the correct labeling of a person with one or more of the developmental disabilities. Not the least of these is a clinical, objective determination of the nature and scope of the problem (see Mercer, 1973). It is not unusual for a person to find it necessary to undergo a series of tests, often spread over a period of time, in order to assess his disability. The acceptance of the existence of the disability by the parents and by siblings is often quite another problem.

For purposes of obtaining funding, most writers of service proposals find it necessary to include an indication of the numbers of persons to be served by the requested funds. Thus, a dilemma arises in accurately estimating the numbers of persons with each of the disabilities and the degree of the disability affecting each one.

Alternative Approaches to Identifying the Developmentally Disabled Population in a Given Area

Various alternative approaches to identifying those who are developmentally disabled within a given area have been employed, not all of which will be discussed at the present time. It is readily recognized that some of these approaches yield more reliable information than others, and that some produce better results with certain subpopulations.

SELF-REPORTING

Some studies have utilized self-reporting as a means of identifying the disabled population. Projects of this particular nature require much general advance publicity of a positive, reassuring nature. For many of the reasons already discussed in this chapter, the self-reporting technique quite often results in notable understatements of the problem. Even if some of the previously mentioned factors are not at work, the lack of an informed populace and of sufficient motivation to self-report is often strong enough to preclude the use of this particular methodology.

PHYSICIANS' REPORTS

Reports by medical doctors have been utilized as one method and are more likely to meet with a greater probability of success in studies of the *incidence* of a disease or disability over short periods of time. Nevertheless, it is often difficult to obtain complete cooperation from doctors, who have so many previous demands on their time. Unless the subject under study is required by law to be reported, many cases are never reported. Even so, many cases would go unreported. Another, different problem is an *absolute verification* of the type and degree of disability. For example, cerebral palsy and epilepsy would be easier for doctors to ascertain than would the degree of mental retardation, because medical doctors are not usually confronted with the latter problem, as such, on a medical basis.

Furthermore, physicians are often hesitant to reveal the names of persons who are afflicted because of a certain sense of loyalty to their patients. In addition, the possible legal complications that may result are another deterrent. The confidentiality of a patient's problems is a barrier for many doctors who may be very sympathetic with the research goals.

If doctors are to be asked to furnish information on *each* developmentally disabled person, as would be the case in a study of prevalence rates, then the task becomes a much more formidable one. Most physicians have such large caseloads that they cannot possibly remember every person who is a victim of one or more of the developmental disabilities. A search of their medical files is precluded because of the inordinate amount of time necessary to devote to the task, not to mention the judgmental decisions that would need to be made.

Nevertheless, in studies where doctors are asked to report cases of one or more of the developmental disabilities (cf. Wolfe and Reid, 1971), a decided advantage is that an absolute clinical verification of the disability is usually available. In general, however, this particular method may not be widely employed because of its problematical nature to the physicians themselves.

AGENCY REPORTS

Another approach utilized to a certain extent is to ask agencies and facilities charged with the treatment of the various disabilities to report their caseloads. Because of heavy workloads, and because many facilities do not maintain their individual case records in such a manner as to permit an easy retrieval of the data in the form in which they are needed, this technique is not without its shortcomings. Nevertheless, the use of this approach is of tremendous value in learning of those persons who are currently receiving services. A further difficulty encountered in using this method is that often the agencies are not permitted to release names of persons on their caseloads without obtaining prior written consent in each case, a process involving an inordinate amount of time and work.

PREVIOUS RESEARCH AS AN INDICATOR

Still other researchers decide to base their estimates of prevalence of a particular developmental disability on rates obtained in previous studies of prevalence or on national estimates from a variety of sources. As revealed in Chapter Six, this method, too, is not without its problems. First is the fact that for each disability, a number of investigations have reported widely divergent rates of prevalence and/or incidence. The interested researcher is in a dilemma because of the differences in estimates of prevalence reported by the various studies.

Reasons for these differences are several. A careful review of the population studied in each previous report may reveal differences caused by the fact that the report deals with only one of the various characteristics that account for differences in prevalence. Age is a good example, while another is the sex of the respondent. Still another problem is that some scientists use one criterion for determining the existence of a disability, while others use a number of different criteria. For example, some define mental retardation as evidenced by an IQ of 84 or below, while others may use an IQ of 70 or below as their basis. The person attempting to base his estimates on previous studies must decide which most specifically meets his needs and which is most applicable to his target population.

Another type of approach to identifying the developmentally disabled in a given population has resulted from a combination of two or more of the above-mentioned techniques. Through the use of large-scale publicity campaigns, citizens in a certain area have been requested to report to a given place for physical and mental examinations if they suffered certain symptoms. There, they have undergone extensive testing in order to permit an evaluation of the symptoms, either confirming or denying the existence of one of the disabilities. This procedure was utilized in Georgia by Wishik (1956).

Problems Associated with the Use of the Reputational Approach in Locating and Identifying the Developmentally Disabled

In Chapter Four of this work, Dr. Alsikafi has discussed the nature, origin, and development of the various types of the reputational method.

Likewise, he has alluded to the most serious problems associated with the technique, namely the verification of the disability, and the technical competence of the average informant. The current discussion shall center on the implications of these problems for the validity and accuracy of the logic of the reputational approach.

Obviously, a major problem in utilizing the reputational method, as outlined above, is the selection of a sufficient number of qualified informants. By entering a given community and talking with key persons in the most functional community roles, this problem is not a serious one in rural areas, such as the ones where the interviews conducted in the present study occurred. Furthermore, the informants must be dispersed (in a geographic manner) in order to assure relatively complete coverage of the area. Additionally, all significant subgroups should be represented. The reputational method, as formulated in this research, would be much more difficult to implement in urban areas.

A problem related to the selection of informants is that of their competence in making the nominations. Many of them are not fully aware of all the ramifications of mental retardation, cerebral palsy, and epilepsy, thus it is often necessary to utilize trait symbolism and status reputation, as discussed in the previous chapter. Furthermore, some potential respondents are somewhat hesitant to reveal names and addresses to strangers on a matter of such sensitivity. Most of them can be persuaded by stressing the confidentiality of their information and by restating the importance of the data for their local region. An associated problem, the thorn in the paw, so to speak, with the reputational method, is that of verification, a matter covered in the previous chapter.

The proper training of the persons conducting the interviews assumes paramount importance. They must be able to probe without meddling, be able to reassure a hesitant informant, etc. For this purpose, persons of a rural background quite often encounter fewer difficulties in dealing with rural people. In the case of the present project, it was found that persons with Southern accents got far better receptions than did persons lacking such a facility or of persons with distinctly Northern accents. Thus, the interviewer must be one with whom the persons being interviewed can relate and must permit the easy establishment of rapport.

Another method of obtaining information on the developmentally disabled population of the three counties, that is, from agencies and facilities which provide services, is not without its problems. First, many agencies maintain their own files using state agency-formulated procedures, many of which do not record the developmental disabilities as such. They more often are set up to meet immediate medical and other physical problems. The retrieval of the names from voluminous files would require a tremendous amount of time and effort, which the personnel of many of the agencies simply do not possess. Compounding the problem is the fact that many agencies do not have the legal authority to release the names of their clients without first obtaining written permission of the parents or guardians of the disabled person.

Finally, another problem encountered in the utilization of the reputational approach is knowing when the interviewing process is complete enough to halt the work. Obviously, if many of the names being obtained on each subsequent day are duplicates of names already placed in nomination, this fact would in itself indicate that perhaps the work has been mostly accomplished. Another matter is to be assured that all geographic areas have been covered thoroughly, as well as all subpopulations.

With all the problems encountered in using the reputational approach, one may wonder why the researchers in the present project decided to use it. In spite of all the difficulties, the method has proved to be a highly reliable one, as will be seen when comparing the results with information obtained from other channels. The drawbacks listed herein are merely intended to advise the potential users of the procedure of some of the difficulties they may encounter.

Evaluation of the Logic of the Reputational Method

It was pointed out in Chapter Four that the reputational method used in this work is a transplant from community studies dealing with power structure. In these studies the reputational method was used either as a comprehensive technique for discovering the distribution of power in the community (e.g., Hunter's Community Power Structure), or as a guide to knowledgeable members of the community who would in turn give the researcher leads to other informants (e.g., Form and Miller's study of industry and business leaders). It is the latter technique (basically similar to the one used in this study) that was subjected to the lesser criticism, although critics like Wolfinger maintain that in its low-keyed technique, this form of reputational method "is little more than a methodologically elaborate variant of the older procedure of asking insiders . . . for a quick rundown on the local big shots in order to identify potentially useful interviewees" (Wolfinger, 1960:637).

The logic of the reputational method has come under strong criticism by statistically minded community researchers. Their argument centers around the fact that informants and leaders are not selected randomly from the larger population of the community; rather they are individuals presumed to be knowledgeable because of the formal positions they occupy in the social structure of the community (Schulze and Blumberg, 1957:290–96). This criticism may well apply to the process of delineation of leaders and informants in the present study. However, the principle of representativeness did not suffer because a form of "snow-balling" was instituted in the early stages of the study whereby first-encountered leaders were asked to name other leaders or knowledgeable informants and those, in turn, were also requested to nominate further knowledgeable persons in the community. Furthermore, since the communities covered in the study were rather small, the likelihood of missing in "sampling" became very minute indeed.

Closely related to the problem of sampling is the tendency of the reputational method to favor selection of the elite members of the community. After all, reputation, by definition, implies that the person is known and has established contacts with other members of the community. This idea is contrasted with "issue studies" methodology in which community leadership is assumed to be pluralistic in structure, and knowledgeable informants tend to shift from one category of the population to another depending on the issue investigated by the researcher. For a detailed analysis of these aspects of community studies see Preston (1969:556–62).

The question remaining to be answered is the gap that might exist between the reputation a person establishes in the community and the actual behavior in which he engages in his daily contacts with other members of the community. An effective reputational approach must confine its contacts to those members of the community whose behavior in the main justifies their repute as knowledgeable informants (Polsby, 1959:796–803).

In one sense the issue in this research project is that of a possible gap between the reputed knowledge or influence of persons or organizations as perceived by others, or defined by the opinions of community members, and the actual influence or knowledge as shown by the roles played by these persons in determining an outcome of significance to the community. In other words, the researcher must be cognizant of the difference between the assumed reputation of a community member as seen by others and the influence that person actually possesses in issues critical to the community's well-being. A methodological solution to this problem is provided by Form and Miller (1960). They suggest the use of "judges" who are asked to evaluate the influence of the reputed persons. Also, the researcher simply tallies the frequency of nominations of a person and assigns higher marks to those who are mentioned more frequently. The assumption being made is that the frequency of nomination is an adequate indicant of the reputed degree of knowledge of a person. Foskett and Hohle (1957:148–54) report a correlation of .83 ± .04 between frequency of nomination and the degree of influence a leader has in the community as estimated by "judges."

The core of the evaluation of the logic of the reputational method lies in the problems of validity and reliability. The former is basically a question of whether the researcher and the informant have identical conceptions of what constitutes the phenomenon they are trying to delineate, and the latter is an account of the application of the definition to a large number of cases. A researcher would ask such questions as: "Are the informant and I dealing with the same thing, and does this same thing apply to all the cases nominated by all informants in all communities covered in the research?"

A survey of literature dealing with the reputational method shows varying results. On one hand critics emphasize the subjective side of the methodology. A researcher asking questions based upon his complicated conception of the object he is seeking to delineate, they maintain, can either inflict his definition of that object on each respondent, or use a simplified analogous question. In either case the validity of the method suffers. Furthermore, differences in the conception of the phenomenon among individuals living in different communities make the consistency of a precise identification of the phenomenon extremely difficult (see for instance Dahle, 1958:463–69). Proponents of the reputational approach, on the other hand, contend that studies in a vast number of communities show that "reputation and action join" (Blankship, 1964: 207–16), and that a considerable overlap exists between reputed and actual realities (Gamson, 1966:121–31).

In conclusion, one must recognize that the reputational logic is essentially subjective but that this subjectivity is also inherent in other, more clinically oriented procedures. Researchers who applied the reputational technique in their community studies seem to be aware of this limitation. Few, if any, make claim to its infallibility.

Nevertheless, checks of other, independent records in the three counties in which the surveys were conducted reveal that, of all the methods that might have been employed, perhaps the reputational method was a good choice. This observation is especially the case when one considers the financial, personnel, time, and other resource limitations involved in this and similar investigations.

References

Blankship, L. V.
   1964   "Community power and decision making: a comparative evaluation of measurement techniques." Social Forces 43 (December):207–16.
Dahle, R. A.
   1958   "A critique of the ruling elite model." American Political Science Review 52 (June):463–69.
Form, W. H., and D. C. Miller
   1960   Industry, Labor and Community. New York: Harper & Row, Publishers.
Foskett, J., and R. Hohle
   1957   "The measurement of influence in community affairs." Proceedings of the Pacific Sociological Society, Research Studies of the State College of Washington (June):148–54.

Gamson, W. A.
    1966   "Reputation and resources in community politics." American Journal of Sociology 72 (September):121–31.

Polsby, N. W.
    1959   "Three problems in the analysis of community power." American Sociological Review 24 (December):796–803.

Preston, J. D.
    1969   "A comparative methodology for identifying community leaders." Rural Sociology 34 (December):556–62.

Schulze, Robert O., and L. U. Blumberg
    1957   "The determination of local power elites." American Journal of Sociology 63 (November):290–96.

Wishik, Samuel M.
    1956   "Handicapped children in Georgia: a study of prevalence, disability, needs and resources." American Journal of Public Health 46:195–203.

Wolfe, W. G., and L. Leon Reid
    1958   A Survey of Cerebral Palsy in Texas. Austin: United Cerebral Palsy of Texas.

Wolfinger, R. W.
    1960   "Reputation and reality in the study of community power." American Sociological Review 24 (October):636–44.

CHAPTER SIX
THE PREVALENCE OF THE DEVELOPMENTAL DISABILITIES IN ALABAMA: ESTIMATES

As was indicated in Chapter One of this book, approximately 5.5 million people currently residing in the United States are said to be mentally retarded, while another 2 million have epilepsy, and some 750,000 persons are affected by cerebral palsy. Thus, somewhere over 8 million people in our country suffer directly the effects of the developmental disabilities. These numbers represent estimates of *prevalence* of these conditions, a term that refers to the total number of persons within a defined area, such as a state, who have the condition at a given time. *Incidence*, another term often used to indicate the numbers of people who have certain conditions and/or diseases, represents the number of new cases reported within a year. This report shall deal specifically with the *prevalence* of the three disabling conditions in Alabama, not with their incidence.

In the state of Alabama, estimates generated by this survey place the prevalence of mental retardation at 109,277, epilepsy at 19,620, and cerebral palsy at 4,718 (Hollingsworth, 1974:30–42). Thus approximately 133,615 persons in the state are affected directly to some degree by the developmental disabilities, according to the estimates. However, the human effects of these conditions are much more far-reaching than a mere recital of the numbers of persons with these conditions would appear to indicate, for all of us bear the tax burden required to provide even minimal services to a small proportion of these people. Additionally, the parents and friends of persons with one or more of the disabling conditions feel the effects much more than do others.

Thus far, the developmental disabilities have been discussed as if they existed separately from each other, although it has been implied that often a person has more than one of the disabling conditions. Conley (1973) estimates that about 2 percent of the mentally retarded also suffer from cerebral palsy; while the United Cerebral Palsy Association (1973) indicates that between 50 and 80 percent of the cerebral palsied are also retarded. Approximately 4 percent of the epileptic population are retarded. Additionally, estimates by Conley (1973) indicate the further involvement of the retarded with other disabilities: 8 to 12 percent of the mentally retarded also have some degree of hearing loss, while

15 percent of the deaf are retarded; and 25 percent of the blind children are retarded.

Why is such an emphasis placed on the numbers of people involved? Why cannot one just "get down to brass tacks," so to speak, and discuss some of the major problems that directly affect developmentally disabled persons and seek their solutions?

Actually, a major concern in efforts of researchers and planners alike in dealing with the problems of mental retardation, cerebral palsy, and epilepsy has been an accurate assessment of the numbers of people who are directly affected by these disabilities. Careful estimates of the numbers of people who are developmentally disabled in a given area are fundamental to the planning of facilities and services. Furthermore, ideas of the demographic, social, and economic characteristics of the indicated population are of added significance. All of this and other information are of the utmost need and importance if people in planning and action positions are to be able to proceed on a sound basis. Indeed, since the inception of the project from which this book is a result, requests have come from agencies and individuals all over the state of Alabama for detailed information regarding the numbers of people with those conditions in their areas.

A knowledge of the numbers of people affected is essential, furthermore, because funding agencies have need of information concerning both the scope and the effects of their endeavors. Legislators appear to be more willing to appropriate monies if they can have an estimate of the numbers of persons to be benefited by their actions. Thus, any group seeking funds to provide services to developmentally disabled persons must have relatively reliable estimates of the numbers of persons likely to be affected in order, first of all, to secure funding, and secondly, to assess accurately the scope of their operations.

An exact and complete census of the population under discussion would be ideal in such cases. Indeed, this kind of information has often been sought, but so far these efforts have not been highly successful, insofar as is known to the present author. Therefore, it has been necessary for planners to devise techniques that carefully and accurately estimate the numbers of such people who reside in any given area.

A major reason why efforts to assess accurately the numbers of persons in a given region who suffer from mental retardation, cerebral palsy, and epilepsy have fallen short of their goals has been the stigma that has traditionally been attached to these and other handicaps. Some parents do not want it known to others that their child is not completely "normal." Agencies involved in assisting this segment of the population are often reluctant to release names and addresses of the persons under their jurisdiction because of the possible legal complications that may result. Yet, this information is exactly the type needed in order to make accurate counts of persons so afflicted. Data revealing a positive identification are of utmost importance since it is a known fact that some individuals receive assistance from more than one source and thus the same names may appear on more than one list, causing some to be counted more than once, if the researcher uses only the *numbers* of persons receiving assistance from each agency or facility. Reliable sources indicate that many of the substantially handicapped do indeed receive assistance from more than one source.

In the case of mental retardation, many scientists believe that it is possible to obtain fairly accurate estimates by using the normal (or bell-shaped curve) distribution. This approximation may not be very far off. Nevertheless, past studies have revealed that certain *types* of populations are more likely than others to be affected in greater proportions by the developmental disabilities. Thus, the need arises to have more accurate detailed information relating to the social, demographic, and economic characteristics of these people and of the prevalence of each disability, which varies according to differences in the compositions of these important factors in any given population.

In the past, persons interested in the developmental disabilities have used various methods in arriving at estimates of the persons so involved. These estimates have varied quite broadly, as may be seen from observing Tables VI-1, VI-2, and VI-3.

The careful observer will note wide discrepancies among the various estimates noted in the tables. For example, estimates of prevalence for the mentally retarded were between 2/1000 and 184/1000; those for cerebral palsy, between 1.1/1000 and 4/1000; while for epilepsy the estimates ranged between .622/1000 and 18.6/1000. What factors account for these great differences? Which are the "best" estimates, the most accurate? Which rates does one utilize in making estimates to be incorporated in plans for a given county, region, or state? If accurate estimates are so basic to health facility planners, then where does one turn in his efforts to assess accurately the magnitude of these problems?

First, it should be noted that the estimates were, by and large, taken of different populations: that is, some covered only limited ranges of ages (the developmental disabilities occur in varying frequencies in different age groups); they were taken in different parts of the country with widely disparate economic and demographic characteristics; some used one criterion, others used quite another (or used sets of them); and they were made at various stages in the development of knowledge about each of the individual disabilities. The researchers furthermore used different criteria for validating the disability; for example, some of the estimates were based on clinical criteria, others on reported cases, and still others utilized a variety of bases.

Table VI–1.
Selected Estimates of the Prevalence of Mental Retardation

Author	Community	Year	Ages	Upper IQ Limit	Population	Prevalence (Rate/1000)
Lemkau, et al.	Eastern Health District, Baltimore	1936	All	70	55,000	12
Gruenberg	Onondaga County, New York	1953	1–17	90+	108,000	35
Jastak, et al.	Delaware	1953–54	10–64	Combination of various factors	2,002	
2% level						4
9% level						20
25% level						83
Wishik	Clarke and Oconee Counties, Georgia	1954	0–20	79	16,082	37
Levinson	Maine	1957	5–20	75	148,000	32
Kennedy, et al.	Five Southeastern states	1960–61	6–14	69	1,800	184
Richardson, et al.	North Carolina:	1961–62				
	Alamance County, Household Study		0–20	70	1,373	79
	Halifax County, Clinical Study		0–20		–	90
	Household Study		0–20		2,600	77
Taylor	Oregon	1962	0–20	75	215,000	19

Table VI-1. (continued)
Selected Estimates of the Prevalence of Mental Retardation

Author	Community	Year	Ages	Upper IQ Limit	Population	Prevalence (Rate/1000)
Inre	Maryland (unspecified county)	1965	1–59	69	14,500	82
U.S. Dept. of HEW	United States	1965–67	All	TMR's	Health Interview Survey	2
Los Angeles Mental Retardation Board	California	1969	All	Unspecified	State Residents Needing Services	1.8

Table VI–2.
Selected Estimates of the Prevalence of Cerebral Palsy

Author	Location	Date	Source	Population	Prevalence (Rate/1000)
Joint Committee	New York State Schenectady County	1948	General Population Known Cases, (10% population sample)	All Ages Under 18	1.52 2.18
Schlesinger, et al.	Upstate New York	1950–52	Reported Cases	Under 18	1.35
Phelps	Maryland	1951	General Population (agencies)	6 years +	4
Connecticut State Dept. of Health	Connecticut	1951	Agencies and Physicians	1200 cases under 21	2.65 to 3.10
Altman	United Cerebral Palsy Association (National)	1955	Composite of New York, Maryland, Chicago, and Connecticut data	–	3.0 to 3.5
Wolfe and Reid	Texas	1958	Known C. P.'s were referred	5,615	1.1
U.S. Dept. of HEW	United States	1965–67	Health Interview Survey	All	2

Table VI–3.
Selected Estimates of the Prevalence of Epilepsy

Author	Community	Date	Source	Population	Prevalence
Malzberg	Nassau County, New York	1916	Population (highly rural)	General total county	.622
Anderson	Michigan	1930	Population Survey	73,056	2.1
Malzberg	United States	1940	Army Draftees	2,000,000	5.15
Lennox	United States	1940	Army Draftees	2,500,000	7.9
Baldwin, et al.	Maryland	1950–52	Population Survey	796,870	2
Lesser and Hunt	United States	1952	Population Survey	1,375,000	5
Zielinski	Not Specified	1972	Review of Literature	General	3.6
Wishik	Clarke-Oconee Counties, Georgia	1956	Population Survey (21 years)	16,082	3.8
Hauser and Kurland	Rochester, Minn.	1940	Population Survey		3.7
		1950			5.3
		1960			6.2
		1965			5.7
Brewis, et al.	Carlisle, England	1966	Household Survey	70,000 (6,960 sample)	5.1
Pond, et al.	English Community	1960	Clinic Patients		6.2
Leibowitz and Alter	Jerusalem, Israel	1958–61	Unspecified	—	4.1
Wajsbort, et al.	Northern Israel	1967	Unspecified	—	2.3
Gudmondsson	Iceland	1966	Unspecified	177,000	4.6
Krohn	Northern Norway	1957–60	Clinic Cases	—	3.6
Levy, et al.	Southern Rhodesian reserve	1964	Unspecified	—	7.4
Bird, et al.	Africa	1962	Bantu gold miners (male)	—	3.7

Lione	Not Specified	1961	Oil refinery employees	58	6.0
U.S. Dept. of HEW	United States	1965–67	Health Interview Survey	—	3.1
Olivares	Mexico City	1971	Government employees and families	2,169	3.5
Weinberg	Not reported	—	8–9½ year old male pupils	319	5.9
Edwards, et al.	United States	1942	Selective Service registrants	121,700	3.7
Bailey, et al.	United States	1929	Selective Service registrants	549,099	3.3
			U.S. Army	3,500,000	2.1
Ueki and Sato	Niigata, Japan	1963	Hospital Records	100,000	1.5
Rose, et al.	Washington County, Maryland	1972	8–9 year old male pupils	2,064	18.6
Logan and Cushion	England-Wales	1955	Unspecified	1,260	3.3
Henrikson and Krohn	Northern Norway	1965	Unspecified	1,750	3.7

It has already been noted that reliable estimates of the prevalence of mental retardation, cerebral palsy, and epilepsy are essential in the planning of services designed to assist people affected by these conditions. This point is painfully clear. Therefore, the senior participants in this project surveyed vast amounts of epidemiological literature related to these conditions in order to find the most suitable prevalence rates that would be applicable specifically to Alabama. Major concerns included the fact that the estimates be based on age, sex, and race. Because these factors were the variables most often reported, and because they have been reported as being accountable for basic differentials, it was felt that they should constitute a minimal basis for any such projections involving people in the state of Alabama.

The vast amount of epidemiological literature related to epilepsy, cerebral palsy, and mental retardation may be divided into two broad groupings:

(1) "Conference table" or "eyeballing." Literature of this nature usually focuses on conferences held with panels of experts who get together and report estimates of prevalence rates based on their own expertise for a given disability. In most of these cases, one rate is projected (frequently numerical) to a "general" population. *Specific* generalizations in connection with the establishment of such a rate are *non-numerical*, e.g., blacks have rates higher than whites, males higher than females, etc.

(2) Empirical studies. These studies may be classified as either household surveys, clinical diagnoses, questionnaire surveys, or a combination of two or more of these approaches. Apart from the strong tendency to examine prevalence in minute detail within a disability (e.g., *types* of mental retardation)—particularly with clinical diagnosis, there is even a stronger tendency to try to generalize to the United States population as a whole.

With the various sources of data on disabling disabilities, the researchers faced several considerations in trying to establish prevalence rates to be applied to Alabama. They concluded that:

(1) The use of "eyeball" rates are of questionable value, or at best, are based on several considerations. Numerical values established simply by one's expert knowledge or by reviewing the literature have little mathematical meaning, although they may be relatively accurate, since they have been elaborated by experts. However, they do not consider variations in the methodology of various studies or changing demographic characteristics of the population. Even if such variations are considered, the fact that they are evaluated (and exactly what those factors are) is rarely reported to the reviewer. National agencies and President's commissions represent only two of many examples. These reports, addressed to a large segment of the American population, highlight many

basic and relevant facts concerning a disorder, *but they do not constitute a basis for sound professional demographic-sociological projections*.

(2) Many empirical studies, although methodologically sound, do not report materials needed for demographic projections. Although the data are undoubtedly there, journal articles report summaries and general rates rather than the specific rates, in sufficient detail, which are needed for projections. This problem is not so acute for mental retardation as it is for the other two disabilities.

(3) Fallacy of "general rates"—general rates represent a mathematical composite of many specific rates. For this reason, the application of a general rate to a small areal unit such as a county assumes complete homogeneity between the areal unit and the total unit upon which the general rate is based. An example would be the application of a general mental retardation rate of 3 percent to a predominantly black-populated county to estimate prevalence there, when it has been widely reported that the disability is much more likely to affect blacks than whites.

The above are only three considerations of importance. Other considerations involve definition and methodology. On the basis of an overall evaluation of the literature on prevalence, several factors must be carefully evaluated.

Estimates of the Prevalence of the Developmental Disabilities in Alabama, Based on Previous Studies

Because most demographic rates vary by at least age and sex, only those rates that have been reported by age and sex at a minimum should be utilized in any attempts at making estimates. In very few instances have these rates been presented jointly. That is, most often the rates are presented by age groupings and then are given separately by sex. This manner of reporting the findings means that *interaction* effects between age and sex are assumed to be negligible. When possible, rates by race should be an additional factor employed in making projections. Once adequate age and sex specific rates have been derived from the literature, they may then be applied to the age, sex, and racial population structure of Alabama, and projected to the 1973 survey year.

If the studies utilized as bases for the Alabama estimates were essentially correct in their major assumptions, then the derived estimates should be basically sound. Likewise, rates of prevalence for any of the disabilities should be the same for a similar class of persons in whatever part of the country they may be found. Thus, in efforts at predicting the rates for lower middle class white persons living in rural areas of Alabama, they should be roughly similar to those of people with the same characteristics living in any other part of the country.

These assumptions constituted the basis for the preliminary estimates, which were derived from previous field studies. A description of the methods for each separate disability is reported. In Chapter Seven, estimates based on the actual field surveys are discussed and evaluated.

The process of applying the rates that best fitted our criteria to the populations of Alabama counties was somewhat involved. The United States Census is taken every ten years, and was last taken in 1970. Since the information needed by planners is enhanced in its utility if it is current, and because it is a known fact that the population of a given area changes from year to year, the populations of each of Alabama's 67 counties were projected to 1973. However, since 1973 was fairly close to the 1970 Census of Population, it was decided that the method of population projection need not be a greatly sophisticated one.

For the period 1960–1970, it was noted that the rate of growth of population in Alabama was 5.4 percent; for the previous decade, the corresponding figure was 6.7 percent. We therefore assumed that during the three-year period in question, on the basis of advice from several consulting demographers, a fairly accurate estimate of the rate of population increase by county would be approximately 2.8 percent. This is, of course, an arbitrary figure, but it is not out of line with the growth patterns exhibited in the state during the past two decades. It has furthermore been assumed that the rate of increase was equal for each county and for each age-sex-race group. It is readily realized that such an assumption is not totally realistic, because it is obvious that some counties are growing faster than others (as are some age, sex, and race groups), while some counties are actually experiencing losses in total population. Nevertheless, it was assumed that the change in absolute numbers on a county-by-county basis would not be greatly different from the estimates.

ESTIMATES OF THE PREVALENCE OF MENTAL RETARDATION

Wishik (1956), in the study of handicaps in two rural Georgia counties, Clarke and Oconee, took a 10 percent sampling of the childhood population, that is, those under 21 years of age. His method included a three-week period of widespread voluntary reporting, followed by an independent sample canvass of the communities by selecting every tenth household. Random sampling techniques were utilized, thus minimizing the likelihood that interviewer bias might enter into the selection of the individual households in which interviews were conducted. Presumptive diagnoses of handicapping conditions, based on the answers to questionnaire items, were then followed by clinical diagnoses. The following are the age-specific prevalence rates of mental retardation reported by Wishik:

AGE GROUPS	PREVALENCE RATE PER 1,000 POPULATION
0–4	8.7
5–9	57.1
10–14	60.8
15–20	19.4
TOTAL	36.6

Wishik notes (n.d.:23), "The age specific rates ... show a disporpor-tionate weighting in the school years, reflecting both the difficulty of early diagnosis and the traditionally poorer reporting if the adolescent or post-adolescent settles into an accepted position of limited responsi-bility." Thus, he correctly observes that the estimated prevalence of mental retardation for persons less than 21 years of age in Clarke and Oconee counties could reasonably be higher than his calculated figure of 36.6 per 1,000.

A shortcoming of Wishik's study, for purposes of the present analysis, is that he failed to report his findings by sex. Other studies have indi-cated that mental retardation is more prevalent among males than among females. In Wishik's survey, higher rates were reported for blacks than for whites, and his study included a canvass of a higher overall proportion of blacks. Nevertheless, clinical diagnoses did not confirm many of the reported cases for blacks, and, after this screening, the rates for the two races were assumed to be basically similar.

In contrast, Oppenheimer, et al. (1965) screened all patients coming to the pediatric outpatient clinics of the Babies and Children's Hospital in the university hospitals for possible mental retardation during a four-week period. While those investigators found sex differences not to be significant, their study did not confirm previous reports of lower prev-alence in the preschool age group. To the contrary, the prevalence rate for the under-five population was *higher* than that for the school group.

Since Wishik's study had been conducted in rural Georgia counties that would not be significantly different from many Alabama counties in their social, economic, and demographic compositions, it was decided to apply his estimates of the age-specific rates in the present study. Nevertheless, it was difficult to ignore the results of the Cleveland study conducted by Oppenheimer. Thus, based on the suggestions of experts in the fields of demography, special education, and psychology, the two methods were utilized in combination, using Wishik's rates basically, but assuming that the prevalence rates for preschool children would be *at least as high* as those found in the school population aged 5–9 years, spe-cifically, that the prevalence rate of 57.1 per 1,000 could be utilized in predicting the numbers of preschool children who are retarded. This assumption implies that mental retardation cases among preschool children have remained largely unsurfaced because of the many cases of nonfunctional retardation at that age, which usually are not located until the child is enrolled in school and psychological testing has been undertaken.

Furthermore, for purposes of the estimates, it has been assumed that the prevalence rate for the population aged 21 and over is the same for the age group 15–19, or 19.4 per 1,000 population. Traditionally, many mildly retarded persons attain adulthood and assume positions commensurate with their mental capabilities, and thus are subsumed into the general population. Based on these estimates, there were approximately 109,277 mentally retarded persons residing in Alabama, a prevalence rate of 30.9 cases of mental retardation per 1,000 population (Hollingsworth, 1974:40).

These rates were applied to each age group in each of Alabama's 67 counties, separately, by age group, sex, and race. Persons interested in obtaining such detailed information may wish to contact the author of this book.

ESTIMATES OF THE PREVALENCE OF CEREBRAL PALSY

On the basis of previous studies that reported the prevalence of cerebral palsy, the rates varied between 1.1 per 1,000 persons to 4 per 1,000 (see Table VI-2). After carefully reviewing the research dealing with the prevalence of cerebral palsy, the panel of experts decided that perhaps the rates most applicable to the people of Alabama were to be found in a survey of the cerebral palsied in Texas (Wolfe and Reid, 1958). The methodology followed in that research included the referral by medical doctors of known cases of cerebral palsy to the investigators by agencies and physicians. The rates of prevalence were reported by age groups as follows:

AGE GROUPS	PREVALENCE RATE PER 1,000 POPULATION
0–4	1.29
5–9	3.45
10–14	3.23
15–19	2.12
20–24	1.48
25–29	1.08
30–34	0.79

(continued from p. 80)

35–39	0.45
40–49	0.27
50–59	0.13
60+	0.04
TOTAL	1.23

Again, the estimates of prevalence of cerebral palsy were made for each county in Alabama and were projected by age group, by sex and by race. Since the Wolfe and Reid study (1958) reported the percentages of male and female cases in each age group, it was possible to refine the estimates further by this factor in order to attain more accuracy. Using the Texas study's age-specific rates and the proportions of cases reported for that group was an involved process. For example, in the age group 0–4, the table just presented indicated that the prevalence rate was 1.29 per 1,000. However, 53 percent of the cases in the same age group were reported for males, while the proportion of males in the age group 0–4 for the entire state was found to be 47 percent. Thus, males were overrepresented in the reported cases of cerebral palsy. Taking this finding into account, the prevalence rate was multiplied by the proportion of reported cases and divided by the percentage which that age-sex group constituted of the total population. In the case of males 0–4 in Texas, it was found that the prevalence rate was actually 1.46 per 1,000, by the following simple formula, derived from the figures just reported:

$$\frac{1.29 \times 0.53}{0.47} = 1.46$$

The same basic formula was applied to each of the other age-sex-race groups in making our estimates. These calculations indicated that there were approximately 4,718 cerebral palsied persons living in Alabama in 1973 (Hollingsworth, 1974:40).

ESTIMATES OF THE PREVALENCE OF EPILEPSY

Table VI-3 indicated an extremely wide range of estimates of the prevalence of epilepsy. Even the Epilepsy Foundation of America's estimates are stated as between two and four million. After a very careful, painstaking consideration of the merits of all the findings in previous studies, and after considering their applicability to the present project, the decision was made to use the prevalence rates found in the studies conducted by Dr. Leonard Kurland (1959) of the Mayo Clinic. It was the opinion that his data were probably the most complete and accurate for a population of the type under observation. Furthermore, the utility of his results to the present investigation was enhanced by the fact that he calculated and reported the prevalence rates by sex and age groups.

In his long-term study, Kurland based his prevalence rates on patients who lived in Rochester, Minnesota, on January 1, 1955. The clinical data were taken from the files of the Mayo Clinic, which maintains an almost complete record of serious illnesses in the resident population of Rochester. The prevalence rates are reported by age in the following table:

AGE GROUPS	PREVALENCE RATE PER 1,000 POPULATION
0–9	5.79
10–19	3.45
20–29	3.47
30–39	4.33
40–49	3.36
50–59	3.59
60–69	1.20
70–79	0.78
80+	1.86
TOTAL	3.65

In making the decision to use Kurland's prevalence rates as a basis for estimates of prevalence in Alabama, he was contacted by members of the research team. He reported that more current, and in his opinion, more complete and accurate findings were available. In 1965, he had subsequently conducted another study of epilepsy in Rochester and found a prevalence rate of 5.69, whereas it was 3.65 per 1,000 in 1955. The later study revealed a rate of 7.77 per 1,000 males and 3.37 for females, a rate twice as high for males as for females. Thus, this correction was made in the present study in order to obtain more nearly accurate rates for the planners. The resulting estimate for the prevalence of epilepsy in Alabama was 19,620 (Hollingsworth, 1974:40).

Thus, it has been estimated, based on the best available data, that approximately 133,615 Alabamians are afflicted with the developmental disabilities. This is an overwhelming statistic. Nevertheless, the field studies give added significance to the estimates of prevalence rates for each of the developmental disabilities. Chapter Seven reports those findings and attempts to derive even more accurate estimates of the prevalence of these three conditions in the state.

Grateful acknowledgment is made to Dr. C. Jack Tucker, Atlanta University, who performed much of the initial search of the literature for prevalence rates and who supervised their computations by age, sex, and race for each county in Alabama, and to Dr. Prithwis Das Gupta, who checked the original computations, analyzed the results, and wrote the corresponding chapter for the initial report.

References

Altman, Isidore
    1955   "On the prevalence of cerebral palsy." Cerebral Palsy Review 16: 4, 25.

Anderson, C. L.
    1936   "Epilepsy in the State of Michigan." Mental Hygiene 20:441–62.

Bailey, P., F. E. Williams, P. O. Komora, T. W. Salmon, and N. Fenton
    1929   The medical department of the United States Army in World War I, Volume 10 (Neuropsychiatry). Washington, D.C.: U.S. Government Printing Office.

Baldwin, R., E. Davens, and V. G. Harris
    1953   "Epilepsy in public health." American Journal of Public Health 43: 452–59.

Bird, A. V., H. J. Heinz, and G. Klintworth
    1962   "Convulsive disorders in Bantu mineworkers." Epilepsia 3: 175–87.

Bremer, J.
    1951   "A social psychiatric investigation of a small community of Northern Norway." Acta Psychiatrica et Neurologie, Supplement 62.

Brewis, M., D. C. Poskanzer, C. Rolland, and H. Miller
    1966   "Neurological disease in an English city." Acta Neurologica Scandinavia 42 (Supplement 24):1–89.

Chen, K. J., A. Brody, and L. T. Kurland
    1968   "Patterns of neurologic diseases on Guam—I: epidemiologic aspects." Archivos Neurologicos 19:573–78.

Conley, Ronald
    1973   The Economics of Mental Retardation. Baltimore, Md.: Johns Hopkins Press.

Connecticut State Department of Health
    1951   The Study of Cerebral Palsy in Connecticut. Hartford, Connecticut.

Cruickshank, William, and George M. Raus (eds.)
    1955   Cerebral Palsy: Its Individual and Community Problems (rev. ed.). New York: Syracuse University Press.

Dada, T. O., B. O. Osuntokun, and E. L. Odeku
    1969   "Epidemiological aspects of epilepsy in Nigeria: a study of 639 patients." Diseases of the Nervous System 30:807–13.

Dingman, H. F., and C. Tarjan
    1960   "Mental retardation and the normal distribution curve." American Journal of Mental Deficiency 64:991–94.

Dumas, M., and R. Virieu
    1968   "Neurologie au Senegal." Association Medica Lengua Française 4:
            112–17.
Edwards, T. I., K. H. McGill, and L. G. Rowntree
    1942   Local Board Examinations of Selective Service Registrants in Peace-
            time. Washington, D.C.: U.S. Government Printing Office.
Goodman, Melvin B., Ernest M. Gruenberg, Joseph J. Downing, and Eugene
            Rogot
    1956   "A prevalence study of mental retardation in a metropolitan area."
            American Journal of Public Health 46:702–07.
Gruenberg, Ernest
    1955   A Special Census of Suspected Referred Mental Retardation in
            Onondaga County. Technical Report of the Mental Health Research
            Unit. New York: State Department of Mental Hygiene.
Gudmondsson, Gunnar
    1966   "Epilepsy in Iceland: a clinical and epidemiological investigation."
            Acta Neurologica Scandinavia 43 (Supplement 25):1–124.
Hauser, W. Allen, and Leonard T. Kurland
    1972   "Incidence, prevalence, time trends of convulsive disorders in Roch-
            ester, Minnesota: a community survey." Pp. 41–43 in Milton Alter
            and W. Allen Hauser (eds.), The Epidemiology of Epilepsy: A Work-
            shop. Washington, D.C.: U.S. Department of Health, Education, and
            Welfare, Public Health Service, National Institutes of Health, Na-
            tional Institute of Neurological Diseases and Stroke Monograph
            No. 14.
Henrikson, G. F., and W. H. Krohn
    1969   The organization of a national system for the medical care of epi-
            leptics. Excerpta Medica, International Congress Series No. 193.
Hollingsworth, J. Selwyn
    1974   Report of Phase II of Survey of the Developmentally Disabled in Al-
            abama: Needs and Resources. Montgomery: Alabama Department of
            Mental Health.
Jastak, J., H. McPhee, and M. Whiteman
    1963   Mental Retardation: Its Nature and Incidence. Newark, Del.: Uni-
            versity of Delaware Press.
Kennedy, W. A., et al.
    1963   A Normative Sample of Intelligence and Achievement of Negro El-
            ementary School Children: The Southeastern United States. Yellow
            Springs, Ohio: Antioch Press.
Kott, Maurice G.
    1968   "Estimating the number of retarded in New Jersey." Mental Retar-
            dation: 28–31.
Krohn, W.
    1961   "A study of epilepsy in northern Norway, its frequency and char-
            acter." Acta Psychiatrica Scandinavia 36 (Supplement 150):215–25.
Kurland, Leonard T.
    1959   "The incidence and prevalence of convulsive disorders in a small
            urban community." Epilepsia 1:143–61.

1973   Tables on prevalence of epilepsy—Rochester, Minnesota, 1953–1967. Preliminary tables. Private correspondence.

Leibowitz, U., and M. Alter
1968   "A survey of epilepsy in Jerusalem, Israel." Epilepsia 9:87–105.

Lemkau, P., C. Tietze, and M. Cooper
1942   "Mental-hygiene problems in an urban district." Mental Hygiene 26:624–46.
1943   "A survey of statistical studies on the prevalence and incidence of mental disorder in a sample population." Public Health Report 58: 1909–27.

Lennox, W. G.
1960   Epilepsy and Related Disorders. Boston: Little, Brown & Co.

Lessell, S., J. M. Torres, and L. T. Kurland
1962   "Seizure disorders in a Guamanian village." Archivos Neurologicos 7:53–60.

Lesser, A. J., and E. P. Hunt
1954   "The Nation's handicapped children." American Journal of Public Health 44:166–70.

Levinson, E. J.
1962   Retarded children in Maine: a survey and analysis. University of Maine Studies, Second Series, No. 77. Orono, Maine: University of Maine Press.

Levy, L. F., J. I. Forbes, and T. S. Parirenyatwa
1964   "Epilepsy in Africans." Central African Journal of Medicine 10: 241–49.

Lione, J. G.
1961   "Convulsive disorders in a working population." Journal of Occupational Medicine 3:369–73.

Logan, W. P. D., and A. A. Cushion
1958   Studies on Medical and Population Subjects, No. 14. Morbidity Statistics from General Practice, Volume 1: General. London: Her Majesty's Stationery Office.

Malzberg, B.
1932   "The prevalence of epilepsy in the United States with special reference to children and adolescents." Psychiatric Quarterly 6:97–106.

Mental Retardation Services Board of Los Angeles County
1969   "Estimated number of retarded in Los Angeles County, 1969." Mimeographed.

Mercer, Jane R.
1973   Labeling the Mentally Retarded: Clinical and Social System Perspectives on Mental Retardation. Berkeley: University of California Press.

Mullen, F. A., and M. M. Nee
1949   "Distribution of mental retardation in an urban school population." American Journal of Mental Deficiency 56:291–308.

New York State Department of Mental Hygiene
1965   A Special Census of Suspected Referred Mental Retardation, Onondaga County, New York. Syracuse, N.Y.: University Press.

New York State Joint Legislative Committee to Study the Problem of Cerebral
    Palsy
    1940   A Survey of Cerebral Palsy in Schenectady County, New York. Leg-
            islative Document No. 55. Albany, New York.
Olivares, Ladislao
    1964   "El paciente neurológico de consulta externa, estudio comparativo
            entre el Centro Hospitalaria '20 de noviembre' y el Hospital Gen-
            eral." Revista Médica del Instituto de Seguros y Servicios Sociales de
            los Trabajadores del Estado 1:311–15.
    1972   "Epilepsy in Mexico: a population study." Pp. 53–56 in Milton Alter
            and W. Allen Hauser (eds.), The Epidemiology of Epilepsy: A Work-
            shop. Washington, D.C.: U.S. Department of Health, Education, and
            Welfare, Public Health Service, National Institutes of Health, Na-
            tional Institute of Neurological Diseases and Stroke Monograph
            No. 14.
Oppenheimer, Sonya, et al.
    1965   "Prevalence of mental retardation in a pediatric outpatient clinic
            population." Pediatrics 36.
Osuntokun, B. O., and E. L. Odeku
    1970   "Epilepsy in Nigerians: study of 522 patients." Tropical Geography
            Medicine 22:3–19.
Phelps, W. M.
    1948   "Characteristic psychological variations in cerebral palsy." Nervous
            Children 7:10.
Pond, D. A., and B. H. Bidwell
    1960   "A survey of epilepsy in fourteen general practices—II: social and
            psychological aspects." Epilepsia:285–99.
Pond, D. A., B. H. Bidwell, and L. Stein
    1960   "A survey of epilepsy in fourteen general practices—I: demographic
            and medical data." Psychiatria, Neurologia, Neurochirurgia 63:
            217–36.
Poskanzer, David C.
    1972   "House-to-house survey of a community for epilepsy." Pp. 45–46 in
            Milton Alter and W. Allen Hauser (eds.), The Epidemiology of
            Epilepsy: A Workshop. Washington, D.C.: U.S. Department of
            Health, Education, and Welfare, Public Health Service, National In-
            stitutes of Health, National Institute of Neurological Diseases and
            Stroke Monograph No. 14.
Rachman, I.
    1970   "Epilepsy in African hospital practice." Central African Journal of
            Medicine 16:201–04.
Richardson, W. P., A. C. Higgins, and R. G. Ames
    1965   The Handicapped Children of Alamance County, North Carolina:
            A Medical and Sociological Study. Wilmington, Del.: Nemours
            Foundation.
Rose, S. W., J. K. Penry, R. E. Markush, L. A. Radloff, and P. L. Putnam
    1973   "Epilepsy in children." Epilepsia 13:1–19.

Schlesinger, E. R., Helen C. Chase, and Clark Le Bouef
 1954 "Evaluation of mandatory reporting of cerebral palsy." American Journal of Public Health 44:1124–31.
Tarjan, G., S. W. Wright, R. K. Eyman, and C. V. Keeran
 1973 "Natural history of mental retardation: some aspects of epidemiology." American Journal of Mental Deficiency 77:369–79.
Taylor, J. L., et al.
 1965 Mental Retardation Prevalence in Oregon. Portland, Oreg.: State Board of Health.
Ueki, K., and S. Sato
 1963 "An epidemiologic study of epilepsy in infancy and childhood in Niigata city." Psychiat. Neurol. Paed. Jap. 3:3–13.
United Cerebral Palsy Foundation
 1973 Rule of thumb prevalence rates. Private correspondence.
United States Department of Health, Education, and Welfare
 1968 Health Interview Survey. Washington, D.C.: National Center for Health Statistics.
Wajsbort, J., N. Aral, and I. Alfandary
 1967 "A study of the epidemiology of chronic epilepsy in Northern Israel." Epilepsia 8:105–16.
Weinberg, Warren
 1972 "Epilepsy: a study of a school population." Pp. 57–58 in Milton Alter and W. Allen Hauser (eds.), The Epidemiology of Epilepsy: A Workshop. Washington, D.C.: U.S. Department of Health, Education, and Welfare, Public Health Service, National Institutes of Health, National Institute of Neurological Diseases and Stroke Monograph No. 14.
Welfare Council of Metropolitan Chicago and the Chicago Association of Commerce and Industry
 1953 Problem of Cerebral Palsy in Chicago. Chicago, Illinois.
Wishik, Samuel M.
 n.d. Georgia Study of Handicapped Children: A Report on a Study of Prevalence, Disability, Needs, Resources, and Contributing Factors —Implications for Program Administration and Community Organization.
 1956 "Handicapped children in Georgia: a study of prevalence, disability, needs and resources." American Journal of Public Health 46:195–203.
Wolfe, W. G., and L. Leon Reid
 1958 A Survey of Cerebral Palsy in Texas. Austin: United Cerebral Palsy of Texas.
Zielinski, J. J.
 1972 "Social prognosis in epilepsy." Epilepsia 13:133–40.

CHAPTER SEVEN
THE PREVALENCE OF THE DEVELOPMENTAL DISABILITIES IN ALABAMA: FINDINGS FROM THE RESEARCH

The preceding chapter emphasized the importance of knowing with some degree of certainty the numbers and geographical distribution of persons with mental retardation, cerebral palsy, and epilepsy. The major objective of this chapter is to present and to discuss the findings of prevalence of the developmental disabilities as actually located in the field studies of Highland, Piedmont, and Plantation counties, Alabama. Included among the specific objectives of this portion of the project was to test further the reliability of the reputational method of locating developmentally disabled individuals, especially in comparison with some of the other methods that may be so utilized.

The prevalence rates presented in this chapter are based upon three methods: (1) the actual canvassing of every community in these three counties to obtain names of the developmentally disabled, (2) data from state and regional agencies, and (3) a thorough review of medical records in one county. Thus the estimates of prevalence reported in the present chapter differ from those furnished in Chapter Six, which were estimates of prevalence based upon previous studies that had been conducted, using widely different approaches, in a variety of geographical and time settings. The use of the current method was pretested in Piedmont County in order to determine whether the correct approach was being used, and whether the interviewers were using the methods and questions that would elicit the needed information. After the pretest, it was decided that the method did indeed perform according to survey specifications and that the results were accurate to the degree that they should not be discarded, as is generally the case with pretests, but rather that they should be used in the final tabulations. The discussion in Chapter Three indicates that the three counties had been chosen originally to represent regional, racial, and rural-urban variations, as well as to represent counties with levels of socioeconomic development distinct from each other, and representing some of the most basic social, economic, and demographic differentials encountered throughout the state.

Briefly, the method used in the initial reputational approach was the following (for more detailed information on the application of this particular technique, the reader is referred to Chapter Four of this volume). In each county the more knowledgeable informants were contacted first. Generally, these persons included county health officials, school officials, and special education teachers, medical doctors, pharmacists, elected county officials, and selected people who were in positions to know a wide variety of the persons living in the county. The second group of persons who were contacted included, but was not limited to: ministers, county commissioners, midwives, black leaders, county sheriffs, city chiefs of police, county agricultural and home demonstration agents, postmasters, rural mail carriers, owners of large landholdings, and, in general, people who had lived in the communities for a long period of time and who were therefore likely to know most of the people residing there. They were asked, first, to give the interviewers the names of persons having one or more of the developmental disabilities. For some of the less technically oriented categories of informants, brief descriptions were given of each of the disabilities in turn. Secondly, they were asked the names of other persons who might be able to supply additional names of the developmentally disabled. Then, the people they had referred were contacted in each community in order to obtain further names and addresses. Finally, family members of the developmentally disabled were asked these same questions in the field interviews that followed in the second stage of the survey, thus expanding the category of informants substantially.

Members of the interviewing team consisted of University of Alabama professors from the Department of Sociology and the Department of Special Education and of selected University students who had attained at least a bachelor's degree. These interviewers were trained extensively in interviewing techniques. During the actual interviewing phase, group meetings of all interviewers were conducted daily in order to review their progress, to discuss problems, and to provide new information and/or to implement slight modifications in the basic approach. Members of the research team were instructed to assure respondents of the confidentiality of their referrals, and to guarantee that neither they nor the persons whom they referred would be embarrassed and that their names would never be revealed.

Cooperation was surprisingly good. Of course, it is to be expected that some persons in any given community might be somewhat hesitant to reveal such personal information to strangers, but this reluctance was not often the case. As a check on the validity of replies, it is worth noting that the same individuals were named as being developmentally disabled by more than one source in almost one of every three cases in Piedmont County. In some instances, it was not unusual for a particularly severely affected person to be named by between 10 to 20 persons.

Findings

GENERAL PREVALENCE RATES FOR THE THREE COUNTIES

In the three counties, a total of 1,500 mentally retarded persons were referred to the interviewers, indicating a rate of 20.1 per 1,000 population. For cerebral palsy, epilepsy, and multiple disabilities, the rates were 3.7, 3.8, and 1.7, respectively. Thus, a combined rate of 29.4 for each 1,000 inhabitants was reported in the three study counties (Hollingsworth, 1974:50). Table VII-1 reports the numbers and prevalence rates per 1,000 for each county separately.

In comparing the findings in the three counties, the rates of prevalence were highest in all instances in Plantation County. A rather thorough, painstaking search of the literature had led the researchers to expect to find higher rates there because of the relatively greater proportions of blacks and poor who reside there. On the other hand, Highland County, with less than 2 percent of its residents who are black and with a higher level of income, would be expected to have fewer numbers, proportionately, of the developmentally disabled. The findings bore out this expectation. However, other explanations may be partially responsible for the different rates. For example, almost three times as many persons lived in Highland County as in either of the other two, a fact that made it more difficult to cover the area as efficiently as in the two smaller counties. Additionally, Highland County's population is growing relatively rapidly because of new people moving into the county and into

Table VII-1.

Reported Numbers and Rates of Prevalence of the Developmental Disabilities, by County, 1973

Disability	County							
	Piedmont		Plantation		Highland		Total	
	No.	Rate	No.	Rate	No.	Rate	No.	Rate
Mental Retardation	335	20.6	391	24.0	774	18.4	1500	20.1
Cerebral Palsy	65	4.0	79	4.8	135	3.2	279	3.7
Epilepsy	70	4.3	87	5.3	126	3.0	283	3.8
Multiple Disabilities*	25	1.5	53	5.3	51	1.2	129	1.7
Total	495	30.4	610	39.4	1086	25.8	2191	29.3

*The term "multiple disabilities" indicates persons with more than one of the developmental disabilities. It does not include those persons with only one developmental disability who also have other substantial handicaps, such as speech and hearing difficulties, blindness, etc., although many of the people in any one of the four categories did have such additional handicaps.

adjoining areas. These two reasons combined indicate that the people living there may not be as well acquainted with their neighbors as those in the two other counties. In sociological terms, what is being said is that the two smaller counties may have many more primary relationships, while secondary relationships are likely to be more predominant in Highland County. Another related reason for the proportionately fewer findings in Highland County may have been the failure of the interviewers to locate enough people in the right positions to name the developmentally disabled in their individual, scattered communities, given the time limitations of the field survey.

In all three counties, the largest numbers of names from a single source came from the superintendents of education. However, the superintendent of the city board of education in Highland County refused to comply with a request to supply a list of the names of persons enrolled in the city's special education classes, although the confidentiality of the information was stressed over and again, and the possible benefits of his cooperation were emphasized repeatedly. This lack of cooperation is, in large part, responsible for the lower percentage of nominations in Highland County. The school lists in the remaining counties were especially beneficial in compiling accurate estimates of prevalence; the students had been tested individually before being admitted to courses of special education. This procedure (requesting names) was also important in eliminating duplications and thus preventing the overestimation of the numbers of persons directly involved.

Differences by Race and Sex. In order to be able to make the most accurate inferences about the prevalence of any one of the developmental disabilities, the researcher must have at hand data concerning the race and sex of the individuals involved. Additionally, age is a significant factor because the disabilities vary according to an individual's age, as well as by his race, sex, and socioeconomic status. However, it was not feasible to collect age data in the present survey, since many informants were not aware of the exact age of their nominees.

Table VII-2 demonstrates the differences in the prevalence of the three developmentally disabling conditions as they occur by sex and by race for Plantation County and Highland County. This information, unfortunately, is not readily available for Piedmont County, as was explained in Chapter Five of this volume. Generally, rates of prevalence were much higher (usually about twice as high) among blacks. About the same difference occurred between the sexes, with the higher prevalences being found for males. These differences were what had been predicted by the literature but did not hold in all cases in the individual findings, many times because the numbers of one group were so small that none or relatively few were found. This situation was especially evident among the blacks in some instances in Highland County, where

Table VII–2.
Reported Numbers and Computed Rates of Prevalence of
Developmentally Disabled Persons, by Sex, Color, and County, 1973

	Males							
	Plantation				Highland			
	White		Black		White		Black	
	No.	Rate	No.	Rate	No.	Rate	No.	Rate
Mental Retardation	41	16.6	168	31.2	349	17.5	27	71.2
Cerebral Palsy	6	2.4	38	7.1	66	3.3	1	2.6
Epilepsy	7	2.8	33	6.1	62	3.1	0	—
Multiple Disabilities*	5	2.0	30	5.6	33	1.7	2	5.3
Totals	59	23.8	269	50.0	510	25.6	30	79.1

	Females							
Mental Retardation	20	7.5	103	17.8	293	13.8	14	31.7
Cerebral Palsy	4	1.5	31	5.4	48	2.3	2	4.5
Epilepsy	6	2.2	41	7.1	46	2.2	0	—
Multiple Disabilities*	4	1.5	14	2.4	10	0.5	0	—
Totals	34	12.7	189	32.7	397	18.8	16	36.2

*See footnote on Table VII–1 for an explanation of the term "multiple disabilities."

it will be remembered that only 2 percent of the population was black
(in fact, the total black population of the county was just above 800).

Estimates of the Rates of Prevalence Based on Previous Studies Versus Rates of Prevalence Established in the Field Survey

Table VII-1 has indicated that a total of 2,191 cases of the developmental disabilities were located in the three Alabama counties in which
field surveys were conducted. Estimates based on previous studies had
projected approximately 2,867 cases of mental retardation, cerebral
palsy, and/or epilepsy. Thus, more than 76 percent of the cases predicted to exist were actually located by employing the reputational technique. In Plantation County, 92 percent of the expected numbers were
found, while in Piedmont County and Highland County, the respective
percentages were 82 and 68 percent.

These relatively high percentages indicate that the reputational method
is a highly effective one in locating individuals who have developmental
disabilities, especially in rural areas, which have not been well studied
in the past. Since the initiation of this project, numerous requests have
been sent to this project director asking for estimates of the numbers of

persons in a given area who were either mentally retarded, cerebral palsied, or epileptic. Many of the requests were for the names of the affected persons in a given area, because names had been requested for the purpose of eliminating duplications that would tend to overestimate the numbers of persons directly involved. Because of the confidential nature of the data gathered, names or addresses could not be released, although estimates of the numbers of persons in any given county or region have been shared frequently. Thus, it is apparent to this writer that this kind of information is desperately needed by planners.

In Plantation and Highland counties, the ratios of expected findings to those actually located were relatively high (see Table VII-3). In fact, they were higher than might be reasonably expected in a study of this kind. This fact leads one to believe that the estimated rates may be somewhat low in comparison to the realities of the situation, because the actual location could never be anticipated to be 100 percent complete.

A further finding that deserves special attention is that almost three times the numbers of the cerebral palsied that had been estimated were found. This result would lead one to suspect that the rates utilized in making estimates based on previous studies (see Chapter Six) were far too low, and that this survey has seriously underestimated the numbers of the cerebral palsied in the state. Another factor is that large numbers of persons possibly were nominated as being cerebral palsied who had in fact some other handicap, which was confused by lay people as being the specified disorder. Certainly, this possibility must be entertained in any attempt to interpret the results of the field survey.

Another important finding is that the comparison between the numbers of those nominated as being developmentally disabled and their expected numbers, according to the estimates, reveals much higher percentages for blacks than for whites, 192 percent versus 57 percent. In most cases, the proportions of blacks nominated were twice as high as those of whites, when one considers the numbers previously estimated. This interesting revelation points up the higher actual prevalence rates for blacks, plus the fact that the previous findings failed to give the researchers sufficient evidence to permit the calculation of separate rates for blacks in this study. Furthermore, with a team of all-white interviewers, one might reasonably expect less cooperation from blacks. This fact underscores the necessity of making separate estimates by race in areas where blacks constitute a significant proportion of the population. Thus, the previous estimates may be significantly low in the case of blacks.

In most cases in this comparison, the proportions of numbers estimated and actually found were greater for males than for females (74 percent versus 58 percent). This finding, too, indicates the necessity of utilizing sex differentials in making estimates. Likewise, it points up the

Table VII–3.

Actual Numbers of the Developmentally Disabled as a Proportion of the Estimated, by Sex, Color, and County, 1973*

| | Plantation County | | | | Highland County | | | |
| | White | | Black | | White | | Black | |
	Estimate	% Found	Estimate	% Found	Estimate	% Found	Estimate	% Found
Males								
Mental Retardation	80	51	189	89	620	56	20	135
Cerebral Palsy	4	150	10	380	28	236	1	100
Epilepsy	19	37	43	77	155	40	5	0
Totals	103	57	242	111	803	64	26	115
Females								
Mental Retardation	78	26	202	51	660	44	17	82
Cerebral Palsy	3	133	7	443	24	200	1	200
Epilepsy	11	55	20	205	76	61	2	0
Totals	92	37	229	86	760	52	20	80

*The reader is referred to Table VII–2 for the record of the numbers actually reported in each instance. See also footnote concerning multiple disabilities in Table VII–1. In the above table, multiple disabilities have been included only in the total percentages because at present there is insufficient evidence on which to base accurate, logical predictions.

fact that, in some instances, males may have been underestimated and females overestimated. In the latter case, it may also be true that females were less likely to be reported.

Overall, in the opinion of the writer, the use of the reputational method was justified by a close comparison of the findings with the estimates based on previous field studies. The reputational method is not without its problems, however, for no clinical verification was possible in most cases. Many of those persons named in the interviews were, nevertheless, nominated by medical personnel, who would possess the necessary information to classify accurately a person as being mentally retarded, cerebral palsied, or epileptic. These professionals provided a verification of many of the nominations by lay people. Additional checks came from the special-education class lists; others came from state and local agencies and facilities specifically charged with the delivering of services to the developmentally disabled populace of the state, from public health personnel, nurses, etc. In fact, in Piedmont County 71 percent of the reported cases of developmental disabilities were confirmed by one or more of these authoritative sources.

A Comparison of Agency Records of Developmentally Disabled Persons Receiving Treatment Versus Prevalence Estimates

Another method of obtaining an estimate of the prevalence of the developmental disabilities in a particular area is to contact the agencies and facilities that offer direct services to people who live in that area. The materials for this section of the discussion come from the result of the research conducted on the statewide survey of such facilities (see Chapter Nine).

This method is one of the most problematical in attempts to establish prevalence rates. First, it is often difficult, if not impossible, to ascertain all of the agencies and facilities that offer direct services to a particular area, and many of them overlap in their responsibilities. Secondly, with the human population being so very mobile, it is often difficult to know the exact number of persons who live in the area being served by a given facility. Furthermore, some individuals, for one reason or another, find it necessary to seek treatment and/or services elsewhere. At times, people go elsewhere because of a desire to hide the existence of a certain disability from friends and acquaintances; at other times, it may be because they are unable to find the necessary services within the immediate local area.

Often problems exist in obtaining the needed information from the individual agencies. The personnel of some facilities are so occupied with the services they provide that little or no time remains in which to cooperate with research entities or persons. Some agencies are prohibited by law from complying to the extent of supplying names and addresses of their clients.

The data used in this report on the numbers of persons receiving services come from several different sources. Questionnaires were sent to state agencies, such as the State Department of Education with its Program for Exceptional Children, State Crippled Children's Service, and Vocational Rehabilitation Services, the Alabama Department of Mental Health; agencies in the counties, such as local, county, and regional chapters of the above; county and city boards of education; local offices of the Department of Pensions and Security; and private organizations, such as local associations for retarded citizens, chapters of United Cerebral Palsy, and the Alabama Council on Epilepsy. Some 74 percent of the questionnaires were returned. It is believed that those agencies replying to the survey constituted the largest providers of treatment and services to the developmentally disabled: those not returning the requested information were, for the most part, small organizations offering only limited services to very small numbers of clients. Table VII-4 presents the numbers of persons reported by agencies as being served

Table VII–4.
Developmentally Disabled Persons Reported by Service Agencies as Being Service Recipients (S), Numbers Estimated (E), and Numbers Actually Located in the Survey (F), for the Three Study Counties, by Disability, 1973

Disability	Piedmont			Highland			Plantation		
	S	E	F	S	E	F	S	E	F
Mental Retardation	127	499	335	511	1310	774	74	549	391
Cerebral Palsy	11	31	65	12	53	135	11	24	79
Epilepsy	10	82	70	23	237	127	16	93	87
Multiple Disabilities*	0	—	25	0	—	51	0	—	53
Totals	148	612	495	546	1600	1087	101	666	610

Percentages of Service Recipients

	S/E	S/F	S/E	S/F	S/E	S/F
Mental Retardation	25.5	37.9	39.0	66.0	13.5	18.9
Cerebral Palsy	37.9	16.9	32.1	12.6	45.8	13.9
Epilepsy	12.2	14.3	9.7	18.3	17.2	18.4
Totals	24.2	29.9	34.4	50.7	15.2	16.6

*See Table VII-1 for the definition of "Multiple Disabilities."

and makes comparisons between those receiving services and those estimated to have one of the developmental disabilities, and between those
reported as receiving services and those who were reported to be victims
of one or more of the disabilities.

Even a casual perusal of Table VII-4 reveals several interesting findings. First, it is evident that the method under discussion would report
much lower rates of prevalence than either of the other two methods,
because of the above-mentioned problems. What the table also means
is that in each of the study counties, many persons with one of the individual disabilities are not receiving *any* agency assistance. Of course,
it is obvious that not all persons who have one of the developmental
disabilities are in need of direct services. However, as was found in the
survey (see Chapter Eight), many of those who were subsequently interviewed reported that they were in need of services which they were
not receiving. Nevertheless, the reporting of names by local, regional,
and state service agencies is of utmost importance in establishing more
accurate rates of prevalence, because some of the names were received
from only these sources, therefore the disabilities had been verified in
each case, before the client was cleared for treatment.

A second important finding from Table VII-4 is that the counties
seem to vary in terms of those actually receiving services in direct proportion to their per capita incomes. Finally, services for the mentally
retarded appear to be more nearly complete than for the other two
disabilities.

Clinical Findings on the Prevalence of Epilepsy
in One of the Study Counties

The importance of possessing factual data on the frequency and distribution of the developmental disabilities within a given area has already been stressed. The totality of efforts in this area has as a major
goal the encouragement and help to the community in meeting the
needs of the disabled. Therefore, information concerning the numbers
of persons who are directly affected may be utilized, in addition to the
uses already mentioned, (1) in alerting governmental bodies, planning
teams, medical personnel, teachers, and other interested agencies of the
severity of a problem such as epilepsy; (2) in guiding the support of the
above-mentioned entities and individuals for the desperately needed
prevention, treatment, research, and education concerning the disability; and (3) in ensuring sound applications of medical and social efforts
on behalf of the afflicted.

A great number of epidemiologists has worked for many years in attempting to establish rates of prevalence for the developmental disabilities. A disability receiving a goodly proportion of those efforts has been

epilepsy. While the disorder has been reported in some of the very ear-
liest of writings, such as the Bible, one will not find a great deal of sound,
empirically based data on its prevalence.

Complicating the great necessity to know the true prevalence of a disorder reported to be as common as epilepsy, various difficulties occur
in attempts to establish the rates. The prejudicial attitudes of many people against the infirmity and the resultant stigma associated with it cause
people oftentimes not to report it. Coupled with these factors are the
laws that discriminate against epileptics. For example, many states do
not issue a driver's license to a person with epilepsy. Quite often, epileptics report that they encounter discriminatory employment practices.

In surveys of the type reported in this book, underreporting is most
often the case. In household surveys, it is often difficult to obtain diagnostic information. The drawbacks of the reputational method have
already been discussed. Not the least of the problems encountered by
researchers is the lack of agreement on the definition and classification
of the disorder. Some studies include persons who have had only one
seizure; others do not. Some include febrile convulsions (those which
originate because of a high fever) as being epilepsy; others do not. Some
studies include epilepsy when the etiology is known (such as in cases of
alcoholism or brain tumors), while other researchers omit such cases
from consideration. Subtle cases of epilepsy are sometimes not recognized as such, especially in infancy and early life, and thus go unreported. Still other researchers have pondered over reporting only the
"active" cases rather than "inactive" ones, because it is not uncommon
for a person to go for several years without an attack, and subsequently
experience convulsions. In evaluating the cases in clinical records, it is
obvious that some persons have "undeclared" cases of the disorder,
while still other patients go elsewhere for treatment.

Because epilepsy is a condition with low mortality, reporting of its
occurrence is not compulsory. If the law required it to be reported, then
much more knowledge of the actual numbers of people involved would
be made available. Nevertheless, all current reports of the disorder must
be regarded as minimal approximations of its true occurrence.

In spite of all the difficulties encountered in determining the true
prevalence of a disorder such as epilepsy, the need for the information
is nevertheless vital. Therefore, the present author launched an attempt
to conduct a semiepidemiological study of the prevalence of epilepsy in
one of the study counties.

METHODOLOGY

During the field phase of the research it became apparent to the project director that a unique research opportunity into prevalence rates of

the developmental disabilities was within easy grasp, if the permission of the proper authorities could be obtained. Piedmont County had only one medical clinic. One of the four physicians who practiced medicine there mentioned that the clinic had been in operation for approximately forty years, it was the only one in the county, and its original founder had insisted on keeping adequate and complete medical files on every patient. He likewise indicated that practically every person in the county had been a patient at the clinic at one time or another. Closer investigation into the matter revealed that the clinic had approximately 26,000 records on file, while the population of the entire county was only about 16,000, an indication that many patients from surrounding counties used the services of the clinic. Because the records were fairly up to date, with reassignments of file numbers of those who moved out of the county or who were deceased, the source of information was one that could not be overlooked, presenting an invaluable opportunity for a study of prevalence based on clinical verifications.

The research into the relevant contents of the medical files in Piedmont County involved a complete examination of all the available medical records contained in the clinic. This phase was begun on March 1 and continued until August 11, 1974. At the beginning, only one researcher was involved. The average number of records he was able to review daily at the outset was between 150 and 200. On becoming more familiar with the format of the records and the information they contained, he was able to increase his speed to between 350 and 400 per day. On May 20, a second researcher was assigned to assist him. Together, they were able eventually to review some 700–800 records daily.

The examination of the records consisted of a thorough search of doctors' entries and diagnoses, reports of tests conducted by specialists, and reports from specialized clinics, such as the State Crippled Children's Service. The doctors' entries contained reports of any visits to the clinic by a certain patient, emergency room reports, and hospital discharge summaries. All of these sources were carefully read for any indication of the existence of a developmental disability. The hospital discharge summaries were especially helpful in that they contained a preliminary diagnosis (the diagnosis upon admission to the hospital) and a final diagnosis, which either supported the first diagnosis or made a new one, depending on the evidence obtained during the patient's hospital course. For example, should a person be admitted to the hospital after having a convulsion, the preliminary diagnosis might read "convulsion, possible epilepsy." During the hospital course, however, should it be found that the patient also had a high temperature, the final diagnosis might change and read "tonsillitis with secondary high fever, rule out epilepsy."

Although the initial purpose of the search of the clinical records was to assess the prevalence of all the developmental disabilities, it soon became apparent that not much information was available for either mental retardation or cerebral palsy. However, relatively higher numbers of cases of epilepsy were found. It is evident that many types of data pertaining to a person's mental and/or physical health are not reported directly to his doctor, unless the physician has specifically sent a patient to a specialist or another clinic in order to permit the administration of specialized tests. For example, when a person was tested in the school system and found to be mentally retarded, the fact usually was not reported to his doctor. This was often true also in the less severe cases of cerebral palsy. On the other hand, because of the nature of epilepsy, it is a disorder about which a local doctor might be more likely to have firsthand information concerning the nature and degree of the problem. Some of the doctors confided to this writer that they knew of some patients who were epileptic but who had never mentioned the fact to them. Thus, the datum was not entered into their clinical records. This situation was likely when a person had a less severe form of epilepsy but did not wish to be stigmatized by having other persons know of its existence.

Thus, this portion of the report will concern only the data on epilepsy, because the information on that particular disability is felt to be more accurate and much more complete. In locating cases of epilepsy through the records, the researchers were instructed to look first for a definite doctor's diagnosis of the disorder. Secondly, they were to be on the lookout for symptomatic and medicinal indicators of its possible existence. Examples of the symptomatic indicators included notations by doctors of seizures, blackouts, fits, spells, and the like. Such entries in a patient's record were used only to alert the researchers that this record required special handling, and not as a verification of the existence of the disorder. Medicines sometimes prescribed to persons who have epilepsy include dilantin, mysoline, mesantoin, and phenobarbital, as well as some dozen others, and revealed that the researchers should look for other indications of epilepsy. Incidences of these types were placed in a "suspected" category and handled separately. Where a specific diagnosis of epilepsy was found in a patient's record, the fact was duly recorded.

These procedures were followed because of the desire to increase the accuracy of the findings. In some cases, blackouts or convulsions were secondary to other causes, such as high fevers or high blood pressure. Some of the drugs mentioned may be used additionally for other purposes. For example, phenobarbital is a mild sedative that may be used in controlling hyperactivity and similar disorders. All such cases were excluded when no further evidence of epilepsy was encountered.

In some instances it was difficult to decide whether to include a given case in the "confirmed" epileptic category because of the lack of suffi-cient information on which to base a firm conclusion. A confirmed case ideally would contain a diagnosis by the doctor and would then include a report of a specialist's follow-up. These reports from specialists differ in content depending on the disability being analyzed. In general, such a report would contain family and personal medical histories, a descrip-tion of the symptoms, and a complete physical examination. After these, an examination concerning the disability was effected. In the case of suspected epilepsy, this latter examination would generally include an electroencephalogram (EEG), skull x-rays, and a brain scan.

In many cases such information was not available, and the researchers had to make the decision themselves. These decisions were based only on relevant information. For example, a case was placed into a "suspect" category if unexplained black-outs or peculiar losses of consciousness were found in the medical history, or if anticonvulsant drugs had been prescribed over long periods of time. When such a case was found, a closer examination was made.

Still, conclusive diagnoses of the disabilities were often difficult to find. Unless an EEG showed marked abnormalities common to the dis-ability, a patient who suffered black-outs and/or convulsions was often diagnosed as having a "convulsive disorder" and many times such dis-orders were termed "etiology unknown" in the patient's medical chart. In cases of this type, unless some fact that would *substantiate* the presence of epilepsy (for example, specific mention of the drugs used in con-trolling seizures, repeated epileptiform seizures, or the doctors' diag-nosis of epilepsy *after* the patient's visit to a specialist) was later found in the record, these were included on the list of "suspect" cases.

If other evidences of epilepsy were found in the closer search but some doubt still remained, the case was set aside until such time as the researchers could confer with the project director. At that time a definite decision was made to dispose of some of the cases, but some still re-mained and were put on a "suspect" list that was submitted to the doctors for their opinion. It was thought that since these doctors had served the community for some time, then they should be more familiar with these special cases than the researchers. Their opinion was sought on ap-proximately 10 percent of the cases.

A major difficulty of this phase was the task of finding records that were not in the files during the primary search. These records were either in use by the personnel at the clinic or by the local hospital and thus were not available or had been taken out of circulation because the patient had died or moved out of the area served by the clinic. It was decided to leave the matter of missing records until finishing the pri-mary search, at which time the researchers' entire effort was concen-trated on finding those records not in the files.

In the initial search of the clinic's 27,599 records, 2,267 were missing. Thus, the second review consisted of seeking those not located in the first one. In the second search, an additional 465 of the missing records were discovered, and after another two days' waiting period, 363 more charts were found. A final search in June 1975 located all except 1,198 files, which were then considered to be permanently vacant. During the intervening period the names of all the confirmed cases were assembled to determine whether they still lived in Piedmont County during the summer of 1974, the time of the research. Members of the staff's clinic were instrumental in making many of the determinations; another helpful person was the public health nurse, who had lived in the county for almost twenty years. Finally, rural mail carriers were asked whether the individuals who had not yet been located geographically lived on their routes. This procedure permitted eliminating the names of all those who lived outside the county, so that more accurate rates of the prevalence of epilepsy could be reported for the residents of the county.

Thus, this study of the prevalence of epilepsy in Piedmont County, Alabama, is referred to as a "diagnostic" survey. Diagnostic prevalence rates, according to Hauser and Kurland (1972:43) "use as a numerator only those patients who had had a *diagnosis* [of epilepsy] prior to the date in question." Furthermore, the present investigation excluded febrile convulsions from its numbers unless further conclusive evidence indicated that the individual in question was definitely a victim of epilepsy. Persons who had experienced only one seizure were likewise excluded from consideration, unless they had been diagnosed definitely as having epilepsy.

Hauser and Kurland (1972) do not specify the "criteria for residency" in their study of epilepsy in Rochester, Minnesota. The present investigation includes those who were residents of Piedmont County, Alabama (and who had been diagnosed as having epilepsy), at the time of the survey. It does not limit the survey only to those who experienced the onset of the disability while actually living in the county, while the Hauser and Kurland study appears to have done so.

Finally, the method employed is what Kurtzke (1972:21) would term a "community survey"—one which draws data from all medical sources within the locality. Some of the data (only 10 percent) were drawn from other authoritative sources, but no confirming information was encountered in their medical files (of those, the clinic files lacked records for only six people). If names from nonauthoritative sources were not confirmed by the medical doctors as having epilepsy, they were excluded from this survey.

These procedures were adopted in order to maximize the likelihood of reporting only those persons who were indeed epileptics and who were residents of the county at the time the research was conducted. It is felt that the reported prevalence rates will therefore be more reflective of the actual situation.

FINDINGS

A total of 153 cases of epilepsy was confirmed through the procedure outlined above for the approximately 16,000 residents who currently live in Piedmont County. Thus, the prevalence of epilepsy for each 1,000 residents calculates to be approximately 9.41. This is the highest prevalence of epilepsy ever reported for an entire population, according to the findings of the present author (see Table VI-3). Only one study, that of Rose, et al., who surveyed 8–9-year-old school boys, has reported a higher rate, and then for a very limited, high-risk group in Washington County, Maryland. Table VII-5 presents the prevalences as they were computed by age, race, and sex for Piedmont County in the summer of 1974.

As was expected, the prevalence for males (12.2) was much higher than was the case among females (6.7). The studies of Kurland (1959), Leibowitz and Alter (1968), Krohn (1961), Crombie, et al. (1960), Gundmondsson (1966), and Logan and Cushion (1958) have all reported that males had higher occurrences of epilepsy than females. Nevertheless, note should be made that Pond, et al. (1960) and Cooper (1965) both reported more epilepsy among females in their studies. Thus, the question is not completely settled, although it does appear that males generally have more epilepsy, proportionately, than do females.

Not unlike many previous findings, Table VII-5 also highlights higher rates of prevalence for blacks (12.9) than for the whites (8.9) of the county. Unfortunately, most past researchers generally have not controlled or reported results by the important variable of race.

Some of the reasons for greater prevalence of epilepsy among blacks have already been enumerated in this volume. However, as Kurtzke, et al. (1971:7) have pointed out, socioeconomic conditions may well be the most important underlying cause of white-nonwhite differences. The differential cause may well be that socioeconomic conditions in turn affect the amount of cerebral injury, as well as differences in medical care. Nevertheless, the possibility still exists that true differences in the prevalence of epilepsy may occur by color. At any rate, these matters require additional research in an effort to explain them. A further examination of the subject by Kurtzke (1972) reveals that, although death rates per 100,000 people caused by epilepsy have declined since World War II, the rate is still 1.2 in the United States. For Alabama, the corresponding figure is 1.6: 0.8 for whites (lower than for U.S. whites) and 3.7 for nonwhites (higher than for U.S. nonwhites).

A major problem in evaluating the age-specific rates from Table VII-

Table VII–5.
Prevalence Rates Based on Confirmed Cases of Epilepsy, by Age, Race, and Sex, Piedmont County, Alabama, 1974

Age Group	Males			Females			Total		
	White	Black	Total	White	Black	Total	White	Black	Total
0–4	1.8	—	1.5	1.9	7.4	3.0	1.8	4.1	2.2
5–9	9.7	24.0	12.1	1.8	6.8	2.3	5.9	14.8	7.5
10–14	7.2	21.4	9.6	6.4	—	5.2	6.8	10.6	7.5
15–19	12.3	6.8	11.3	7.1	—	5.9	9.9	3.9	8.8
20–24	18.3	44.1	21.8	2.3	—	1.9	10.3	19.7	11.7
25–29	7.8	40.8	11.5	11.6	30.8	14.1	9.8	35.1	12.9
30–34	12.9	27.0	14.2	7.1	22.7	8.5	9.9	24.7	11.2
35–39	13.5	—	12.2	20.3	—	17.5	16.8	—	15.0
40–44	13.4	—	11.8	4.8	16.1	6.3	8.9	8.9	8.9
45–49	11.2	22.7	12.4	9.1	—	8.1	10.0	10.5	10.1
50–54	12.6	52.6	16.1	2.5	—	2.2	7.5	21.1	8.9
55–59	2.5	—	2.2	13.5	—	11.9	8.2	—	7.2
60–64	14.4	15.4	14.5	2.1	33.9	5.6	7.9	24.2	9.8
65–69	6.6	—	5.8	5.7	—	5.0	6.1	—	5.4
70–74	13.9	—	12.3	—	—	—	6.4	—	5.7
75–79	6.5	—	6.0	10.2	62.5	14.1	8.6	33.3	10.5
80–84	33.7	200.0	42.6	7.6	—	7.2	18.1	83.3	21.5
85+	—	—	—	—	—	—	—	—	—
Totals	11.2[a]	18.9[b]	12.2	6.6[c]	7.5	6.7	8.9	12.9	9.4
Age Categories									
0–19	7.9	15.4	9.2	4.4	3.7	4.3	6.2	9.5	6.8
20–64	12.5	24.7	13.8	7.9	11.1	8.3	10.1	17.3	10.9
65+	12.3	10.9	12.2	4.9	8.3	5.3	8.2	9.4	7.8

[a] Includes 6 whose ages were not reported.　[b] Includes 2 whose ages were not reported.　[c] Includes 2 whose ages were not reported.

5 is the fact that some of the age groups were so very small, especially among blacks, whose total population is only about 2,200. The reader should be cautioned against indiscriminate interpretation and use of the prevalence for age-sex-race groups in which the individual rate is disproportionately high when compared to the rates in adjoining columns. Often very high rates were based on extremely small base populations.

Because the numbers in some of the age groups are extremely small, especially with blacks and the very old people, they have subsequently been grouped roughly into school age, working age, and retired age categories as an aid in analysis and interpretation. It is believed that this procedure will reveal the more critical differences. Furthermore, it smooths out the peaks and valleys of the smaller age, race, and sex groups. Nevertheless, this procedure does not obscure the basic differences of higher rates for males and for blacks.

The age group with the highest prevalence is the 20–64 age group, in all cases. Normally, one might expect to find more cases in the school age group, as is the situation with mental retardation. In the present example, the author believes the explanation to be that many cases among preschoolers have not yet been diagnosed, as is hinted at by looking at the younger age groups in the top portion of the table. Additionally, many infants and very young children perhaps have cases that have not yet surfaced.

The middle group, those of working age, may be somewhat higher than the younger group because of trauma, arteriosclerosis, and the like being the precipitating factors in the original occurrence of the disorder. For each group, the rate for the retired group drops below that of the working age group. Why this decline should take place is not certain, but it holds in each of the races and by sex. Speculation might lead into several avenues of thought. First, among young blacks of both sexes and among young white females, epilepsy is among the top 15 causes of death, which is a surprising finding (U.S. Department of Health, Education, and Welfare, 1968). Another puzzling fact is that often alcoholism, arteriosclerosis, and the like, including trauma, may be the precipitating causes of epilepsy. It would appear that more, not fewer, cases would be found in this group of advanced age. It may be that people who are epileptics in the middle years of life die off faster from epilepsy or from other primary impairments, while these latter causes may be reported more often as the primary cause of death. Likewise, epileptics who live until the older ages may die more often of illnesses associated with old age as the primary cause of death than they do of epilepsy. The attending physician thus may be more likely to report the age-associated illness, rather than epilepsy, as the cause of death.

In considering the types of epilepsy reported in the records, it should be pointed out that a substantial number of our cases were not reported in terms of the type of epilepsy. In 64 of the total 153 cases, 41.8 percent, no report was included as to type; 67, or 44 percent, were gran mal; 11 cases of petit mal were reported, 6 described as psychomotor; 2 of Jacksonian; and 1 each of temporal lobe, "clinical," and nocturnal.

AN EVALUATION OF THE CLINICAL FINDINGS

In the opinion of this writer, the number of cases of epilepsy confirmed by clinical diagnosis in Piedmont County is still an understatement of the true prevalence of the disorder there and must be regarded as a minimal estimate at best. Several reasons are offered for stating this belief, after carefully reviewing the findings of the researchers. For example, one of the doctors in the clinic was opposed to labeling a person as epileptic. Thus, he would record "convulsive disorder," but not epilepsy, as his diagnosis. Often, other findings provided insufficient evidence for the researchers to include the person in the epileptic category. Secondly, it is apparent that many persons are prone to hide this particular disability, even from their doctors. If the disorder is fortunately of a mild nature and poses no particular overriding difficulties to the person affected, then perhaps the underestimate becomes less a problem in actuality. Thirdly, it is entirely possible that many cases exist that are largely unsurfaced because of their relatively mild nature. Especially among infants and children, it is quite possible that many of these cases have not yet been discovered. Another possibility is that with better prenatal care and better medical care in general, the numbers of young with epilepsy may actually be on the decline. However, the only prevalence data based on long-term estimates do not support this suggestion, and it must be rejected, since Kurland (and others) found greater numbers of epileptics among the younger age groups. Merlis (1972), reviewing several studies, concluded that approximately 65–75 percent of epileptics have onset of epilepsy before age 20. Thus, it is likely that they have not yet been discovered in Piedmont County. Another unexplored possibility is that the epileptics are not so mobile in terms of job flexibility as are other people and perhaps have remained in Piedmont County, while nonepileptics have moved away in greater numbers.

Table VII-6 permits a closer comparison of the findings by age group and sex with those of Kurland for two time periods, 1955 and 1965, and for Hauser, et al. Dr. Kurland was one of the coworkers of Hauser in the latter report, and it is most likely that the findings, although reported separately, actually come from the same data. The prevalence rates found in Piedmont County, Alabama, are higher than those in Rochester, Minnesota. This finding holds for all except the very youngest age group and is especially noticeable in the oldest group.

Several factors may be potentially explanatory for the higher preva-

Table VII-6.

A Comparison of Survey Prevalence Rates with those of Kurland and Hauser, et al., by Age Group and Sex, Piedmont County, Alabama

Age Groups	Piedmont Co.	Kurland, 1955	Hauser, et al., 1966
0–9	5.01	5.79	4.4
10–19	8.46	3.45	6.6
20–29	12.27	3.47	4.4
30–39	12.92	4.33	7.6
40–49	11.13	3.36	6.4
50–59	8.04	3.59	8.2
60–69	7.96	1.20	8.2
70–79	8.78	0.78	7.8*
80+	12.82	1.86	
Totals	9.41	3.65	4.5

	Males		Females	
	Piedmont Co.	Kurland, 1965**	Piedmont Co.	Kurland, 1965**
0–9	7.04	12.37	2.91	5.33
10–19	10.44	7.37	5.54	3.17
20–29	17.04	7.41	7.87	3.19
30–39	13.21	9.25	12.64	3.98
40–49	12.11	7.18	7.21	3.09
50–59	8.90	7.67	7.24	3.30
60+	12.27	2.00	5.37	1.31
Totals	12.24	7.77	6.73	3.37

*Age group 70+
**These rates are figured on our projection of Kurland's reported rates, adjusted by sex, based on private correspondence with him. The procedure was described in Chapter Six of this volume.

lence rates in the Alabama study. First, Kurland included only those individuals who experienced the onset of their convulsions while living in the study city. The present investigation, however, in an attempt to represent the current situation in the most accurate manner possible, consists of all epileptic persons living in Piedmont County at the time of the study, regardless of where they lived at the time of the onset of their disorder. The author is not absolutely certain that the procedure attributed to Kurland is an entirely accurate reading of his approach, but it does appear from published reports to be the case.

Another factor that cannot be ignored is the rural nature of Piedmont County in contrast to the urban setting of Rochester, Minnesota. Other investigators have felt that rates of prevalence should be higher in rural areas, because medical and other prenatal care is usually not so adequate there. However, Kurtzke (1972:34) has noted that there is " . . . essentially no difference between [prevalence of epilepsy in] metropolitan and non-metropolitan counties in the United States as regards epilepsy frequencies. This suggests that there is no appreciable rural-urban difference in the frequency of epilepsy."

The possibility exists that differences between socioeconomic conditions in the two areas may have a greater influence than rural-urban differences on variations in the findings. While it has long been felt that the lower socioeconomic groups experienced greater proportionate occurrences of epilepsy, an excellent article by Hauser (1972), in which he draws on all relevant past studies, indicates that actually not much research into the subject has been conducted and that the results of the individual studies are somewhat inconclusive on this matter. The current writer hopes to delve into the matter further in his study of Piedmont County.

Another puzzling difference in the prevalence rates encountered in Piedmont County and those reported for Rochester, Minnesota, are the much larger figures encountered in Alabama among the oldest age groups. Even Kurland and Hauser report the possibility of better case ascertainment for the elderly, thus causing a relatively small evaluation for the most elderly group, but the findings in Piedmont County were of much greater magnitude for that particular group. It has not been possible to determine, from examination of Kurland's methodology, whether he included cases of epilepsy in which the onset occurred in late life as a result of strokes, arteriosclerosis, trauma, and the like. It should be noted that the rates from Piedmont County were based on relatively small population bases, and that this reason may be at least partially explanatory.

The method used in the research being reported (reviewing medical records) was not the most effective method for finding prevalence rates for mental retardation and cerebral palsy. Most of these cases were not found in the clinical records since their cases had been referred to state institutions and facilities. A better method to find such a rate would be to contact said state institutions and facilities, *plus* a survey of the population of the area. In the case of epilepsy, the medical survey method was probably the most effective and accurate approach to the task. Considering the stigma attached to the disability, a survey of the population could not be used effectively. The victims of epilepsy and their families would be prone to try to keep the disability hidden and would not be willing to cooperate with the surveyors. Also, because epilepsy can be well controlled with drugs, many people could have the disorder without any suspicion on the part of even the closest associate unless a seizure was witnessed. In all, a close investigation of medical records is perhaps the best method of establishing a prevalence rate for epilepsy.

Although the existence of the medical records in itself presented an invaluable source of information, they were not without their limitations, not the least of which was the difficulty involved in reading the doctors' handwriting, in some instances. A difficulty with somewhat more serious consequences was the fact that for many years, the records were not diagnostically oriented, that is, the doctors often listed complaints and test results, and then listed the prescribed medications. It should be noted that these doctors have recently been more apt to include their diagnoses in a patient's record, that is to say, that they have become more diagnosis-oriented.

References

Cooper, J. E.
    1965   "Epilepsy in a longitudinal survey of 5,000 children." British Medical Journal:1020–22.
Crombie, D. L., et al.
    1960   "A survey of the epilepsies in general practice: a report by the Research Committee of the College of General Practitioners." British Medical Journal:416–22.
Gudmondsson, Gunnar
    1966   "Epilepsy in Iceland: a clinical and epidemiological investigation." Acta Neurologica Scandinavia 43 (Supplement 25):1–124.
Hauser, W. Allen
    1972   "Sex and socioeconomic status." Pp. 89–93 in Milton Alter and W. Allen Hauser (eds.), The Epidemiology of Epilepsy: A Workshop. Washington, D.C.: U.S. Department of Health, Education, and Welfare, Public Health Service, National Institutes of Health, National Institute of Neurological Diseases and Stroke Monograph No. 14.
Hollingsworth, J. Selwyn (ed.)
    1974   Report of Phase II of "Survey of the Developmentally Disabled in Alabama: Needs and Resources." Montgomery: Alabama Department of Mental Health.
Krohn, W.
    1961   "A study of epilepsy in northern Norway, its frequency and character." Acta Psychiatrica Scandinavia 36 (Supplement 150):215–25.
Kurland, Leonard T.
    1959   "The incidence and prevalence of convulsive disorders in a small urban community." Epilepsia 1:143–61.
Kurtzke, John F.
    1972   "Mortality and morbidity data on epilepsy." Pp. 21–36 in Milton Alter and W. Allen Hauser (eds.), The Epidemiology of Epilepsy: A Workshop. Washington, D.C.: U.S. Department of Health, Education, and Welfare, Public Health Service, National Institutes of Health, National Institute of Neurological Diseases and Stroke Monograph No. 14.

Kurtzke, John F., et al.
   1971   Convulsive disorders, unpublished manuscript by L. T. Kurland,
           John F. Kurtzke, and I. D. Goldberg, Epidemiology of Neurologic
           and Sense Organ Diseases (American Public Health Association
           Monograph), to be published by Cambridge: Harvard University
           Press.
Leibowitz, U., and M. Alter
   1968   "A survey of epilepsy in Jerusalem, Israel." Epilepsia 9:87–105.
Logan, W. P. D., and A. A. Cushion
   1958   Studies on Medical and Population Subjects, No. 14. Morbidity Sta-
           tistics from General Practice, Volume 1: General. London: Her Maj-
           esty's Stationery Office.
Merlis, Jerome K.
   1972   "Epilepsy in different age groups." Pp. 83–86 in Milton Alter and
           W. Allen Hauser (eds.), The Epidemiology of Epilepsy: A Workshop.
           Washington, D.C.: U.S. Department of Health, Education, and Wel-
           fare, Public Health Service, National Institutes of Health, National
           Institute of Neurological Diseases and Stroke Monograph No. 14.
Pond, D. A., B. H. Bidwell, and L. Stein
   1960   "A survey of epilepsy in fourteen general practices–I: demographic
           and medical data." Psychiatria, Neurologia, Neurochirurgia 63:217–
           26.
United States Department of Health, Education, and Welfare
   1968   Health Interview Survey. Washington, D.C.: National Center for
           Health Statistics.

CHAPTER EIGHT
PROBLEMS AND TREATMENT OF THE DEVELOPMENTALLY DISABLED IN THREE RURAL ALABAMA COUNTIES

DAVID W. COOMBS

In this chapter is a straightforward account of the information obtained from the interviews in Highland, Piedmont, and Plantation counties. The presentation is descriptive rather than analytical or technical in order to facilitate understanding.

A careful review of the 450 interviews completed showed that in 46 cases the subject of the interview either appeared definitely to the interviewer not to have any of the disabilities being surveyed or the subject and/or guardian denied the presence of the handicap. (Subsequent checks of some of the cases where a parent denied the existence of one or more of the developmental disabilities revealed an unequivocal diagnosis by a competent authority that the person did have the disability in question. However, the interviews were usually terminated in such cases.) This left a total of 404 usable interviews. Of these, reliable confirmation for the presence of the disability(ies) in question existed in 318 cases. Evidence of professional diagnosis was not clear-cut in the remaining 86 interviews although the interviewers felt that the subjects were in fact handicapped by the disability(ies) for which they had been nominated. Nevertheless, in order to strengthen the validity of the results, a decision was made to limit presentation of data to the 318 cases for which there was confirmation.

In view of these problems the sample's representativeness may be somewhat impaired, especially with regard to the more isolated and inaccessible groups in the three populations. However, because of the great care exercised in selecting sample replacements, along with the relatively small size and homogeneity of the populations sampled, the findings probably portray with a fair degree of accuracy the conditions and problems surrounding these disabilities in rural Alabama.

Characteristics of the Sample

In order to understand connections between the life circumstances of the 318 disabled subjects surveyed and the problems they and their families have confronted with the occurrence of a developmental disability, it is necessary to describe what these life circumstances were. Accordingly, the first findings presented are of the social characteristics of the individuals and families surveyed.

Table VIII-1 describes the entire sample in terms of disability, race, and sex. The multiple disability category refers to cases in which the victim had two or all three of the disabilities surveyed. Following are tables that give the same information separately for the three counties.

SEX

Although the nominees from which the sample was drawn were not stratified in advance according to sex, race, or in any other way, males surveyed outnumbered females in all disability categories and for both races (Tables VIII-2, VIII-3, and VIII-4). Among the confirmed epileptics and the cerebral palsied the difference was slight, but for the confirmed mentally retarded and multiply handicapped, it was especially prominent. When the sample is broken down by county, the same pattern holds except for Piedmont County, where the sexes were sampled about equally.

The high ratio of males to females encountered in the samples of the retarded and multiply handicapped has also been found by most other investigators, although the differential varies. Mumbauer and Miller (1970), for example, found that 77 percent of the mentally retarded children referred to agencies in their study were boys, while in Mercer's (1973:73) review of 687 previously identified retardates in Riverside, California, 57 percent were males. Yet Mercer's field survey of mental retardation in Riverside (1973:74) showed almost no difference between the number who were male or female. Conley (1973:18) remarks that, while most agency studies show a male-female ratio of 2 to 1, household surveys like Mercer's show much smaller differences. Mercer (1973:74) believes that males often outnumber females in all but the most careful surveys because the normal-bodied female with a low IQ is not expected to do intellectually demanding work as often as the male and is therefore not labeled by people as retarded.

Although possible with regard to adults, this explanation is inadequate for male-female differences among school age children because boys and girls are expected to do the same work in schools and are given the same tests of intellectual ability. The present findings, based on research in three rural, poor, Southern counties, where intellectually demanding roles are likely not common for either males or females, lend credence to the accuracy of data showing the predominance of male retardates. Mumbauer and Miller (1970) also found in their study of 2,928 exceptional children that boys outnumbered girls by about 3 to 1 for other kinds of physical and emotional disabilities.

Table VIII-1.

Sample of Developmentally Disabled, by Disability, Sex, and Race, All Counties, 1973

Sex and Race	Total		Epilepsy		Cerebral Palsy		Mentally Retarded		Multiply Disabled	
	Number	Percent	Number	Percent	Number	Percent	Number	Percent	Number	Percent
Total	318	100.0	46	100.0	12	100.0	177	100.0	83	100.0
Males	201	63.2	24	52.2	7	58.3	116	65.5	54	65.1
Females	117	36.8	22	47.8	5	41.7	61	34.5	29	34.9
White	175	55.0	31	67.4	9	75.0	87	49.2	48	57.8
Males	108	34.0	16	34.8	5	41.7	54	30.5	33	39.8
Females	67	21.1	15	32.6	4	33.3	33	18.6	15	18.1
Black	97	30.5	9	19.6	1	8.3	63	35.6	24	28.9
Males	64	20.1	5	10.9	1	8.3	42	23.7	16	19.3
Females	33	10.4	4	8.7			21	11.9	8	9.6
Other	2	.6					1	.6	1	1.2
Males	2	.6					1	.6		
Females										
Unsure of Race	1	.3					1	.6		
No Information on Race	43	13.5	6	13.0	2	16.7	25	14.1	10	12.0

Table VIII-2.
Sample of Developmentally Disabled, by Disability, Sex, and Race, Piedmont County, 1973

Sex and Race	Total		Epilepsy		Cerebral Palsy		Mentally Retarded		Multiply Disabled	
	Number	Percent	Number	Percent	Number	Percent	Number	Percent	Number	Percent
Total	87	100.0	15	100.0	4	100.0	41	100.0	27	100.0
Males	49	56.3	8	53.3	3	75.0	20	48.8	18	66.7
Females	38	43.7	7	46.7	1	25.0	21	51.2	9	33.3
White	52	59.8	11	73.3	4	100.0	18	43.9	19	70.4
Males	31	35.6	6	40.0	3	75.0	7	17.1	15	55.6
Females	21	24.1	5	33.3	1	25.0	11	26.8	4	14.8
Black	18	20.7	2	13.3			14	34.1	2	7.4
Males	10	11.5	2	13.3			7	17.1	1	3.7
Females	8	9.2	2	13.3			7	17.1	1	3.7
Other										
Males										
Females										
Unsure of Race										
No Information on Race	17	19.5	2	13.3			9	22.0	6	22.2

Table VIII-3.

Sample of Developmentally Disabled, by Disability, Sex, and Race, Plantation County, 1973

Sex and Race	Total		Epilepsy		Cerebral Palsy		Mentally Retarded		Multiply Disabled	
	Number	Percent	Number	Percent	Number	Percent	Number	Percent	Number	Percent
Total	98	100.0	15	100.0	2	100.0	56	100.0	25	100.0
Males	68	69.4	8	53.3	1	50.0	41	73.2	18	72.0
Females	30	29.6	7	46.7	1	50.0	15	26.8	7	28.0
White	9	9.2	4	26.7	1	50.0	3	5.4	1	4.0
Males	6	6.1	2	13.3			3	5.4	1	4.0
Females	3	3.1	2	13.3	1	50.0	3	5.4	1	4.0
Black	73	73.5	7	46.7	1	50.0	44	78.6	21	84.0
Males	49	50.0	3	20.0	1	50.0	31	55.4	14	56.0
Females	24	23.5	4	26.7			13	23.2	7	28.0
Other	1	1.0					1	1.8		
Males	1	1.0					1	1.8		
Females										
Unsure of Race										
No Information on Race	15	15.2	4	26.7			8	14.3	3	12.0
Males	12	12.2	3	20.0			6	10.7	3	12.0
Females	3	3.0	1	6.7			2	3.6		

Table VIII-4.
Sample of Developmentally Disabled, by Disability, Sex, and Race, Highland County, 1973

Sex and Race	Total		Epilepsy		Cerebral Palsy		Mentally Retarded		Multiply Disabled	
	Number	Percent	Number	Percent	Number	Percent	Number	Percent	Number	Percent
Total	132	100.0	16	100.0	6	100.0	80	100.0	30	100.0
Males	80	60.6	8	50.0	3	50.0	53	66.3	16	53.3
Females	52	39.4	8	50.0	3	50.0	27	33.7	14	46.7
White	109	82.6	16	100.0	4	66.6	64	80.0	25	83.3
Males	67	50.8	8	50.0	2	33.3	43	53.7	14	46.7
Females	42	31.8	8	50.0	2	33.3	21	26.3	11	36.7
Black	4	3.0					4	5.0		
Males	3	2.3					3	3.7		
Females	1	.8					1	1.3		
Other	1	.8					1	1.3		
Males										
Females	1	.8					1	1.3		
Unsure of Race	1	.8					1	1.3		
No Information on Race	18	13.6			2	33.3	11	13.7	5	16.7

Assuming this difference is real, its cause is not clear. Most of the retarded in our sample, whether male or female, were from lower class backgrounds, and neither sex was disproportionately black or white. One is unable to ascertain from the data whether boys are systematically given less intellectual stimulation than girls in rural Alabama or whether boys are normally exposed to circumstances that could result in traumatic head injuries more than are girls. Impressionistically, the latter would seem to be true and may at least partially explain the predominance of males among the retardates sampled.

RACE

Most research on the psychosocial correlates of epilepsy and mental retardation in the United States shows that blacks are more likely to be afflicted by those disabilities than are whites. Little racial difference has been found nationally in the prevalence of cerebral palsy. In the present study, the proportion of confirmed black epileptics interviewed in the three counties was either the same as or less than the proportion of blacks in their respective populations. Thus, 20 percent of the confirmed epileptics interviewed in the three counties were black while 19 percent of their total population was black in 1970. In Plantation County, 27 percent of the epileptics interviewed were presumably white as is 30 percent of the population. The qualifier, "presumably," has been used because, as the figures in Table VIII-3 show, only 47 percent of the remaining epileptics interviewed in Plantation County were categorized as black. This result is due to the unfortunate fact that race was not specified in 26 percent of the interviews. Nevertheless, blacks did not constitute a disproportionate number of the epileptics drawn from Plantation County as was expected in view of their inferior living and health conditions. The possibility exists that epileptic seizures are not labeled as such to the same extent among blacks as among whites. This supposition would seem unlikely, however, given the ease with which black respondents identified epileptic seizures as epilepsy.

As Table VIII-1 shows, only 1 of the 12 cerebral palsy victims interviewed in the three counties was black. The small size of the total sample of palsy victims does not permit statements or inferences about the normality of this distribution.

Among the mentally retarded surveyed in the three counties, blacks were, as in most other American studies, disproportionately represented. Of all confirmed mental retardates interviewed, 36 percent were black whereas 20 percent of the combined populations of the three counties were black. In Plantation County, where 68 percent of the population was black, 78 percent of the mental retardates sampled were black.

Racial differences in the sample of multiply disabled showed roughly the same pattern. Heber (1970:10), as well as Lapous and Weitzner (1970:197), in reviewing the American literature on mental retardation, comment on the consistency of findings that show disproportionate numbers of blacks and other nonwhites among the mentally retarded. The differential generally holds across regions and in cities as well as rural areas although it is somewhat narrower in cities (Heber, 1970:11). Mercer (1973:78–79) found in Riverside that when social class was taken into account, these differences were minimized, that is, the proportion of lower class blacks who were mentally retarded was about the same as the proportion of lower class whites. Because so many more blacks than whites *were* lower class in Riverside, blacks in general were overrepresented in the population of retardates to the same degree they were overrepresented in the lower class.

Curiously, accounting for or "controlling" social class did not eliminate the differences between whites and Mexican-Americans in Riverside (Mercer, 1973:79). Mercer (1973:83–95, 171–82) attributes her finding, that more Mexican-Americans than whites are identified as retarded at all social class levels, to the marked cultural differences between the two groups. That is, she believes Mexican-Americans at any class level are at a disadvantage in performing on intelligence tests standardized for middle class white Americans. Because the adaptive behavior and occupational performance in the "real world" of Mexican-Americans in Riverside were about the same as those of whites (of the same educational and social class level), it appears that Mercer's conclusions are correct.

It is not possible to determine whether social class, race, and mental retardation are related in the same way among the Alabama sample as in Riverside because our entire sample of confirmed black mental retardates was, by any criteria, lower class. About 75 percent of the confirmed white retardates were also of the lower class. This finding is not surprising, given that almost all of the black population in the three counties and, except for Plantation County, most of the white population are, in terms of income and occupation, lower class (see Chapter Two). However, the larger proportion of black mental retardates sampled may be due to the fact that more blacks than whites are lower class and the fact that the black lower class is even poorer than the white.

There may be other reasons for the racial difference. One of these is likely to be the difference in age structure between the black and white populations. The median age of the black population in predominantly black Plantation County was 18 in 1970 versus a median age of 32 for that county's white population (U.S. Bureau of the Census:1972a). Similar age differences were recorded in the other two counties. The predominantly black counties of the Black Belt in general had the highest proportions of their population below age 18. The prevalence of mental retardation all over the United States is highest during the school years because school children are regularly given IQ tests that enable testers to identify and label retarded children, whereas many mildly retarded adults escape the label in undemanding jobs and disappear into lower class subcultures. Thus, any group in a population with a relatively high proportion of school-age children should have a higher proportion of labeled mental retardates. Absence of one or more parents is also a contributing factor in the occurrence of mental retardation, and the frequency of female-headed households is much higher for blacks all over the United States. In predominantly black Plantation County, the U.S. Census for 1970 (1972b) reported that an extraordinary 40 percent of all persons under 18 years of age were not living with both parents.

Other important factors contributing to the prevalence of mental retardation (all linked, however, to socioeconomic status as well as race) are environmental deprivation and acceptance of the label itself. It is probable that the black population of the three counties, being "poorest of the poor," will have experienced environmental deprivation to a greater extent than whites. It is also known that blacks are, in general, more accepting of the label "mental retardate" than whites and less reticent about identifying family members as such.

Unfortunately our survey data do not enable us to determine whether these factors contribute to the black-white differential. Nevertheless, it is the overwhelming impression of those professionals who helped carry out the survey that such is the case.

SOCIAL CLASS

A great debate exists at present as to whether a low level of intelligence is primarily a result of one's biological inheritance or whether it stems mostly from environmental learning (or lack of learning). Those who take the latter position see low social class status, with the environmental deprivation that often accompanies it, as a principal cause of mental retardation. There is no disputing the fact that intelligence test scores directly correlate with social class position and that the highest rates of mental retardation in the United States are found among lower class groups (see Heber, 1970:13–23). Moreover, this particular relationship is not peculiar to this country. In a 1967 survey of English school children, about 1 percent of those classified as upper class scored in the 50 to 79 range on IQ tests while 10 percent of the children from lower class families scored in that range (Lapous and Weitzner, 1970).

The incidence of epilepsy in the United States shows a similar pattern according to most studies, with lower class groups usually (but not always) being disproportionately affected (see Hauser, 1972).

The debate as to the causes of these patterns is still unresolved, but if the side effects of lower class status such as poor schooling, lack of mental stimulation in the home environment, absence of parents, poor nutrition and health care, large family size, etc., do in fact contribute to the incidence of mental retardation and epilepsy, then the rural, poor populations reported on here should be more subject to these disabilities than the American population in general. Our data do not provide a reliable base for making prevalence estimates of confirmed cases in the three counties, but the data do indicate that 85 percent of our total sample of confirmed cases in all three disability categories were of lower class status. This finding was expected because all types of mental retardation, except severe retardation of known organic origin (see Heber, 1970:34–35), and epilepsy occur more frequently among the lower class. We also know that the incidence of poverty in all three counties is extraordinarily high, although it does not characterize 85 percent of their populations (see Chapter Three). Nevertheless, census reports (U.S. Bureau of the Census, 1970b) indicate that the proportion of families with incomes of $10,000 a year or more in 1969 in the three counties ranged between 15 and 20 percent (in comparison with 31 pecent of all families in the state of Alabama). Thus, it would appear that the disabled in our sample did not come *disproportionately* from the lower classes but that nevertheless, it is primarily the lower classes, least equipped in terms of material resources, which must deal with the problems of these disabilities.

AGE

The handicapped individual's age also affects the kinds of adjustments which the disabled and his or her family make. Most of the epileptics, the palsied, and the multiply handicapped in our survey were adults between the ages of 19 and 64. However, 69 percent (or 123 of 177) of the mentally retarded surveyed were between 6 and 18 years of age. The fact that only two were younger than 6 years is probably because most of the mentally retarded are not positively identified until they enter school and are tested. But why were so few (relatively) older than 19? Most members of the population in the three counties are over 20. Few have been institutionalized outside the counties. The answer may be that the mentally retarded *tend* to "disappear" after leaving school in that many (probably the mildly retarded) obtain jobs and are no longer thought of as retarded. This phenomenon is known to happen in urban areas, and it is entirely plausible that the same thing occurs in poor rural areas like the ones studied here. In fact, it may happen with even greater frequency in rural areas because educational levels are lower, demands are less exacting, and life in general is less complicated. The mildly retarded adult in Plantation or Highland counties is not required to learn subway routes or otherwise deal with the ever-changing exigencies of city life. Yet, we cannot tell from our data whether this has happened in the counties surveyed.

MARITAL STATUS

Few adults in the sample (other than the epileptics) had ever married. Specifically, only 2 out of 8 eligible (in terms of age) cerebral palsied and 6 of 70 eligible mentally retarded had ever married. Barely half of the 40 epileptics over 18 were or had been married. Nevertheless, most of the disabled adults were extraordinarily dependent on others. This lack of personal autonomy is shown by the finding that only 5 of the mentally retarded adults surveyed and none of the palsied or multiply handicapped lived in their own homes. Practically all lived with parents or other relatives. Of the adult epileptics, more than half—57 percent— were living independently.

JOB STATUS

A similar pattern of dependence emerges when job histories are ex- amined for the 118 disabled adults for whom this information was ac- quired. Of this group, only 22 were formally employed in full or part- time jobs. This pattern held true for all disability categories, even the epileptic who surprisingly fared little better than the mentally retarded or cerebral palsied in finding employment. In numbers, 8 of 31 adult epileptics held jobs while 7 of 38 adult retardates, 2 of 7 palsied adults, and 5 of 41 multiply handicapped adults were employed at the time of the survey. There was no variation in this pattern among the three counties. '

In spite of the rural and economically underdeveloped character of the three counties, the Center for Business and Economic Research at The University of Alabama (1973) reports that unemployment rates in the three counties were little different from the state's unemployment rate during 1973 (about 3.8 per 100 employable adults). Thus, the ex- traordinary paucity of employment among the disabled cannot, on the face of it, be attributed to economic conditions or a generalized lack of job opportunities. The Epilepsy Foundation of America (1972) esti- mated that, nationwide, up to 25 percent of medically controlled, nor- mally intelligent epileptics are chronically unemployed because of per- sonal apprehension (of the epileptics themselves), the resistance of other employees, discriminating work compensation laws, and a generalized lack of training, counseling, and placement services for epileptics. It is easy to imagine that all of these reasons may help explain why so few of the adult epileptics surveyed in the three counties were employed. Lack of placement services is certainly a factor.

Concerning employment of the mentally retarded, Conley (1973:187) cites studies in diverse communities which show that given normal economic conditions about 90 percent of all mildly retarded adults are employed and self-supporting at any given time. Yet he feels that many of these individuals are still marginally dependent on families and friends because of low salaries and poor budget management. Moreover, after age 40 many mentally retarded workers evince great difficulty in retaining their jobs (Conley, 1973:195). Conley found that few retardates with an IQ level below 50 were employed or earned enough to be self-sufficient (1973:189). Of course, the severely retarded are also likely to be multiply handicapped and this further reduces their employability.

Conley (1973:195) believes that the mentally retarded living in rural areas may have an employment advantage in that work of a rural nature is typically less intellectually demanding. In his view such an advantage should hold in spite of the generally higher levels of unemployment and the relative inferiority of rehabilitation programs in rural areas. This finding may indeed apply in the three counties studied here as far as the *mildly* retarded are concerned. It would appear, however, that most of the confirmed retardates sampled in this study were unable to work (in the formal sense) because of the severity of their handicap. Although only 5 of 177 retardates interviewed reported noncerebral physical disabilities, less than half could reportedly carry on a normal conversation or were functionally literate. In fact, 80 percent of the 96 unemployed adults in all disability categories reported severity of the handicap as a reason for their unemployment. The remaining 19 cited a variety of reasons including discrimination (against the disability itself). Epileptics, who possessed the greatest functioning ability, also reported that they were more subject to discrimination. Epileptics constituted half of all the disabled surveyed who had ever been fired from a job.

About 90 percent of those disabled who did work in the three counties were, aside from the epileptics, laboring in lower-level jobs—as farm or nonfarm manual laborers, service workers, or operatives. In the nation as a whole Conley (1973:215–16) found that even the mildly retarded usually held semiskilled or unskilled jobs (though many did work themselves up into skilled positions). Moreover, their average earnings were about 14 percent below earnings for the labor force in general during 1970.

Problems of Adaptation: The Disabled

Defining or measuring "adaptation" is somewhat difficult and even arbitrary given the many cultural and personal definitions of this concept. For purposes of the survey, it seemed logical to use a widely accepted cultural definition, applicable to the disabled individual, in order to maximize understanding and agreement. Accordingly, a modification of a definition from Conley (1973:8) has been utilized. For the disabled adult, adaptation is defined as the degree to which the individual is able to maintain himself independently in his community, meet his own needs as well as those of significant others, and fulfill those personal and social responsibilities set by the community. The adaptation of disabled children could be measured by the same criteria except for independence in the community, since children are not expected to be fully independent in that sense.

Adaptation of the disabled person to his or her social environment is, of course, not a unilateral process. The family and friends of the disabled must also adapt in their relationships with the disabled. Their adaptation can also be measured by the degree to which they maintain autonomy, by the extent they meet their own needs as they help the disabled, and by costs incurred in doing so. For the family of the disabled, especially a poor family, tangible costs must be paid as adaptation occurs. Leisure and even work time that would otherwise be available are reduced. Money may be spent on the disabled, depending on the extent of the handicap. Psychological stress may result from dealing with the needs and behavior of the disabled and from perceptions of the "stigma" that is placed on them.

Conceivably there are benefits too. In some cases the disabled may work and contribute income to his or her family or at the very least contribute to the accomplishment of household and farm chores. Pleasure may be derived from selflessly meeting the needs of others, and some may even enjoy having others dependent on them.

ADAPTATION OF THE DISABLED

The manner in which both the disabled individual and significant others adapt to each other depends on a number of factors, including the nature and extent of the disability itself, the amount of help received (both professional and informal), race, social class, interpersonal relations within the family, and the personalities of all involved. Zigler and Harter (1969) found that for the mildly retarded (IQ scores ranging from 50 to 75) social competence, or adaptation, was more influenced by personality and motivation than by the intellectual deficit itself.

Nevertheless, the type and degree of disability are obviously important. In our sample, the multiply handicapped and the cerebral palsied were, in terms of physical mobility and functioning, the most disabled. On the level of intellectual functioning, the multiply handicapped and mentally retarded were the least able. Epileptics were least afflicted, both in mind and body. In spite of this variation, relatively few of the disabled individuals sampled in any category had failed to develop very basic self and motor care abilities—for example, feeding and dressing oneself, being able to sit, stand, and walk. Even among the cerebral palsied, about 75 percent were to some degree self-sufficient.

Most of the sample could also communicate their needs, though 17 percent of the mentally retarded and 21 percent of the multiply disabled could do so only within the family. Thus, few were so disabled that they were not independent at the level of basic bodily care and mobility.

Moving to higher levels of adaptation, such as reading and writing, only about one third of the retarded and less than one quarter of the multiply handicapped were able to perform. Of the 195 disabled persons between the ages of 5 and 20, 112 (or about 60 percent) were attending school. Most of those not in school were retarded or multiply handicapped. Strangely, the poorest of the three counties, Plantation, had the highest proportion of school age retardates in the sample who were attending school (89 percent). In Highland County only 40 percent of the school age retarded who were sampled were reportedly in school while in Piedmont County the proportion was 60 percent. Of those not in school 28 percent of the mentally retarded children and 38 percent of the multiply handicapped children in all three counties were reportedly excluded by parents and/or doctors from school due to the severity of their disability. Most of the remaining parents providing reasons for exclusion kept handicapped children at home because special classes or programs were not available. A footnote to these findings is that, of those retarded children attending special classes at school (77 percent), most were between the fourth and ninth grades. If these results are typical, it may be that mentally retarded children are often not diagnosed as such until they reach the third or fourth grade.

Earlier in this chapter it was stated that most of the disabled between 20 and 64 years of age in our sample were unmarried, unemployed, and living with parents or other relatives. Thus, at the level of adult adaptation, few could perform independently. Except for the epileptics, severity of the disability itself kept most of them from assuming these adult roles.

Conley (1973:12) classifies dependent mentally retarded adults in three ways, according to overall level of adaptation or functioning capability. The highest level is represented by the marginally dependent adult who is capable of self-support and independent living but needs special assistance when accomplishing complex or stressful goals such as finding a job or budgeting funds. The semidependent adult can work and perform under sheltered conditions but needs guidance in most day-to-day activities. The dependent adult requires constant care and supervision. Aside from the epileptics, the great majority of the subjects surveyed, both adults and children, fall in the intermediate category of semidependence. Relatively few—27 in all—3 epileptics, 13 mental retardates, and 11 multiply disabled—had even been institutionalized because of inability to perform basic functions. Most of the group had adapted fairly well in carrying out basic self-care tasks and communicating their needs to others. Few of the adults surveyed, however— about 20 percent—had been able to adapt to normal social responsibilities of economic self-support or marriage.

In the realm of interpersonal relations practically all of the subjects appeared to be well adapted. Only 18 percent reportedly had difficulties in their relations with siblings and peers, and these were attributed to a lack of understanding on the part of friends or relatives. Acceptance by siblings was even more widespread, there being only 10 subjects in the entire sample of confirmed cases who reportedly had been rejected. Epileptics had more difficulties adapting in this sphere than did other disabled in contrast to their relatively high levels of adaptation in other areas.

Unfortunately, there is no way of directly determining the role played by social class, personality factors, and outside help in the adaptation of the 318 disabled individuals surveyed. The importance of these factors is made apparent by the recent emphasis on helping the mentally retarded with personality and environmental assets rather than through formal teaching methods (Klapper, 1970). The survey data do indicate, however, that degree of disability and race do markedly influence adaptation. Overall, blacks in the present study were better adapted to their environment than whites, as were those disabled with higher physical and intellectual capabilities. In addition it would seem that good interpersonal relations have been a positive factor in helping the disabled to adapt.

A comment on the contemporary trend toward deinstitutionalization of the mentally retarded in Alabama is called for here. In spite of the care with which the program is carried out, severe problems of adaptation for those being released can be expected unless they are placed in appropriate jobs with professional supervision, or unless the work ethic expectations about the productive-work obligation of adults are changed. The latter may be necessary in many areas given the difficulties our largely noninstitutional groups have had in obtaining and holding jobs outside the home.

Problems of Adaptation: The Family of the Disabled

For family members (as well as peers), adaptation involves more than learning to perform familial roles while coping with the extraordinary needs of a disabled member. It also entails acceptance—of having a positive attitude toward the disabled person and allowing him or her active participation in the family. Acceptance is subjective adaptation. The degree of adaptation by family members and peers is a consequence of several factors including the nature and extent of the disability; personalities and motivations of parents, siblings, etc.; amount of knowledge about the disability; community or cultural definitions of the disability; and family income. Several studies of adult epileptics reveal that the less frequent and severe the convulsions, the greater the likelihood they would marry and experience marital stability (Pond, et al., 1960; Zielinski, 1972).

Acceptance of epilepsy has increased markedly over the past 25 years. In 1949, 24 percent of American parents questioned objected to having their children play with epileptics. By 1969, barely 9 percent objected. Of the employers polled in a 1949 study, 35 percent said they would not hire epileptics under any circumstance, whereas only 12 percent said they would refuse to hire them in 1969 (Caveness, et al., 1969). Unfortunately, greater resistance was encountered in the South in 1969 where 11 percent of the parents and 19 percent of the employers surveyed were still unaccepting of epileptics.

Nevertheless, epilepsy is no longer labeled a hopeless or dangerous disease as it was in the recent past. Undoubtedly, recent advances in drug therapy, which permit a high degree of seizure control for many epileptics, have made acceptance easier. Zielinski (1972) found that epileptics with employment and/or familial problems invariably were either subject to severe, frequent convulsions or suffered from associated problems such as emotional instability or mental retardation. Otherwise, the degree of effective disability for the epileptic whose seizures are controlled is, in reality, minimal, and more a consequence of lingering public fears and prejudice than of the condition itself.

In the survey it was found that families of epileptics with controlled seizures were minimally inconvenienced in the performance of daily, routine activities. Two families felt a need for special training for the disabled and in only one case was there a felt need for specialized, professional day care or, failing this, institutionalization. The most common problem for families of epileptics was the necessity and expense of providing medication. Some of the adult epileptics, however, believed that they were victims of job discrimination (and in fact only half were employed at the time of the survey). Some resentment was also expressed at the Alabama law that requires an epileptic to be declared competent in court before he is permitted to drive.

In spite of the epileptics' minimal interference with day-to-day family functioning, they were relatively less accepted by siblings than were subjects with other disabilities. This difference may be due to the fact that epilepsy inspires more fear because of the suddenness and unpredictability of its onset. In the rural setting of the survey such fears and the myths that accompany them have likely remained strong.

By way of contrast, the few confirmed cerebral palsy victims were entirely accepted in the family setting, yet in almost all cases they caused far greater problems of adaptation because of demands for special attention and care, expense, and time. Whereas in only one of the epileptics' families was there a significant reduction of leisure time, discretionary income, shopping, and other activities outside the home; in most instances where the disabled was palsied or multiply handicapped normal activities and income were negatively affected. For example, in all 12 families where the subject was palsied, extra medical expenses of all kinds, as well as expenses for special equipment, existed. Sixty-seven percent of the 83 families that cared for a multiply handicapped person incurred extra expenses of this nature. Thus, it would appear that levels of adaptation for families of the palsied and the multiply handicapped were much lower than was the case for epileptics. This observation is not to deny that, subjectively, family members may feel very positive toward their charges.

Problems of adaptation to a mentally retarded child or adult are perhaps more difficult, not only because of differences in the nature of the disability but also because the label mentally retarded evokes such a negative image with implications of genetic inferiority for the family. In other words, the social stigma of mental retardation induces more culpability and shame for parents and, as a result, studies show that parents tend to evaluate their retarded children much less favorably than normal children (see Adams, 1971; Self, 1970) or even emotionally disturbed children (Ricci, 1970). Jano (1970) also found a direct relationship between social class level and negative evaluations, that is, the higher the class level of parents, the higher the level of rejection. A related finding in a sample survey by Meyers, et al. (1966) showed that nonwhite families demonstrated more acceptance of mentally retarded children than did white families.

Despite verbal nonacceptance, most American families prefer not to institutionalize their retarded members (Wilson, 1970). Tizard (1968) found the same thing to be true in England. Conley (1973:173) points out that only about 5 percent of the known retarded population in the United States is in special institutions. Conley (1973:167) also notes that in 1960 the percentage of nonwhites in American institutions for the mentally retarded was about that of whites, despite the higher prevalence rates of mental retardation for the nonwhite population. This finding illustrates the fact of more acceptance among nonwhites and perhaps greater ignorance about the availability of institutional care.

The data collected in this survey indicate great reluctance to institutionalize a mentally retarded family member (only 13 of 177 confirmed cases in the sample had ever been institutionalized). Institutionalization was (reportedly) prompted only by the inability of the family to provide the special education or training needed. Moreover, acceptance of the retarded member was reported to be well-nigh universal within the rural families interviewed. Adams (1971) believes that acceptance is a consequence of the capacity of the environment—social and physical—to "contain" the mentally retarded person. It was noted previously that, except for nonagricultural employment opportunities, rural environments with their slower pace, less complex life style, and fewer demands are relatively high in their capacity to contain the mentally retarded. The same may be said for lower class, and especially black lower class, familial environments. Thus, it is likely that because most of the retarded in our sample were rural, lower class, and in many cases, black, levels of acceptance were high.

In other respects, an overwhelming number of families with mentally retarded members also manifested high levels of positive adaptation. Only 4 percent of the respondents said that the presence of the disabled had had major adverse effects on the marriage of the parents or the integration of the family. This finding is consistent with those of a study by Fowle (1968), comparing the effects on marital integration of having a severely retarded child in or out of an institution. In Fowle's study of 70 families, presence or absence of the affected child had no measurable impact on marital integration.

Here and there individual families reported specific problems of adaptation, including: (1) added difficulties in arranging activities outside the home such as vacations, shopping trips, visits to relatives, or church; (2) the inability of working mothers to work outside the home (28 percent of the families in the sample cited this problem); (3) added difficulties in securing better employment outside the immediate area for working fathers (15 percent); (4) extra monetary expenses; and (5) excessive demands on time and physical energy.

In short, the major problems derived from lack of money and reduction of time and mobility. Blacks were even less likely than whites to report adverse effects on familial operations, possibly because of the greater prevalence of large, extended families among blacks. However, as money expenditures went up, complaints about problems in general increased irrespective of race.

Although some problems of adaptation in the fulfillment of normal familial duties were in evidence, it is remarkable how few complaints of this kind were voiced given the very limited economic resources of most families. On the other hand time may be on their side in comparison with urban families in the sense that demands are fewer and less regulated by the clock. It is said that the presence of a disabled person in a household can bring family members together or increase cohesiveness as well as lessen it. In the three counties studied the evidence suggests that the disabled had neither a positive nor negative effect on the closeness of the family or its day-to-day functioning but was integrated and accepted with a minimum of subjective discomfort. Adaptation was accomplished with limited material resources. Yet as heartening as these findings may be for the overall well-being of the disabled and his family, it is also clear that objectively and relative to middle class standards, greater material aid and professional help would make the burden (they deny) much lighter.

Orientations toward Assistance

By and large, outside assistance to the disabled and/or their families was minimal and less than what they might expect today. Rural people are notably independent and this may have been a factor, although in many cases felt needs existed for several kinds of assistance. Impressionistically, it also appeared that many respondents were simply unaware of existing services. Only 1 out of 10 reported having contact with professional private agencies such as the Epilepsy Foundation, United Cerebral Palsy Chapters, or even local associations for the mentally retarded.

ASSISTANCE RECEIVED

Financial aid and special education were primarily the types of assistance received. Sixty percent of the total sample reported they were receiving money or some type of service from the state welfare agency (the Alabama Department of Pensions and Security). Thirty-five percent of the families with a mentally retarded member and a few of the multiply handicapped were beneficiaries of special education and transportation from the public schools of their county. Almost half of the 12 cerebral palsied individuals in the sample and 25 percent of the multiply handicapped were receiving medical assistance from the State Crippled Children's Service. A handful of the retarded and the epileptics also were obtaining some medical help from this agency. Yet almost *40 percent* of the mentally retarded in our sample reported incurring extra expenses for medicine.

Other state and public agencies such as local mental health centers were reportedly providing aid to only a handful of the disabled. In the crucial area of employment only 10 percent of the employed disabled said they obtained their job through an agency or through Vocational Rehabilitation Services. The remainder were employed through either their own efforts or familial assistance. In some instances lack of assistance was likely due to ignorance of its existence, while in others resources were probably inadequate. Whatever the reason, it appears that care of the disabled was principally a family affair. Given help that is or should be available, this situation should receive special attention.

FELT NEEEDS FOR ASSISTANCE

The fact that greatest perceived needs were for types of assistance already being received lends credence to the hypothesis that the respondents were to some extent unaware of other available assistance. The most oft-mentioned need was for more and better educational and training services. Fifty-five percent of the total sample listed this service as their primary need. Families with mentally retarded and multiply handicapped members most often expressed the need for special education and training. More financial assistance was desired by 30 percent of the sample and practically all of the respondents with a cerebral palsied person in their charge. Transportation to and from treatment centers was mentioned by about 20 percent, with the families of epileptics and multiply handicapped expressing this need most frequently.

Finally, more medical services and special medication were reportedly needed by about 15 percent of the total sample including 40 percent of the epileptics and 20 percent of the multiply disabled. Relatively few families with retarded members showed interest in these services.

All of these needs are for basic items that would enable both the disabled and his or her family to better adapt to each other and to their environment. In some cases these items are available through agencies such as mental health centers. Others, such as new educational programs, were not available. There are still services (such as job placement) that have been unmentioned and would be highly valuable. Provision of these and other services would markedly lighten the burden of families and disabled individuals who carry on with few complaints and few economic resources. Fortunately, they appear to have an even greater resource, the ability or will to accept the burden.

In essence, the respondents in this survey appear to have adapted to the problems created by a developmentally disabled member in the household, probably because of the high levels of acceptance and familial help characteristic of these rural areas, rather than outside help. Objectively, many are carrying a heavy burden of expense and time lost in caring for the disabled person. Direct provision of medication and services at lower cost by state agencies, as well as cash payments in some cases, would do much to alleviate this burden.

References

Adams, Margaret
    1971   "The social evaluation and its significance for mental retardation."
            Pp. 114–50 in Margaret Adams (ed.), Mental Retardation and Its Social Dimensions. New York: Columbia University Press.

Caveness, W. F., H. Houston Merritt, and G. H. Gallup
1969   "A survey of public attitudes toward epilepsy in 1969 with an indication of trends over the past twenty years." Epilepsia 10:429–40.
Conley, Ronald
1973   The Economics of Mental Retardation. Baltimore, Md.: Johns Hopkins Press.
Epilepsy Foundation of America
1972   Epilepsy: Recognition, Onset, Diagnosis, Therapy. Washington, D.C.
Fowle, C.
1968   "Effect of the severely retarded child on his family." American Journal of Mental Deficiency 73:468–73.
Hauser, W. Allen
1972   "Preface." P. vii in Milton Alter and W. Allen Hauser (eds.), The Epidemiology of Epilepsy: A Workshop. Washington, D.C.: U.S. Department of Health, Education, and Welfare, Public Health Service, National Institutes of Health, National Institute of Neurological Diseases and Stroke Monograph No. 14.
Heber, Richard
1970   Epidemiology of Mental Retardation. Springfield, Ill.: Charles C Thomas.
Jano, Richard
1970   "Social class and parental evaluation of educable retarded children." Education and Training of the Mentally Retarded 5:62–67.
Klapper, Zeus
1970   "Developmental psychology." Pp. 1–113 in Joseph Wortis (ed.), Mental Retardation: An Annual Review—Volume I. New York: Grune and Stratton.
Lapous, Renia, and Martin Weitzner
1970   "Epidemiology." Pp. 197–221 in Joseph Wortis (ed.), Mental Retardation: An Annual Review—Volume I. New York: Grune and Stratton.
Mercer, Jane R.
1973   Labeling the Mentally Retarded: Clinical and Social System Perspectives on Mental Retardation. Berkeley: University of California Press.
Meyers, C. E., E. G. Stitkei, and E. H. Watts
1966   "Attitudes toward special education and the handicapped in two community groups." American Journal of Mental Deficiency 71:78–84.
Mumbauer, Corinne C., and J. O. Miller
1970   "Socioeconomic background and cognitive functioning in pre-school children." Child Development 41:471–79.
Pond, D. A., B. H. Bidwell, and L. Stein
1960   "A survey of epilepsy in fourteen general practices—I: demographic and medical data." Psychiatria, Neurologia, Neurochirurgia 63:217–26.
Ricci, Carol
1970   "Analysis of child-rearing attitudes of mothers of retarded, emotion-

ally disturbed, and normal children." American Journal of Mental Deficiency 74:756–61.

Self, Helen H.
   1970   The Relationship Between Parental Acceptance and Adjustment of Mentally Retarded Children. Unpublished Ph.D. Dissertation, The University of Alabama.

Tizard, Jack
   1968   "Social psychiatry and mental subnormality." Pp. 50–64 in Micheal Shepherd and D. L. Davis (eds.), Studies in Psychiatry. London, England: Oxford University Press.

United States Bureau of the Census
   1972a   Census of Population: 1970. General Population Characteristics. Final Report PC(1)-B2: Alabama. Washington, D.C.: U.S. Government Printing Office.
   1972b   Census of Population: 1970. General Social and Economic Characteristics. Final Report PC(1)-C2: Alabama. Washington, D.C.: U.S. Government Printing Office.

University of Alabama, Center for Business and Economic Research
   1973   Alabama Business. University, Ala.: Center for Business and Economic Research.

Wilson, Warner
   1970   "Social psychology and mental retardation." Pp. 229–62 in Norman R. Ellis (ed.), International Review of Research in Mental Retardation: Volume 4. New York: Academic Press.

Zielinski, J. J.
   1972   "Social prognosis in epilepsy." Epilepsia 13:133–40.

Zigler, Edward F., and Susan Harter
   1969   "The socialization of the mentally retarded." Pp. 1065–1102 in David A. Goslin (ed.), Handbook of Socialization Theory and Research. Chicago: Rand McNally.

CHAPTER NINE
SPECIALIZED TREATMENT AND PROGRAMS FOR THE DEVELOPMENTALLY DISABLED IN ALABAMA

M. H. ALSIKAFI

The objective of this chapter is to report on a survey of facilities and programs available to the developmentally disabled population in Alabama and to identify types of services provided. Specifically, the chapter, drawing heavily on a report by Alsikafi and Palk (Hollingsworth, 1974), presents results of data collected over a period of time concerning the existing services and facilities, as well as a documentation of some of the unmet needs for services that may lead to plans and recommendations as to how facilities may be developed, improved, or expanded.

To achieve these objectives a two-stage program for collection of data and material about facilities existing throughout the state of Alabama was developed. The first stage involved a pilot project primarily designed to test the effectiveness of the method and the feasibility of the techniques employed by the researchers. The second stage, on the other hand, involved collection of information from specific agencies and obtaining details about the particular services they provided to their clients.

The Pilot Project

Work on the pilot project started in the fall of 1972 and was completed in early spring of 1973. It involved mailing questionnaires to two types of agencies: those which were service-oriented and those which might possibly refer clients to other agencies or facilities for special services. In the first questionnaire, detailed information about the nature of services, number of professional personnel, sources of funds, and case loads was requested. Some 251 agencies and facilities fell in this category. When the pilot study was completed, replies were received from 174 agencies, approximately 70 percent of the total number. On the other hand, questionnaires mailed to the potential referral agencies requested information as to the type of facilities they recommended to persons with mental retardation, cerebral palsy, or epilepsy; therefore the researchers could locate any agencies offering direct services to the target population, if such agencies had been missed by primary informants and other sources. Some 254 agencies belonged to this category. When results were tallied, 145 agencies (approximately 57 percent of them) replied. The findings of the pilot survey were included in Hollingsworth (1973). The report was submitted in February 1973 to the Alabama Department of Mental Health, Montgomery, Alabama.

The pilot project provided the researchers with three important sets of information that proved to be useful in preparing the questionnaire for the next stage of conducting the final survey. These are as follows:

(1) The questionnaire form was relatively long and required a great deal of time and effort from the person in charge of responding to the request. In addition, many facilities did not have their records in a format which we had hoped would be available in order to obtain the information requested.

(2) Instructions related to information about the case load of the facility and the distribution of disabilities among clients were not clear.

(3) A relatively large number of facilities included on the mailing list of the survey proved to be either uninvolved in providing the type of services researchers were surveying, or did not make any referrals to other agencies.

Survey of Facilities

In light of these shortcomings the project staff developed in the spring of 1973 a new questionnaire to obtain more specific information from agencies and facilities. Based on the number of agencies responding to the requests in the pilot stage the new set of questionnaires was mailed to 117 agencies and facilities. In addition, nine sets were personally taken to agencies in the Tuscaloosa metropolitan area. Through extensive follow-up, returns were received from a total of 86 agencies.

In this stage a more systematic effort was made to include information about services provided by state agencies to the developmentally disabled. Thus questionnaire forms were mailed to the State Department of Education, Vocational Rehabilitation Services, Crippled Children's Services, and such state-wide voluntary organizations as the Association for Retarded Children. A sample questionnaire form has been appended (Appendix II) to give the reader an idea about the type of information collected from these agencies.

The geographical distribution of the agencies and facilities surveyed in this study is shown in Figures 1 and 2. A close look at these maps reveals that these agencies tend to cluster in certain counties and/or regions. Figure 1 shows county locations of only the state agencies. The reader is reminded that no attempt was made to locate the symbols in the exact geographical locations within each county, because in some counties this would involve piling symbols on one another to the extent that they would be totally undistinguishable. In Figure 2 state agencies located within a given county are denoted by a single "S," no matter how many there may have been. The reader should interpret the two maps as if they were superimposed on one another.

Turning to an examination of the questionnaire form itself (see Appendix II), notice that the information requested from each agency dealt with the size and specialties of staff, services rendered to clients, sources of financial support, number of clients served (residential and day), number of individuals on waiting lists, admission requirements, diagnostic and evaluation capacities, and specific types of disabilities currently on the case load. It was impossible for some of the facilities responding to the requests to provide specific data on case loads because these agencies' record-keeping systems were not compatible to the retrieval of the survey's specific objectives. When this was the case, facilities often provided approximate figures for each category or gave information regarding the primary handicap(s) they served. Returned questionnaires have been reproduced in Hollingsworth (1974), Volume II.

STATE-WIDE AGENCIES AND FACILITIES

A brief discussion of the functions of the state agencies will help the reader to relate the scope of operation of the two levels of organizations to one another. As the ensuing discussion reveals, these agencies provide a myriad of services, all touching on the daily life of the developmentally disabled in some way or another.

The Alabama Department of Mental Health provides services including diagnosis of, treatment of, rehabilitation for, follow-up care of, prevention of, and research into the causes of all forms of mental or emotional illness. Services include Bryce Hospital, Partlow State School and Hospital, Searcy Hospital, Brewer Developmental Center, Lurleen B. Wallace Developmental Center, and a number of other mental health adjustment centers, schools, and the like.

The Alabama Department of Education has three major divisions that offer services to the developmentally disabled. These are: Vocational Rehabilitation Services, State Crippled Children's Service, and the Exceptional Children's Program. The first division is involved in providing services for the physically disabled in the areas of evaluation, counseling and guidance, physical restoration, training, help in finding a job, and the like. The other two divisions concentrate on the needs of children in clinical and hospital care and classroom curriculum and instructional services.

The Alabama Department of Pensions and Security provides financial assistance and social services to needy residents who are eligible for assistance within a variety of categories including anyone who has a per-

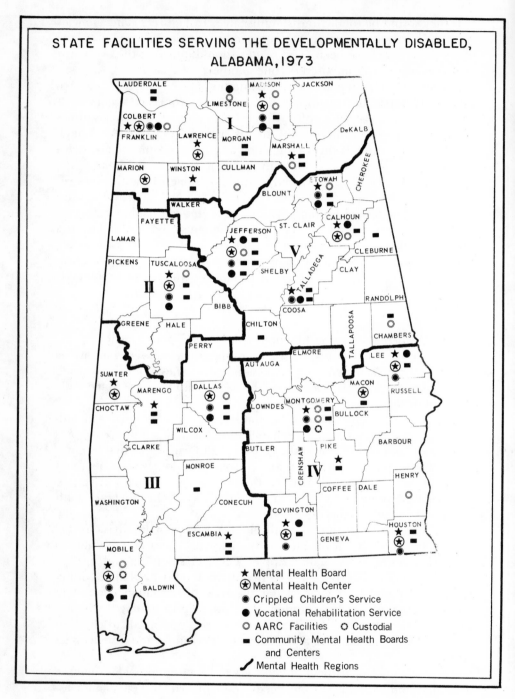

Figure 1

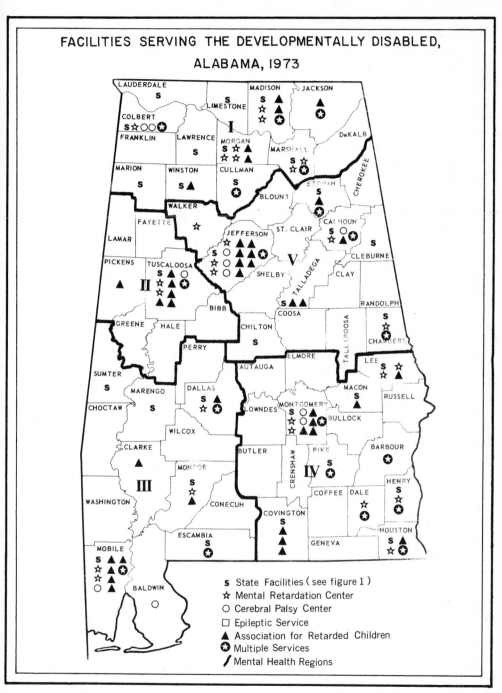

Figure 2

manent impairment that is totally disabling. Also the Department of Public Health contributes indirectly to the needs of the developmentally disabled by providing services in the areas of hospital inspection and licensing and administering the Medicaid program through which some developmentally disabled persons receive benefits.

The State has three major educational institutions that provide significant services to the developmentally disabled. These are: The University of Alabama in Birmingham, The University of Alabama in Tuscaloosa, and the Alabama Institute for the Deaf and Blind. The first two institutions provide services in the form of diagnosis and evaluation of the mentally retarded child. The Birmingham facility extends its services to complete social work services, physical and neurological work-up, psychological evaluation, psychiatric consultation, and public health nurse home visitation. The Center for Developmental and Learning Disorders of the University's Tuscaloosa campus provides services, consultation, and training to personnel of all levels who will be involved in services to the disabled population. On the other hand, the Alabama Institute for the Deaf and Blind is mainly an educational institute where people with multiple disabilities from the southeastern region of the United States are provided services.

Turning to the private sector of facilities and organizations providing services to the developmentally disabled population, we can identify two levels of organization: the state level and the nationally based facilities. On the state level, Alabama Goodwill Industries, Incorporated, with its rehabilitation services for the handicapped includes such services as training, employment, and opportunity for personal growth as an interim step toward helping the client to be absorbed in competitive industry. Also on the state level are both the Alabama Association for Retarded Children and the Alabama Society for Crippled Children and Adults. The former is an incorporation of local associations supporting classes for "trainable" retarded children with an IQ of 50 and below from the ages of 5 to 18 years. The latter, on the other hand, provides services such as treatment, transportation, appliances, education, and therapy for crippled people, and aids communities in building and staffing clinical centers. To these two systems of services must be added the Alabama Council on Epilepsy, which specializes in referring epileptics to physicians for treatment, defraying drug expenses for the impoverished, and assisting in job placement, and United Cerebral Palsy, which provides a developmental program for cerebral palsied children and sponsors daycare, recreation, arts and crafts, family counseling, and summer camp.

On the national level the Muscular Dystrophy Association and the National Foundation of the March of Dimes occupy a prominent place in the area of services to the developmentally disabled. These agencies provide services for persons with neuromuscular disorders and have regional offices in Birmingham.

Finally, a relatively large number of local religious and fraternal organizations provide a variety of services, both systematic and intermittent, that may be of help to the developmentally disabled population.

Findings from the Survey of the Regional, County, and Local Facilities

This section presents the findings based upon returns of the questionnaires sent to the different agencies and facilities throughout the state. The nature of the questionnaire and the rates of return were discussed earlier in the chapter. The objective in this section is a systematic discussion of the distribution of facilities in the different regions, counties, and communities of the state and a somewhat detailed analysis of their functions and activities.

A number of observations must be made prior to the discussion. First, the survey received part of the data from which the findings are derived from such state agencies as the Alabama Department of Mental Health, the State Department of Education (including Crippled Children's Services, Vocational Rehabilitation Services, and the Exceptional Children's Program), and statewide organizations such as the Association for Retarded Children, United Cerebral Palsy, and Alabama Council on Epilepsy. Second, data received from the Department of Education did not include a diagnosis of cerebral palsy. The authors were advised by authorities in the Department, however, that most persons listed as being multiply handicapped did, in fact, have cerebral palsy. Third, data provided by the State Department of Education concerning the number of developmentally disabled and special education units are mostly from the 1973–74 published figures. On the other hand, data received from Partlow State School, Bryce and Searcy Hospitals, Vocational Rehabilitation Services programs, and the Crippled Children's Services are based on 1972 figures.

A look at Figures 1 and 2 reveals that the state is divided into five mental health regions. Each region was given a number indicating its relationship to the others. The ensuing discussion will focus on each region and discuss its major facilities and services for the developmentally disabled.

REGION I: NORTHERN REGION

The 13 counties of this region in the northern portion of the state include: Colbert, Cullman, De Kalb, Franklin, Jackson, Lauderdale, Lawrence, Limestone, Madison, Marion, Marshall, Morgan, and Winston.

In 1973 this region had a population of approximately 717,229, or about 20 percent of the total population of the state; about one person of every five in Alabama lived in this region. Situated above the "Black Belt" of the state, the population included 646,659 whites and 70,570 nonwhites, indicating that 9.8 percent of the region's residents were classified as nonwhite, while the average in the state was 26.1 percent (U.S. Bureau of the Census, 1972).

The total case loads of the different facilities surveyed in this study indicate that at least 8,636 developmentally disabled people were served in the region, or roughly 1.2 percent of the total population. This figure does not include all those actually under treatment. Rather, it shows only those who are being served in some form or fashion by one of the reporting facilities.

The data gathered from facilities in this region also indicate that most persons being served are receiving assistance from special education classes in the region's 28 school systems—one system in each of the 13 counties and 15 additional city school systems. In each of the systems, classes are provided for the educable mentally retarded at both the elementary and secondary levels. The Exceptional Children's Program presently allots 339 units for the educably retarded to this region. Eight systems are providing a total of 23 classes for the trainable mentally retarded. Two special units for the physically handicapped and two classes for the multiple handicapped are situated in the largest city in the region, Huntsville. Seventy-one other units are allocated to serve a variety of handicapped persons including those with learning disabilities, emotional disturbances, and hearing and speech problems. There are no special units, as such, for the epileptic child. For the region, special education services are provided for approximately 4,258 educable mentally retarded and 34 cerebral palsied children.

In this region, as in all other regions of the state, data received from homeroom teachers show that school children "nominated" as potential developmentally disabled far exceed the number presently enrolled in special education classes. In many instances this reaches two or three times the number of those already in special education classes. As far as this study is concerned those "nominated" by homeroom teachers, but who have not been tested and verified with a battery of psychological tests, have not been included in the total number of developmentally disabled persons reported in this chapter.

Turning to the share of this region in the developmentally disabled population of state-operated facilities, we find that every county of this region has residents who are provided services and/or treatment by Bryce and/or Searcy Hospital, Vocational Rehabilitation Services and/or Crippled Children's Services. These facilities provide services for a total of 3,330 developmentally disabled, which include 2,535 mentally retarded, 373 cerebral palsied, and 405 epileptics. Other reporting agencies in this region provide for 722 cases, which include 554 retardates, 25 cerebral palsied, 41 epileptics, and 102 multiply handicapped. Of these agencies, facilities are located in six counties, with the majority being in Limestone, Madison, and Colbert counties. The most prominent of these agencies and facilities include: Centers for Cerebral Palsy, Centers for the Mentally Retarded, Mental Health Centers, Rehabilitation Centers, Lurleen B. Wallace Developmental Center, an achievement school, a learning foundation, and an association for learning disabilities. Table IX-1 (pp. 144–45) provides totals for the different disabilities served by the various agencies of this region.

REGION II: MIDDLEWESTERN REGION

This mental health region is the smallest of the five regions, both in population and in number of counties. It comprises 7 counties: Bibb, Fayette, Greene, Hale, Lamar, Pickens, and Tuscaloosa.

According to 1973 population estimates, approximately 211,009 persons live in this region, or about 6 percent of the total population of the state. This estimate means that only about 1 of every 16 Alabamians lived there at that time. Racially, nonwhites accounted for slightly more than 30 percent of the total population of the region, or roughly 4 percentage points higher than that of the state (U.S. Bureau of the Census, 1972).

Questionnaires returned from the agencies and the facilities in this region show that a total of 2,692 disabled, or 1.3 percent of the people of this region, were provided services (the resident populations of all state hospitals were allocated to their home counties for purposes of this analysis).

The region includes seven county and one city school systems. All these systems provided classes for the educable mentally retarded. All but one system reported providing these classes at both the elementary and secondary levels, with a total of 98 classes being taught for the educable retardates. Three systems in two counties have 9 units for the trainable retardates. Two systems were providing training for the mentally retarded at the preschool level, and three systems specialized in services for cerebral palsied children. As in Region I, no programs or units were designed especially for the epileptic school-aged child. However, the region had 21 units providing services for other types of learning disabilities, emotional disturbances, and speech problems. All in all, the region provided special education services for 1,345 mentally retarded children and for an estimated 10 cerebral palsied children.

State-operated agencies assisted a total of 1,252 developmentally disabled residents of this region. Other reporting agencies provided services for 95 developmentally disabled, including 67 mentally retarded, 4 cerebral palsied, 5 epileptics, and 19 multiply handicapped. Of the other agencies, services were provided for children from four counties, most of them from Tuscaloosa.

Agencies surveyed in this region provided almost all the services listed in the questionnaire form. These agencies include the Hearing Center at The Univeristy of Alabama, the Adult Activity Center, the Infant Development Program, West Alabama Rehabilitation Center, Ridgecrest Children's Center, Tuscaloosa Association for Retarded Children, Opportunity Center, Center for Developmental and Learning Disabilities, Office of the State Crippled Children's Services, the Mental Health Board, the Mental Health Center, a Vocational Rehabilitation Center, Partlow State School for the Retarded, and Bryce Hospital for the Mentally Ill. See Table IX-1 for details of the case load and the agencies providing the services.

REGION III: SOUTHWESTERN REGION

In the southwestern region are 13 counties: Baldwin, Choctaw, Clarke, Conecuh, Dallas, Escambia, Marengo, Mobile, Monroe, Perry, Sumter, Washington, and Wilcox. Demographically, in 1973 this region had an estimated population of 657,967, accounting for 18.6 percent of the state's total (U.S. Bureau of the Census, 1972). Reporting agencies of this region indicated that 6,749 persons, slightly above 1 percent of the population, were receiving services as a result of a developmentally disabling condition.

Focusing on services provided by public schools, this region has 19 systems: 13 county systems and 6 city systems. All 19 systems provided classes for the educable mentally retarded. Of these, all but 4 had classes at both the elementary and secondary levels. Furthermore, some 29 classes for the trainable mentally retarded were being provided. Four classes were designated for the physically handicapped—most likely to have been serving the cerebral palsied child. Also, 53 other units were providing classes for other types of handicapped persons, such as children with learning disabilities, hearing and speech problems, and emotional disturbances. Special education classes were provided for approximately 5,521 educable retardates, 336 trainable mentally retarded, and 364 cerebral palsied.

The southwestern region has residents representing each country in the state schools and hospitals for retardation and such facilities as Bryce and/or Searcy Hospital, Vocational Rehabilitation Services, and the Crippled Children's Services. All in all, these facilities provided services for a total of 2,492 developmentally disabled, which included 1,829 mentally retarded, 293 cerebral palsied, and 370 epileptics. Other reporting agencies in this region provided services for 454 developmentally disabled, which included 223 mental retardates, 71 cerebral palsied, 14 epileptics, and 146 multiply handicapped.

All services included in the questionnaire forms were provided by the agencies of this region. Facilities included special schools for the handicapped, rehabilitation centers, mental health centers, Goodwill Industries, and special centers for cerebral palsy and the retarded. Table IX-1 summarizes the details of the case loads and the various agencies of this region.

REGION IV: SOUTHEASTERN REGION

This region comprises 18 counties: Autauga, Barbour, Bullock, Butler, Coffee, Covington, Crenshaw, Dale, Elmore, Geneva, Henry, Houston, Lee, Lowndes, Macon, Montgomery, Pike, and Russell. The estimated population of the region in 1973 was 692,812, or about 19.6 percent of all the people living in the state (U.S. Bureau of the Census, 1972). The total number of developmentally disabled included 9,529 people, or 1.4 percent of the total inhabitants of the region.

Region IV included 32 school systems—17 county systems and 15 city systems. All school systems provided special education classes for the educable type of mental retardation, but only 18 classes, located in 11 school systems, provided education for the trainable type. Almost all classes for the educable retarded were provided at both the elementary and the secondary school levels, constituting a total of 417 units. On the other hand, 2 school systems provided classes for the physically handicapped and/or multiply handicapped, but no special units for the epileptic child were reported in the region. Twenty-nine other units serving children with learning disabilities, emotional disturbances, speech problems, hearing difficulties, and similar disabilities were provided. For the region as a whole, services existed for a total of approximately 4,738 educable retardates, 179 trainable mentally retarded, and 82 cerebral palsied.

As in the preceding regions, each county in the southeastern region has residents in state-operated facilities such as Bryce and/or Searcy Hospital, Vocational Rehabilitation Services, and Crippled Children's Services. These facilities provided services for a total of 3,461 developmentally disabled, which included 2,709 retardates, 317 cerebral palsied, and 435 epileptics.

Services provided by other reporting agencies in this region were rather limited. There were only 1,143 developmentally disabled persons served by these agencies. Furthermore, these facilities are in six counties, with the most being in Montgomery County. Returns from the agencies of this region showed that they varied in their functions. Their facilities

Table IX-1.

Findings from the Survey of the Regional Facilities Serving
the Developmentally Disabled in Alabama

Region	Mentally retarded	Cerebral palsied	Epileptic	Multiply disabled
Region I				
City and county school systems	4,563	34		
Partlow State School and Hospital*	180			
Bryce and/or Searcy Hospital*	116			
Vocational Rehabilitation*	2,239	47	173	
Crippled Children		343	232	
Other facilities	554	25	41	94
TOTAL	7,652	449	446	94
Region II				
City and county school systems	1,345			
Partlow State School and Hospital*	235			
Bryce and/or Searcy Hospital*	72			
Vocational Rehabilitation*	660	13	72	
Crippled Children		107	93	
Other facilities	67	4	5	19
TOTAL	2,379	124	170	19
Region III				
City and county school systems	3,805	28		
Partlow State School and Hospital*	334			
Bryce and/or Searcy Hospital*	147			
Vocational Rehabilitation*	1,348	31	168	
Crippled Children		262	202	
Other facilities	223	71	14	146
TOTAL	5,857	392	384	146
Region IV				
City and county school systems	4,917	28		
Partlow State School and Hospital*	356			
Bryce and/or Searcy Hospital*	144			
Vocational Rehabilitation*	2,209	36	127	
Crippled Children		281	308	
Other facilities	954	7	4	159
TOTAL	8,580	352	439	159
Region V				
City and county school systems	6,372	83		
Partlow State School and Hospital*	791			
Bryce and/or Searcy Hospital*	263			
Vocational Rehabilitation*	2,272	62	240	
Crippled Children		583	302	
Other facilities	980	26	28	222
TOTAL	10,678	754	570	222

Table IX-1 (continued)

Region	Mentally retarded	Cerebral palsied	Epileptic	Multiply disabled
State Totals				
City and county school systems	21,002	173		
Partlow State School and Hospital*	1,896			
Bryce and/or Searcy Hospital*	742			
Vocational Rehabilitation*	8,728	189	780	
Crippled Children		1,576	1,137	
Other facilities	2,778	133	92	640
TOTAL	35,146	2,071	2,009	640

*Data from 1972 figures

included centers for cerebral palsy, mental retardation centers, mental health centers, rehabilitation centers, Goodwill Industries, and special schools. Table IX-1 gives the details of the services rendered by these agencies and their case loads.

REGION V: MIDEASTERN REGION

The 16 counties in the mideastern region are Blount, Calhoun, Chambers, Cherokee, Chilton, Clay, Cleburne, Coosa, Etowah, Jefferson, Randolph, St. Clair, Shelby, Talladega, Tallapoosa, and Walker. Although not the largest region in size in the state, the mideastern region had an estimated population of 1,262,695 in 1973—almost twice as many as any of the other regions, or approximately 36 percent of the total population of the state. The Birmingham metropolitan area is the center of population concentration in this region (U.S. Bureau of the Census, 1972).

The region has 38 school systems—16 county and 22 city school systems. Of these, all but one provided special education classes at the elementary level. On the other hand, a total of 4 secondary schools reported no such classes. A total of 24 classes for the trainable mentally retarded were being provided. Regarding other types of disabilities, the region includes 120 units for such disabilities as hearing difficulties, speech problems, emotional disturbances, and visual impairment. For special education, classes were provided for approximately 6,088 educable retardates, 284 trainable retardates, and 82 cerebral palsied.

Every county in the mideastern region had official residents at one or more of the state-operated schools and hospitals for the developmentally disabled. In 1973 Partlow State School had 791 residents who came from a county in the region. Bryce and/or Searcy Hospitals claimed some 263 developmentally disabled residents from this region, and more than 2,200 of its retarded residents received services from Vocational Rehabilitation Services. The State Crippled Children's Services provided assistance to approximately 583 cerebral palsied and 302 epileptics. Other reporting agencies provided services for 980 mental retardates, 26 cerebral palsied, 28 epileptics, and 219 multiply handicapped.

Agencies responding to the questionnaire provided a variety of services to their clients. These agencies included rehabilitation centers, children's development centers, Goodwill Industries, United Cerebral Palsy centers, Workshop Incorporated, Opportunity Centers, Training Schools, the Center for Developmental and Learning Disorders, Mental Health Centers, and the Alabama Institute for the Deaf and Blind. Table IX-1 shows the total of developmentally disabled served by the different agencies of this region.

Conclusions

A quick glance at the number of agencies and the size of their loads as presented in every region of the state should help the reader to formulate a number of tentative conclusions regarding the status of specialized treatments and programs available to the developmentally disabled. (See Table IX-1 for the totals of all the developmentally disabled and the agencies rendering services to them in the state.) These conclusions may be summarized in the following points:

First, each of the five regions contains a variety of services. These services include evaluation, diagnosis, treatment, day-care, training, education, sheltered employment, recreation, personal care, domiciliary care, special living arrangements, counseling, information and referral, follow-along, protective care, and transportation. This study did not assess the claim to these services made by each agency nor did it attempt to evaluate the quality of the service. Such undertakings would have been monetarily prohibitive and not within the scope of the survey. However, after an examination of the number of specialists and the level of training of personnel employed in these facilities, it may be concluded that services provided for the developmentally disabled vary considerably from one agency to another.

Second, special education services for developmentally disabled children are provided in practically every school system. Most of these services are designed for the mentally retarded, with the largest number served falling in the educable mentally retarded category. Generally speaking, few classes are provided for the trainable retardate. Also, special education classes for the cerebral palsied are provided in conjunction with classes for the physically handicapped and multiply handicapped and programs for the homebound. Practically no special classes are provided for the epileptic child.

Third, both Vocational Rehabilitation Services and Crippled Children's Services provide indispensable services to the developmentally disabled population of the state. While the former engages in activities that serve both adults and children who are mainly retardates, the latter is designed primarily for the cerebral palsied. Furthermore, services of the former are rehabilitative whereas the latter tend to be of the diagnostic and evaluative types.

Fourth, there is an apparent lack or even absence of services provided for the severely disabled and those who are in need of special care. Specifically, those persons with profound mental retardation and/or multiple disabilities have few facilities geared to their needs. Furthermore, as Figures 1 and 2 clearly indicate, most facilities are in the more populated areas of the state. The result is that disabled persons in rural counties have fewer services available to them and fewer trained personnel capable of handling their problems.

References

Alsikafi, Majeed, and Bobby Palk
  1974   "Survey of facilities serving the developmentally disabled in Alabama." Pp. 6–29 in J. Selwyn Hollingsworth (ed.), Report of Phase II of "Survey of the Developmentally Disabled in Alabama: Needs and Resources." Montgomery: Alabama Department of Mental Health.
Hollingsworth, J. Selwyn (ed.)
  1973   Report of Phase I of "Survey of the Developmentally Disabled in Alabama: Needs and Resources." Montgomery: Alabama Department of Mental Health.
  1974   Report of Phase II of "Survey of the Developmentally Disabled in Alabama: Needs and Resources." Montgomery: Alabama Department of Mental Health.
United States Bureau of the Census
  1972   Census of Population: 1970. General Social and Economic Characteristics. Final Report PC(1)-C2: Alabama. Washington, D.C.: U.S. Government Printing Office.

Part IV: Recommendations and Future Plans

CHAPTER TEN
THE FUTURE OF THE DEVELOPMENTALLY DISABLED IN ALABAMA

The existence of problems concerning the rendering of services to the developmentally disabled population in Alabama is not new. However, the research on which the present volume is based has pointed out, in a quantitative manner, a great deal of knowledge concerning this specific segment of our population on which existed heretofore only some conjectures and some "educated guesses" as to service needs. Using the data collected in the "Survey of the Developmentally Disabled in Alabama: Needs and Resources" as a basis, as well as other available data, intelligent, knowledgeable planning for the offering of treatment and services for the immediate and long-range future is under way.

This chapter proposes to look into some of the plans currently being made for the benefit of the mentally retarded, cerebral palsied, and epileptic people of the state. In recent years, treatment and facilities for persons with problems of mental health and the developmental disabilities have been undergoing rapid change in Alabama. Needless to say, the case of Wyatt *vs.* Stickney has been a precipitating factor in the most recent upgrading of services. However, it should be pointed out, as did Buckley and Lee (1974), that efforts at improving treatment and services for the developmentally disabled actually began in earnest in the state in the 1960s. Interested people throughout the state were aware of many of the problems concerning the disabled population prior to this time, but none had had the far-reaching effects of the report to the governor and state legislature of the Alabama Planning Project, issued in 1965, which reflected many issues and programs currently being supported. Along with a follow-up report submitted in 1968, these two reports together made many recommendations that were far ahead of their time in terms of the concepts elaborated. Lack of funds and manpower has, nevertheless, prevented the implementation of many of the proposed plans. It remained for the decisions of the aforementioned court case to force the implementation of many facets that would upgrade significantly the services offered to the state's developmentally disabled, as well as to the mentally ill.

Bearing these occurrences in mind, the present chapter shall deal primarily with the efforts and planning activities of the Alabama Department of Mental Health and of the Governor's Planning and Advisory

Council on the Developmental Disabilities in Alabama. It is recognized
that many local, regional, and state citizens' groups are confronting
many of the problems which they see on these various levels, and failure
to attempt to enumerate their efforts should not be viewed as an effort
to downgrade their invaluable assistance, but rather as a reflection of
the tremendous and perhaps insurmountable difficulties in attempting
to catalog them.

Strong efforts for aiding the developmentally disabled in the state are
being made by such state agencies as the Alabama Department of Mental
Health, the State Crippled Children's Service, Vocational Rehabilitation,
the State Department of Education (through the Council for Exceptional Children, and special education classes in schools in every county
throughout the state), the Department of Pensions and Security, and the
State Department of Health. State, regional, and local centers of such
client-related organizations as the Alabama Association for Retarded
Citizens, United Chapters of Cerebral Palsy, and the Epilepsy Foundation of America are bringing much effort to bear on the problem, and
without the invaluable services rendered by these and other agencies,
the task would be even more awesome.

Major attention in the present chapter shall focus on the efforts of
the Governor's Planning and Advisory Council on the Developmental
Disabilities in Alabama and of the Alabama Department of Mental
Health. The planning efforts of the two, for purposes of this report, are
largely inseparable. It should be remembered that the Council constitutes only a minute portion of the undertakings of the Department.

It is not the purpose of this chapter to attempt to outguess what future
changes will come about as a result of legislation yet to be enacted.
Nevertheless, it should be pointed out that the state legislature has been
appropriating ever-greater sums of funds for the alleviation of the suf-
ferings of the developmentally disabled in Alabama, and for the mentally ill as well. Rather, what will be attempted in this chapter is a brief
glance at plans for the future of some of the agencies in their efforts to
serve more adequately the developmentally disabled population of
Alabama.

The Governor's Planning and Advisory Council on
the Developmental Disabilities in Alabama

Public Law 91-517, the Developmental Disabilities Facilities and Construction Act, was passed in 1970 by the federal government. Basically,
the Act was designed to "plug the gaps" in services being offered to
persons with mental retardation, cerebral palsy, and epilepsy. The Act
provided for the designation of one state agency to oversee the provisions of the Act. In Alabama, that was the Board of Mental Health of

the Alabama Department of Mental Health. Therefore, the Council works under the aegis of the Department of Mental Health. Additionally, the Department of Public Health was given specific responsibilities to supervise the construction of facilities through their Bureau of Health Facilities Construction.

The Act likewise provided for the appointment, by the governor's office, of a planning and advisory board to make the plans for these services. The Council, comprising 24 members in this state, is divided equally among (1) representatives of principal state agencies that administer specified programs, such as special education, vocational rehabilitation, residential services for mentally retarded persons, social services for the disabled and for families and children, diagnostic and treatment services for crippled and/or retarded children, health services or long-term care programs for adults with chronic neurological disorders such as epilepsy and cerebral palsy, medical assistance and maternal and child health, and health facilities construction; (2) representatives of other state agencies and local governmental groups, such as university-affiliated facilities, university-associated services, university speech and hearing clinics, nursing, local schools, local departments of Pensions and Security, special legislations, the legislature, and The University of Alabama Council on Human Resource Training; and (3) representatives of nongovernmental organizations and groups (this category represents the "consumers," or the developmentally disabled, directly), such as local and national associations for retarded citizens, chapters of United Cerebral Palsy of Alabama, the Alabama Society for Crippled Children and Adults, chapters of the Epilepsy Foundation of America, and individuals who are themselves consumers of the services.

As a minimum the Act provides that the Council shall submit annually modifications of the State Plan, which reflect budgetary and expenditure requirements of the next fiscal year; incorporate changes in the quality, scope, and extent of services to be provided and facilities programmed; update priorities; and update any assurances or other information requirements included in the State Plan.

The functions of the Council are to: plan activities on behalf of all developmentally disabled individuals of the state; set the pace for the direction, development, and growth of the developmental disabilities program; establish goals and objectives and set service and construction priorities for Alabama's developmentally disabled persons; plan for a statewide service delivery system developed and maintained for the developmentally disabled by governmental and private agencies; conduct needs assessment, analyses, and data gathering; plan the effective coordination of other major activities and programs in the state for the developmentally disabled and assure that the public is aware of Developmental Disabilities Services Act programs and the services available to them; plan for in-state technical assistance to public and nonprofit private agencies in providing services and facilities for developmentally disabled persons; at least annually, review and evaluate the state plan and submit appropriate revisions to the administrator; at least quarterly, receive programmatic and fiscal reports from administering agencies for the purpose of evaluation; and monitor the deinstitutionalization process within the state (Alabama Department of Mental Health, 1975:23).

Objectives of the Council are to be met through the elaboration of short-range and long-range goals. In the following sections, they are reproduced largely in the form in which they were presented in the 1975 DDSA State Plan (Alabama Department of Mental Health, 1975).

SHORT-RANGE GOALS

The general goals of the Alabama DDSA Council are oriented to the support of the broad federal goal of reducing the institutional developmentally disabled caseload by one third by 1979. Each state goal is intended to help developmentally disabled citizens lead a life as normal as possible by satisfying quantitative and qualitative features of the overall federal goals. State goals intend additional quality community services or enhanced institutional care for those who require it. The Council's short-range goals are dictated by need, priority, and short-term feasibility.

Specific short-range goals were:

To complete regional and local planning for the development of quality community services for one third of the state's developmentally disabled population by June 1975.

As a part of this regional and local planning, to increase public awareness and, by June 1975, to inform private and professional segments of the population concerning the availability of services for the state's developmentally disabled persons.

To contract for and commence further regional and local planning for the development of quality community services for an additional one half of the state's developmentally disabled population by June 1975.

By June 1975, to train and provide approximately 175 qualified personnel to diagnose, evaluate, train, and otherwise serve developmentally disabled people, thus improving the quality of community and institutional services for developmentally disabled citizens of Alabama.

To contract for the training of approximately 230 additional qualified personnel during FY1975 to serve developmentally disabled citizens of Alabama.

To facilitate deinstitutionalization by: (1) providing "gap filling" community services for the State's developmentally disabled persons and (2) completing the Institutional Reform and Deinstitutionalization Plan by October 1974 (Alabama Department of Mental Health, 1975:54).

The coordinator of planning for deinstitutionalization of the developmentally disabled for Alabama under the Institutional Reform and Deinstitutionalization Plan has developed a plan for deinstitutionalization in consonance with Council planning and that of the Department of Mental Health. Background data have been acquired and deinstitutionalization planning is being coordinated with the Council and representatives of other state and federal programs to achieve the following objectives:

To create qualitative standards for community alternatives to institutionalization where standards are deemed appropriate.

To develop numerical projections as to services necessary to succeed in deinstitutionalizing those developmentally disabled individuals inappropriately institutionalized.

To develop long-range projections as to overall service systems related to preventing inappropriate placement in institutions.

To develop budgetary estimates through 1977 to provide alternatives to institutionalization (Alabama Department of Mental Health, 1975:62).

LONG-RANGE GOALS

The Alabama Planning and Advisory Council for Developmental Disabilities has the following long-range goals:

To decrease the resident institutional population by one third (to 1500 residents) by the end of FY1979.

To complete community plans for the development of integrated community service systems for the entire state by the end of FY1976.

To train and/or employ an estimated 4,100 additional qualified professional and nonprofessional personnel by the end of FY1979 to meet the needs of the state's developmentally disabled population.

To provide a system of quality community services throughout the state that will satisfy the service needs of an estimated 25,000 mentally retarded, cerebral palsied, and epileptic persons by the end of FY1979.

To assure public education and/or training opportunities for approximately 935 additional developmentally disabled persons of school age by the end of FY1977, commensurate with that afforded every other citizen of the State.

To provide a client follow-along system by the end of FY1979 for the state's developmentally disabled individuals that will increase placement options, assist in deinstitutionalization, and aid in the normalization process of every developmentally disabled person.

To provide sufficient daycare services throughout the state so that by the end of FY1979 no developmentally disabled person in need of this service will have to travel more than 20 miles to a daycare facility (Alabama Department of Mental Health, 1975:63).

STATE PRIORITIES

General. The Council's expression of state priorities for FY1975 demonstrates support for the federal and state goals of deinstitutionalization. Hence, a degree of interdependence and coincidence among priority items should facilitate the achievement of this goal. The initiation of community services, for example, implies planning, the development of programs, public information, the availability of trained, qualified personnel, and adequate facilities. Accordingly, the Council intends to support each of the following stated priorities, but none to the exclusion of any of the others.

Planning for the Development of Community Services. The continuation of community planning for the development of programs to serve developmentally disabled individuals was a Council priority for FY 1975. Additional and appropriately situated, quality community programs integrated in a system of services will provide alternatives to institutionalization and serve to reduce institutional caseloads. Elements incorporated as part of this ongoing planning effort include:

Identification of specific service needs at the local level.

Coordination of public and private agencies in meeting needs of the developmentally disabled.

Increasing public awareness and informing the public of available services.

Planning the development programs for the developmentally disabled, including preschool and postschool age daycare, special living arrangements, domiciliary care, and vocational education and training opportunities to reduce dependency.

Developing community human and financial resources to support program requirements.

Public Information. The need for informing the public of services available for developmentally disabled persons is well substantiated by Phase II of the Alabama Survey (Hollingsworth, 1974) and other sources. In addition to increasing public awareness through the medium of planning and other similar grants, the Council supports proposals for community education to assist the general public to understand and accept the developmentally disabled.

Training Personnel. The development of human resources within the state will promote quality care for those with developmental disabilities both in the institution and in alternative residential settings. The Council in its allocation of resources indicates support of training programs for

those who provide direct service for the developmentally disabled population. This training includes areas of therapy, social work, management, administration, education, and those to implement the sixteen
basic services for developmentally disabled persons.

Community Services. The provision of community services is a priority
statewide requirement. Daycare, domiciliary care, special living arrangements, transportation (particularly in rural areas), diagnosis, evaluation,
and counseling for those areas remote from existing facilities, and employment for the developmentally disabled are prerequisites to quality
deinstitutionalization.

Construction and Renovation of Facilities. The Alabama Planning and
Advisory Council recognizes the extensive need for renovation and construction based on projections made under the provisions of prior legislation and statewide inventories of existing programs and facilities.
Few funding sources allow for renovation or construction, and DDSA
construction funds are limited. Therefore, this plan is intended to en-
compass the needs of the developmentally disabled as associated with
private nonprofit programs or any of the federally assisted programs
that support the developmentally disabled and make application for that
purpose in conjunction with other funding. An approved program of
service is a prerequisite to application for construction or renovation so
that services and facilities will be complementary (Alabama Department
of Mental Health, 1975:66–68).

Conclusions

The brief overview of the plans for the future of Alabama's developmentally disabled indicates that considerable thought and effort are
being expended on behalf of the people involved. Again, it should be
made explicit that this report has not enumerated the efforts of other
public and private entities, although the Council attempts to coordinate
services offered by the various agencies. A summary of these plans is
included in the *1975 DDSA State Plan* (Alabama Department of Mental
Health, 1975:55–56).

While it is not the primary purpose of this volume to assess the planning efforts of the Governor's Council and of other agencies offering
services to the state's developmentally disabled, it must be concluded
that the efforts being made are indeed impressive. Only through responsible, knowledgeable planning can the lot of these people improve.
Perhaps the data gathered in the "Survey of the Developmentally Disabled in Alabama: Needs and Resources," on which this volume is based,
will present a sound basis for making careful plans for the future of our
developmentally disabled citizens.

References

Alabama Department of Mental Health
    1975   1975 State DDSA Plan. Montgomery, Alabama.
Buckley, Richard E., and William E. Lee, Jr.
    1974   "Deinstitutionalization of the developmentally disabled in Alabama."
            Report submitted to the Alabama Department of Mental Health.
Hollingsworth, J. Selwyn
    1974   Report of Phase II of "Survey of the Developmentally Disabled in
            Alabama: Needs and Resources." Montgomery: Alabama Depart-
            ment of Mental Health.

CHAPTER ELEVEN
SUMMARY AND CONCLUSIONS

Great investments of time, resources, and effort have been expended in the completion of the project upon which this book has been based. During this time, voluminous amounts of data concerning the developmentally disabled population of Alabama have been gathered and compiled. However, this volume cannot include all the information collected during the course of the research-gathering endeavor. Nevertheless, we have attempted to point up some of the most salient findings in the present book. It is hoped that the publication and subsequent distribution and reading of it by interested laymen and professional people alike will prove to be beneficial to those who must spend their lives as the developmentally disabled.

The material reported in this book may be considered "applied sociology," that is, sociologically sound studies conducted with practical applications in mind. Too often, projects using a great deal of expertise and the latest techniques have been carried out, then allowed to gather dust on library shelves because no use was ever made of them. Happily, that is not to be the fate of the data from this research project. As was indicated earlier in Chapter One, the developmentally disabled people of Alabama are *already* reaping the benefits of grant proposals that have obtained funding using information gathered during the course of this project.

At this point, no attempt will be made to summarize the major findings of the investigation. Rather, it is thought that perhaps it might be more advantageous to examine some of the findings in closer detail, to consider carefully some of their implications and to make some limited recommendations for consideration.

Magnitude of Needs

Table XI-1 combines data from Chapters Six and Nine in order to reveal, geographically, some of the gaps in service to the state's developmentally disabled population. As we should point out again, to estimate that Alabama has approximately 133,615 developmentally disabled individuals is not to imply that each one is in immediate need of treatment or of other services. Nevertheless, as was indicated in Chapter Eight, many of the families of mentally retarded, cerebral palsied, and epileptic persons revealed that they were in need of certain services which they were not receiving. It should be noted, likewise, that the *estimates* are just that. As was mentioned in Chapter Seven, the much

Table XI-1.

Estimated Numbers of the Developmentally Disabled, Numbers Receiving Services, and Numbers Not Being Served, by Disability, County, And Region, Alabama, 1973

REGION I

County	Number Reported As Receiving Services					Number Estimated To Have Each Disability				Number Affected But Not Receiving Services			
	MR	CP	Ep	Multi.	Total	MR	CP	Ep	Total	MR	CP	Ep	Total*
Colbert	443	26	28	20	517	1575	68	286	1929	1132	42	258	1412
Cullman	669	30	33	—	732	1712	72	298	2082	1043	42	265	1350
De Kalb	511	17	23	—	551	1310	53	237	1600	799	36	214	1049
Franklin	278	15	14	—	307	606	23	100	729	328	8	86	422
Jackson	483	20	27	—	530	1221	52	225	1498	738	32	198	968
Lauderdale	528	41	35	—	604	2142	92	383	2617	1614	51	348	2013
Lawrence	254	24	26	—	304	893	39	169	1101	639	15	143	797
Limestone	817	45	60	42	964	1345	57	243	1645	528	12	183	681
Madison	1891	123	106	27	2147	6112	278	1127	7517	4221	155	1021	5370
Marion	151	20	14	—	185	727	29	130	886	576	9	116	701
Marshall	608	37	33	—	678	1691	74	313	2078	1083	37	280	1400
Morgan	827	39	45	—	911	2484	107	450	3041	1657	68	405	2130
Winston	192	12	2	5	211	513	23	94	630	321	11	92	419
TOTAL	7652	449	446	94	8641	22,331	967	4055	27,353	14,679	518	3609	18,712**

REGION II

County	MR	CP	Ep	Multi.	Total	MR	CP	Ep	Total	MR	CP	Ep	Total
Bibb	160	11	10	—	181	442	18	80	540	282	7	70	359
Fayette	127	11	10	—	148	499	20	82	601	372	9	72	453
Greene	86	3	8	—	97	350	14	57	421	264	11	49	324
Hale	127	10	16	—	153	529	23	86	638	402	13	70	485
Lamar	370	9	12	—	391	439	19	77	535	69	10	65	144

County	MR	CP	Ep	Multi.	Total	MR	CP	Ep	Total	MR	CP	Ep	Total
Pickens	193	16	12	—	221	654	28	120	802	461	12	108	581
Tuscaloosa	1316	64	102	19	1501	3470	156	649	4275	2154	92	547	2774
TOTAL	2379	124	170	19	2692	6383	278	1151	7812	4004	154	981	5120
REGION III													
Baldwin	289	17	18	—	324	2120	86	390	2596	1831	69	372	2272
Choctaw	72	10	6	—	88	545	23	92	660	473	13	86	572
Clarke	209	19	19	—	247	893	39	156	1088	684	20	137	841
Conecuh	212	6	12	—	230	498	20	86	604	286	14	74	374
Dallas	877	47	63	—	987	1832	81	320	2233	955	34	257	1246
Escambia	332	10	13	—	355	1089	49	200	1338	757	39	187	983
Marengo	62	21	18	—	101	791	34	131	956	729	13	113	855
Mobile	2971	204	167	145	3487	10,269	449	1817	12,535	7298	245	1650	9048
Monroe	322	13	14	1	350	675	30	118	823	353	17	104	473
Perry	124	13	13	—	150	496	22	83	601	372	9	70	451
Sumter	61	9	10	—	80	549	25	97	671	488	16	87	591
Washington	252	12	15	—	279	542	25	95	662	290	13	80	383
Wilcox	74	11	16	—	101	549	24	93	666	475	13	77	565
TOTAL	5857	392	384	146	6779	20,848	907	3678	25,433	14,991	515	3294	18,654
REGION IV													
Autauga	63	12	16	—	91	826	37	151	1014	763	25	135	923
Barbour	386	12	13	—	411	721	33	127	881	335	21	114	470
Bullock	120	1	4	—	125	390	18	70	478	270	17	66	353
Butler	210	11	7	—	228	695	29	118	842	485	18	111	614
Coffee	497	24	22	—	543	1116	50	201	1367	619	26	179	824

(continued)

*Includes multiple disabilities, while "estimated" totals do not.

**This section totals correctly across the rows only if the multiple disabilities in the first section are taken into account.

Table XI-1. (continued)

REGION IV

County	Number Reported As Receiving Services					Number Estimated To Have Each Disability				Number Affected But Not Receiving Services			
	MR	CP	Ep	Multi.	Total	MR	CP	Ep	Total	MR	CP	Ep	Total*
Covington	504	16	11	2	533	1046	43	186	1275	542	27	175	742
Crenshaw	117	8	5	—	130	403	18	76	497	286	10	71	367
Dale	500	12	16	13	541	1623	79	331	2033	1123	67	315	1492
Elmore	341	16	22	—	379	1063	44	193	1300	722	28	171	921
Geneva	114	14	14	—	142	676	28	123	827	562	14	109	685
Henry	206	9	11	—	226	408	21	78	507	202	12	67	281
Houston	781	29	30	—	840	1761	76	314	2151	980	47	284	1311
Lee	748	11	31	4	794	1871	84	357	2312	1123	73	326	1518
Lowndes	84	12	16	—	112	430	20	71	521	346	8	55	409
Macon	201	14	15	—	230	754	34	134	922	553	20	119	692
Montgomery	2778	111	150	140	3179	5390	235	953	6578	2612	124	803	3399
Pike	478	28	36	—	542	771	35	135	941	293	7	99	399
Russell	452	12	20	—	484	1476	64	259	1799	1024	52	239	1315
TOTAL	8580	352	439	159	9530	21,420	948	3877	26,245	12,840	596	3438	16,715

REGION V

County	MR	CP	Ep	Multi.	Total	MR	CP	Ep	Total	MR	CP	Ep	Total
Blount	61	12	19	—	92	830	34	149	1013	769	22	130	921
Calhoun	967	67	43	75	1152	3460	142	597	4199	2493	75	554	3047
Chambers	249	13	21	—	283	1167	46	205	1418	918	33	184	1135
Cherokee	208	6	10	—	224	505	23	90	618	297	17	80	394
Chilton	415	14	39	—	468	769	33	142	944	354	19	103	476
Clay	122	5	6	—	133	394	16	69	479	272	11	63	346
Cleburne	91	4	9	—	104	339	17	63	419	248	13	54	315
Coosa	124	8	6	—	138	335	14	61	410	211	6	55	272

	MR	CP	Ep	Multi.	Total	MR	CP	Ep	Total	MR	CP	Ep	Total
Etowah	902	54	65	5	1026	2892	120	523	3535	1990	66	458	2509
Jefferson	4733	386	181	139	5439	20,035	849	3560	24,444	15,302	463	3379	19,005
Randolph	162	11	15	—	188	558	23	100	681	396	12	85	493
St. Clair	299	13	18	—	330	892	39	198	1129	593	26	180	799
Shelby	272	26	22	—	320	1203	54	228	1485	931	28	206	1165
Talladega	936	70	51	—	1057	2115	92	376	2583	1179	22	325	1526
Tallapoosa	323	20	33	—	376	1061	43	187	1291	738	23	154	915
Walker	814	45	32	3	894	1740	73	311	2124	926	28	279	1230
TOTAL	10,678	754	570	222	12,224	38,295	1618	6859	46,772	27,617	864	6289	34,548

STATE TOTALS

Region	MR	CP	Ep	Multi.	Total	MR	CP	Ep	Total	MR	CP	Ep	Total
I	7652	449	446	94	8641	22,331	967	4055	27,353	14,679	518	3609	18,712
II	2379	124	170	19	2692	6383	278	1151	7812	4004	154	981	5120
III	5857	392	384	146	6779	20,848	907	3678	25,433	14,991	515	3294	18,654
IV	8580	352	439	159	9530	21,420	948	3877	26,245	12,840	596	3438	16,715
V	10,678	754	570	222	12,224	38,295	1618	6859	46,772	27,617	864	6289	34,548
STATE TOTALS	35,146	2071	2009	640	39,866	109,277	4718	19,620	133,615	74,131	2647	17,611	93,749

*Includes multiple disabilities, while "estimated" totals do not.

**This section totals correctly across the rows only if the multiple disabilities in the first section are taken into account.

greater numbers of cerebral palsied persons who were actually located by interview than had been previously estimated to exist may be an indication that their numbers have been seriously underestimated, both in this study and in earlier research endeavors. From the findings on the prevalence of epilepsy in Piedmont County, the earlier estimates may have to be elevated by as much as half, if the same rates of prevalence hold true for the rest of the state (there is no sound basis for believing that such is not the case). Actually, such a procedure would have to take into account the age-sex-race distribution of the areas involved to reflect the picture more precisely.

If the previous rates appear to be inordinately high, then simply by applying to the total population of Alabama the prevalence rates of those who were *actually located* in the three-county survey, approximately 65,000 remain in the untreated category. This figure must also be regarded as an underestimate, since *all* the cases would be identified only through time-consuming and tedious methods. Nevertheless, it is painfully clear that massive inputs of manpower and finances are necessary to alleviate this bleak picture. We are not implying that the situation in Alabama is any worse than anywhere else in the United States. Indeed, the present author has been greatly impressed by the efforts of both individuals and agencies throughout the state in attempting to mitigate the problem. It appears that, so far, we are seeing only slightly more than the tip of the iceberg. However, the yeoman efforts currently under way in Alabama will probably provide an ever-growing sphere of treatment and service to our developmentally disabled.

Referring back to Table XI-1, if we compare the numbers of developmentally disabled persons who are reportedly receiving services with those we have estimated to exist, then slightly less than 30 percent of those estimated are actually receiving some kind of service. Regions III and V are below the state average in this respect, while the others are above it. Comparisons on a county basis are somewhat shaky, ranging from a 9 percent coverage in Autauga County to more than 73 percent in Lamar County. These comparisons for individual counties vary, perhaps because of the more complete reporting of agencies serving certain counties than others. It should be noted that these figures are, at best, tenuous, largely because of differences in reporting. For regions, however, they are regarded as being somewhat more complete and therefore more reliable.

The numbers who are estimated (by whatever means) to be affected directly by one of the developmental disabilities, but who are not receiving any services, are much too great to bypass without comment. Nevertheless, it must be noted that efforts to assist ever greater numbers are already in progress throughout the state. The Alabama Department of Mental Health is receiving larger budget appropriations by far than ever before. Local and regional agencies are increasing the scope of their services; new centers for treatment and services are being established on the basis of a great deal of planning, and only after careful, painstaking assessments of existing resources with relation to the needs of this segment of our population. Indeed, one of the implications of the findings of this research effort is that even more financial and personnel resources are going to be needed if we are to meet the tremendous challenges posed by the great numbers and the variety of needs remaining unmet.

Types of Needs

It might be advantageous at this point to refer once again to Figures 1 and 2, which were presented in Chapter Nine. The maps are useful in assessing the distribution of agencies and facilities throughout the state and within regions. It will be noted that a number of counties are without any facilities that serve the developmentally disabled, except the school systems. Other counties appear to have a multiplicity of facilities and agencies. Nevertheless, there is not a single county without such a facility in an adjoining county. However, many school systems serve only the mildly mentally retarded and do not provide any services for the more severely handicapped.

Careful study of the maps indicates that, in order to obtain certain kinds of services, long trips are necessary. Schrag (1973:8) indicated that parents were often unwilling to travel more than 20 miles (on a regular basis) for special programs to aid their children. If this statement is true, then more widely spread facilities need to be considered. The regional treatment centers, situated locally within each region, are examples of this type of endeavor.

Since they are found in all the counties, school systems may well become an optimal unit for program development for benefit to most of the school-aged children (Renzaglia and Shafter, 1969). The Alabama Department of Education, through the Exceptional Children's Program, instituted in 1972 a survey of school children who were identified by their teachers as potentially having some kind of disability or learning disorder. Large numbers were located, and once proper evaluations of the individuals named have been accomplished, then the provision of the indicated additional special education units would appear to pose a partial remedy to the problem.

A careful evaluation of the types of services provided in each county, along with a computation of the distances that would have to be driven in order to obtain special services, as well as the numbers of individuals to be served (and the types of services needed), would be a useful procedure. These steps would pinpoint areas where additional facilities are most likely to be needed. Careful use and interpretation of the detailed tables stored in the Department of Sociology at The University of Alabama in Tuscaloosa would aid also in locating the populations whose needs are likely to be greatest.

The need for transportation to and from facilities for the treatment of mental retardation, cerebral palsy, and epilepsy was indicated as among the greatest of all needs. It is not uncommon for poor people living in urban areas to lack a means of getting to one or another of these centers. The problem is compounded in rural areas, where distances are greater and family resources may be meager. Our data indicate that transportation needs should receive a relatively high priority in the state plan. An added dimension of the problem is that it appears that higher rates of prevalence of the developmental disabilities tend to be associated with lower economic ability.

Our investigations identified facilities where epileptics are currently receiving treatment, medicine, and assistance, but apparently no facilities are charged *specifically* with aid to epileptics. Careful consideration should be given as to whether there is a real need for such entities, and if so, how many and where they should be located.

Similarly, persons with more than one of the developmental disabilities reported difficulty in finding adequate assistance in one agency. The facilities surveyed reported that at least 637 such individuals were served by them. Furthermore, countless numbers of mentally retarded, cerebral palsied, and epileptics also are affected by other nondevelopmental handicapping conditions.

Many mentally retarded persons leave school and are gradually absorbed into the labor market. Follow-up efforts are suggested in order to ensure their well-being and their better adjustment.

In the in-depth surveys conducted in the homes of the developmentally disabled persons, a tremendous lack of awareness of services being provided to developmentally disabled persons was in evidence; great numbers of handicapped persons were not making use of available facilities. In many cases people simply did not know of the facilities or of the services rendered, or how to go about obtaining the needed services. This finding suggests that more public relations and public education programs for reaching the developmentally disabled and their families should be considered.

One way of implementing the previous suggestion would be to establish information and referral agencies within local communities throughout the state. Such centers would need to be well publicized in order to function to the fullest extent. Furthermore, reassurances would need to be given to ensure safeguards of confidentiality. An organization of this nature would appear to alleviate many of the problems faced by the developmentally disabled, by their families, and in their relations with others.

The research also indicates that children with mental retardation problems often are not located until after they are enrolled in public schools, after they have lagged behind, and then usually in about the fourth grade. More efforts should be made to locate the preschool, non-functional mentally retarded child and to begin his treatment at an early age, not just when he has trouble in school.

When they were interviewed in the survey conducted in the three counties, families of the developmentally disabled indicated that they needed (1) more and better educational and training facilities, (2) more financial assistance, and (3) transportation to and from treatment centers. These were the greatest needs for the developmentally disabled population as a whole. Families of persons with cerebral palsy stated that their greatest need was financial assistance, especially with special medicines and special equipment. Approximately 40 percent of the epileptics indicated a need for more adequate medical services.

All groups stressed the need for financial assistance. The presence of a family member who is handicapped often adds a great financial burden on the family budget. It will be remembered that the population most affected by the problems of mental retardation, cerebral palsy, and epilepsy, was the poor. Thus, the necessity of taking from an already stretched budget to aid a disabled child creates even greater economic burdens.

Several of the parents interviewed indicated a need for more services for the noninstitutionalized, profoundly retarded, and severely affected cerebral palsied persons. Normally, these individuals would be placed in an institution, but for one reason or another, their parents decided to care for them at home. Such parents indicated that more daycare facilities would permit them to engage more freely in needed family activities with their other, nonretarded children. In many school systems with special education classes, there are no classes specifically offered to meet the urgent needs of these children. An additional suggestion for the aid of families who prefer to keep their severely affected children at home instead of placing them in a state institution would be for the state to provide them direct financial assistance. This procedure would greatly reduce the financial burdens on the families and would likewise result in a saving to the state, if the cost of institutionalizing that child were compared with such payments.

Another need indicated in the in-depth interviews was for counseling services for individuals with mental retardation, cerebral palsy, and epilepsy, and for members of their families as well. Many parents or guardians indicated that they would welcome counseling for themselves and for their families in trying to assist the handicapped individual.

For future endeavors of the type reported in this volume, as well as for planning and program operations, a unified record-keeping system should prove to be of great value. The Alabama Department of Mental

Health has already begun efforts at developing such a system, which is used within the Department. However, when one is seeking information on a given population, such as the developmentally disabled, many different governmental agencies are involved, and the data are not kept in a form in all agencies that is compatible with the needs of those seeking it. The cost in time, effort, and finances would be great, but if it were kept in computerized files, the necessary information would be instantly retrievable. Built-in safeguards to ensure the confidentiality of information identifying individuals would be required, of course.

An integral part of any planning team should be empirically trained social scientists to assist in determining the social implications of planning decisions. The institution of a research-coordinating group at the state level would help to eliminate many of the repetitive research efforts presently occurring. Such duplication of effort not only is wasteful of manpower and money but also increases the likelihood of the failure of agencies and facilities to take the time to provide the necessary information, since they are so often asked for the same or similar information. In formulating such a group, again, well-trained, empirically oriented social scientists should be included in order to evaluate the methodological adequacy of the proposed research, since any research worthy of funding should be well planned and methodologically sound.

For the following suggestions, I am indebted to Mr. Billy Jackson "Butch" Ray, who is a former member of the Executive Committee of the Governor's Planning and Advisory Council on the Developmental Disabilities in Alabama and who currently serves on the National Advisory Council on Services and Facilities for the Developmentally Disabled.

More regional and state diagnostic centers are needed in order to locate the developmentally disabled as early in their lives as possible. Even prenatal and perinatal testing needs to be instituted in order to achieve the goal of early identification and intervention, especially in rural areas. Such agencies need to be staffed with well-trained specialists who know what to look for and are not afraid to make the diagnosis (it appears that some physicians have not been trained in recognizing mental retardation at an early stage and that many others are afraid of revealing the diagnosis to parents).

The laws of the state provide for education for all. For many of the developmentally disabled, special education classes are provided. However, it may be that the law is not implemented to its full extent. Many school systems are not equipped with sufficient numbers of adequately trained personnel. When they are, they tend to deal mostly with the educable mentally retarded. Although the law mandates that the trainable mentally retarded shall be taught also, no provision has been made for them in many systems. Severely affected victims of cerebral palsy have numbers of problems in the public schools, not the least of which are architectural barriers. An idea here would be the shifting of classes so that wheelchair cases would have all their classes on ground floors in buildings where no other provisions had been made for them.

Personal and financial independence is the goal of many of the developmentally disabled. However, when they begin seeking employment, the picture is often quite bleak. Area vocational and trade schools and junior colleges should consider developing programs in conjunction with such entities as the Vocational Rehabilitation Services in order to train the disabled for a variety of job descriptions, depending on their abilities and their professional potentials.

Already mentioned has been the problem of transportation. Where transportation facilities are available, they often have no provision for the handicapped. Common carriers, such as airlines, need to be adapted to be able to handle severely disabled individuals who are in wheelchairs. Furthermore, integrated use of the multitude of transportation facilities provided for all sorts of needs would greatly reduce the cost of this item.

Another major consideration should be low-cost housing designed specifically with the handicapped individual in mind, and especially for those who have low or moderate incomes. Such housing would need to be barrier-free for all kinds of disabilities, including the blind, hard of hearing, etc.

Easy personal identification for the handicapped and epileptics is a definite need and should be a relatively easy accomplishment. Currently, epileptics and severely handicapped persons are not issued drivers' licenses in Alabama, although many establishments require them as a means of identification. Thus, a drivers' license issued and clearly stamped *for nondriving purposes only* would greatly assist these people in such routine matters as cashing checks, checking into motels, and the like. Some places will accept draft cards as means of identification when one does not have a drivers' license, but women do not receive draft cards.

Conclusions

Finally, it is the feeling of the author that if we are to be able to assist the developmentally disabled to the fullest extent possible, then we must conduct well-planned, well-executed research in order to *know* with a great deal of precision who and where the developmentally disabled with unmet needs are and what their most pressing needs are. For example, the study conducted in Piedmont County on the prevalence of epilepsy needs further funding in order to study the socioeconomic characteristics of the people with mental retardation, cerebral palsy, and epilepsy; the more we know about such matters, the more precise becomes our knowledge about who and where they are and what their needs may be. Many statements in the published literature make reference to the alleged connection between different levels of socioeconomic status and levels of prevalence of the developmental disabilities. However, the present author knows of no research which has studied the situation carefully.

Of course, we are not contending that research holds all the solutions to all the problems. Nevertheless, it does occupy an important position and should be utilized wisely in the never-ending search for answers. Furthermore, research is making new inroads into the battle we are waging to benefit the disabled population. For example, we now have the capability of discovering before birth the existence of various congenital disorders. By extracting a sample of the amniotic fluid from a woman at approximately 16 weeks of pregnancy, irregularities in the chromosomal configuration indicate that birth defects are likely to occur. Certain types of mental retardation may be discovered by this method. Also, advances in perinatal care (care for the newborn) can reduce by about 85 percent the deaths and/or deformities that would have occurred, with an original investment of $20–25,000. Both are currently available in Alabama.

In the opinion of the author, Alabama has come a long way in meeting the most pressing needs of its developmentally disabled citizens. However, the research on which this volume is based has pointed up other, equally urgent necessities. It is the hope of the present writer that the research data collected and the recommendations made herein will help to make the lives of our residents who are the victims of mental retardation, cerebral palsy, and epilepsy more meaningful and, in the process, easier.

References

Alter, Milton, and W. Allen Hauser (eds.)
  1972   The Epidemiology of Epilepsy: A Workshop. Washington, D.C.: U.S. Department of Health, Education, and Welfare, Public Health Service, National Institutes of Health, National Institute of Neurological Diseases and Stroke Monograph No. 14.
Holton, Wilfred E., Bernard M. Kramer, and Peter Kong-ming New
  1973   "Locational process: guidelines for locating mental health services." Community Mental Health Journal 9:270–79.
Renzaglia, G. A., and A. J. Shafter
  1969   "Satellite programs for the retarded in rural areas." In R. C. Scheerenberger (ed.), Mental Retardation. Springfield: Illinois Department of Mental Health.
Schrag, Howard L.
  1973   "Program planning for the developmentally disabled: using survey results." Mental Retardation (October):8–10.

APPENDIX I
QUESTIONNAIRE USED
IN THE IN-DEPTH FIELD STUDIES

SURVEY OF THE DEVELOPMENTALLY DISABLED IN ALABAMA:
NEEDS AND RESOURCES

DEPARTMENT OF SOCIOLOGY
UNIVERSITY, ALABAMA 35486

Name of handicapped person _____

Address or Directions_____

_____

City_____ County_____

Telephone Number _____

NUMBER OF CALLS:

	Calls	Date	Hour	Initial
1.				
2.				
3.				
4.				

REASON FOR NON-COMPLETION OF INTERVIEW

_____ non-existent address   _____ refusal

_____ vacant house   _____ broke off interview

_____ not home after three calls   _____ other, explain

DATE_____   TIME INTERVIEW BEGINS _____

                                      TIME INTERVIEW ENDS   _____

Interviewer _____

Interviewer's Comments:

Edited by: _____

Editor's Comment:

Director's Verification   _____

1. What is your child's (handicapped person's) full name?

2. Sex: (By observation or question): Male _____ Female _____

3. How old is _____?

4. What is his birthdate? _____

5. What is your name? _____

   a. Age (if not parent)   _____

   b. Sex (by observation)   _____

   c. Race (by observation)   _____

6. (If respondent is not handicapped person himself) What is your
   relationship to _____?

   _____ Handicapped person (subject)   _____ Foster parent

   _____ Mother (ask if natural mother)   _____ Step parent

   _____ Father (ask if natural father)   _____ Relative (specify)

   _____ Sister   _____ Guardian

   _____ Brother   _____ Wife

   _____ Grandmother   _____ Husband

   _____ Grandfather   _____ Other (specify)

                                             _____

7. a. Is _____'s natural father living? Yes_____ No_____

   b. Is _____'s natural mother living? Yes_____ No_____

   c. Are his natural parents:

                        Separated?   Yes_____ No_____

                        Divorced?   Yes_____ No_____

   d. If divorced, has either remarried?

                        Father   Yes_____ No_____

                        Mother   Yes_____ No_____

8. What was his mother's age when _____ was born? _____

    a. Was he born in a hospital, clinic, or at home?

        hospital _____   clinic _____   home _____

    b. Was the child delivered by a midwife or by a doctor?

                        midwife _____   doctor_____

9. Where does _____ live most of the year?

    _____ Parent's home   _____ Own home

    _____ Special school   _____ Other (specify)

    _____ Institution   _____

10. Has _____ ever had convulsions, fits, seizures or falling out
    spells? (Probe for trances, twitching or rolling his eyes and staring
    into space.) (If No, go to 11).

                            Yes _____ No _____

    a. Did the seizures occur only in connection with a fever?

                            Yes _____ No _____

    b. How often does he have convulsions (or other appropriate
       terms)?

            _____ per month (or _____ per year)

    c. How old was he when he had his first seizure?

    d. When was the most recent one? _____

    e. Do you know what caused these convulsions?

                            Yes _____ No _____

11. Has he been diagnosed by a physician as being epileptic?

   NOTE: (If No, proceed to 12).   Yes _____ No _____

   a. What was the diagnosis?

          Grand Mal _____   Petit Mal _____

          Other (specify)_____

   b. Is he taking medicine for his seizures? Yes _____ No _____

   c. Do you know the name of the medicine? _____

   d. Where do you get this medicine?_____

12. Is _____ crippled in any way?   Yes _____ No _____

   (If No, skip to 13)

   a. What caused him to be crippled? _____

   b. Has the doctor diagnosed him as being cerebral palsied?

          Yes _____ No _____

   c. If cerebral palsy, did he give you a special name for the type of cerebral palsy _____ has such as

         _____ Spastic   _____ Ataxic

         _____ Athetosis   _____ Other (specify)

         _____ Don't know   _____

   d. What parts of _____ 's body are affected?

         _____arms   _____left side only

         _____legs   _____entire body

         _____right side only   _____other (specify)

                                          _____

   e. Does _____ use

         _____braces   _____crutches

         _____wheelchair   _____other (specify)

                                          _____

13. Has he ever been tested to find out his IQ or intelligence?

(If No, go to 14)   Yes _____ No _____

   a. Where was he tested? _____

   b. Do you know the results of the test? Yes _____ No _____

   c. (If Yes) What were they? _____

14. Is _____ a slow learner?   Yes _____ No _____

15. (If Yes) Who made this diagnosis? _____

NOTE: If this person is epileptic only, skip to number 20; otherwise ask
      questions 16-19 when appropriate.

16. Can he:

	No	With help	Without Help
Sit	__	__	__
Stand	__	__	__
Walk	__	__	__
Dress	__	__	__
Feed	__	__	__

17. Can he read?

   (If Yes) How well?

         Few words _____   Sentences _____   Very well _____

18. Can he speak clearly?

   (If Yes)

	No	With Family	With Everyone
Can say what he wants or needs	__	__	__
Can carry on a conversation	__	__	__
Talks like everyone else	__	__	__

19. Is _____ toilet trained?   Yes _____ No _____

NOTE: Question 20 refers to public or private regular day school.

20. Does he go to public school?

    a. (If No) Why isn't he in school? _____

                                                  _____

    b. Would you like for him to be in school?   Yes _____ No _____

    c. (If in school) Is he in special or regular classes?

                special classes _____   regular classes _____

    d. Has he ever been in a special class? Yes _____ No _____

    e. Do you want him to be in a special class? Yes _____ No _____

21. Does he attend any special school or training place?

                                                Yes _____ No _____

NOTE: If handicapped is a child, go to question 26

22. Does _____ have a job?

    a. (If No) Why not? _____

        _____

    b. (If Yes) What is he doing? _____

        _____

    c. How many hours a week does he work? _____ hrs/week

    d. How did he get his job?

        _____ Vocational Rehabilitation

        _____ Local employment agency

        _____ Private employment agency

        _____ Self

        _____ Other (specify)

        _____

        _____

    e. Has he ever been discharged from a job? Yes _____No _____

    f. (If Yes) Why was he discharged?

        _____

        _____

23. Has _____ ever been married?   Yes _____ No _____

    (If No, proceed to 26)

    a. How many years has he been married? _____

    b. Is he

        Separated   Yes _____ No _____

        Divorced   Yes _____ No _____

    c. If divorced, has he remarried?   Yes _____ No _____

24. Does he have any children?   Yes _____ No _____

(If No, proceed to 25)

a. (If Yes) How many? Male _____ Female _____

b. Are the children in good health?   Yes _____ No _____

c. (If No) What's wrong with them? _____

_____

25. Has the wife/husband of _____ been diagnosed as

cerebral palsied   Yes _____ No _____

mentally retarded   Yes _____ No _____

epileptic   Yes _____ No _____

26. Have you had to spend extra money on _____ during the past
year because of his handicap?

Yes _____ No _____

a. (If Yes) About how much extra? _____

b. (If Yes) What items have caused this expense?

_____ Medicine

_____ Special school

_____ Physical therapy

_____ Medical (doctors, hospitals)

_____ Special equipment (including special shoes, braces, glasses, etc.)

_____ Extra help at home

_____ Other (specify)

_____

_____

27. Have any groups or agencies helped you with _____?

a. (If Yes) Who?

    (1) _____ Pensions and Security ("welfare")

    (2) _____ State Vocational Rehabilitation

    (3) _____ Crippled Children's Service

    (4) _____ Church

    (5) _____ Diagnostic center

    (6) _____ Mental health center

    (7) _____ Public schools

    (8) _____ Parent organizations

    (9) _____ United Cerebral Palsy

   (10) _____ Association for Retarded Children

   (11) _____ Society for Crippled Children and Adults

   (12) _____ Epilepsy Foundation

   (13) _____ Private agency (specify) _____

   (14) _____ Other (specify) _____

28. How has the agency helped?

      <u>Agency Number</u>   <u>Manner of Help (Probe)</u>

            _____   _____

                                                          _____

                                                          _____

            _____   _____

                                                          _____

                                                          _____

            _____   _____

                                                          _____

                                                          _____

29. Who's helping now?

      <u>Agency Number</u>

            _____

            _____

            _____

30. Have any individuals helped you with _____? Yes _____ No _____

a. (If Yes) Who?

Neighbors	Relatives	Ministers	Others
_____	_____	_____	_____
_____	_____	_____	_____
_____	_____	_____	_____

(Interviewer: If answer to question 9 is "institution," go to question 32)

31. Has _____ ever been in an institution? Yes _____ No _____

32. Why did you decide to place _____ in an institution?

_____ Marital disruption   _____Community problems

_____ Child too hard to handle   _____Advice of professionals

_____ Too much care demanded   _____Advice of friends/relatives

_____ Sibling adjustment   _____Other (specify)

_____

33. Have you ever considered placing _____ in a residential institution?

Yes_____ No _____

Why?

_____

34. Have you planned for the time when you will no longer be able to care

for _____?

Yes _____No_____

a. (If Yes) What have you considered or planned for _____?

Put in an institution   _____

Leave care to relatives   _____

Other (specify)_____

35. Are you in contact with any associations for promoting the welfare of the handicapped?

Yes _____ No _____

a. (If Yes) What are they?

_____

_____

_____

36. What has been your greatest problem in getting help for _____

_____

Probe in following areas:
1. Lack of services or no services: medical, dental, educational, day-care, and recreation

2. Getting to and from help source: no transportation, and distance.

37. What is the occupation of the man of the house? (Be specific)

_____DNA_____

a. Where does he work? _____

b. Is he working? Full time _____ Part time _____

38. Does the woman of the house work? Yes _____ No _____ DNA _____

a. What is her occupation? _____

b. Is she working? Full time _____ Part time _____

c. Where does she work? _____

39. How many years of school has the man of the house completed? _____

40. How many years of school has the woman of the house completed?_____

41. How long have you lived in this community? _____ Total years.

42. Where did you live before you lived here? _____

43. What is the age of the man of the house? _____

44. What is the age of the woman of the house? _____

45. Could you give me the age and sex of each child living in this home? (Include the handicapped)

Male		Female	
Age	Sex	Age	Sex
____	____	____	____
____	____	____	____
____	____	____	____

46. Are there children of this household living elsewhere (such as army, college, institution)?

Yes _____ No _____

   a. (If Yes) Where are they living?

Sex	Age	Where
___	___	_____
___	___	_____
___	___	_____
___	___	_____
___	___	_____
___	___	_____

47. Are there any other handicapped persons living in this household?

Yes _____ No_____

Disability	Name	Age	Relationship
_____	_____	___	_____
_____	_____	___	_____
_____	_____	___	_____
_____	_____	___	_____
_____	_____	___	_____
_____	_____	___	_____
_____	_____	___	_____

48. Who do you go to for help around the house when you have sickness in the family?

_____Nobody--do it myself   _____Church or church members

_____Nuclear family members   _____Hire extra help

_____Extended family members   _____Don't know

_____Friends and neighbors   _____No response

_____Public agency (specify) _____

_____Other (specify) _____

49. Who do you turn to for help when you have money problems?

_____Nobody--solve it myself

_____Nuclear family members

_____Extended family members

_____Friends and neighbors

_____Public welfare agency (specify)_____

_____Other (specify)_____

_____No response

50. When you're feeling sad or low, who do you turn to?

_____ Nobody   _____ Church or church members

_____ Nuclear family members   _____ Other (specify)

_____ Extended family members   _____

_____ Friends and neighbors   _____ Don't know

_____ God   _____ No response

NOTE: The "a" portion of questions 51-57: Interviewer rates -3,-2, 0, +1, +2, +3 from negative to positive effect, in addition to writing down what respondent said.

51. Would you say _____'s handicap has had any effect on whether your family will take a trip, go on vacation, or visit relatives?

Yes_____ No_____

a. How has he affected your doing things like that?

-3, -2, -1, 0, +1, +2, +3

_____

_____

52. Would you say _____'s handicap has had any effect on the family's getting out to do things such as going shopping, going to the movies, or going to church?

Yes_____ No_____

a. How has he affected your family outings?

-3, -2, -1, 0, +1, +2, +3

_____

_____

53. Would you say _____'s handicap has had any effect on your marriage?

a. How has he affected your marriage?

-3, -2, -1, 0, +1, +2, +3

_____

_____

54. Would you say _____'s handicap has had any effect on the closeness or happiness of your family?

                                        Yes _____ No _____

   a. <u>How</u> has he affected the closeness of your family?

            -3 -2 -1 0 +1 +2 +3

       _____

       _____

55. Would you say _____'s handicap has had any effect on deciding where the family will live?

                                        Yes _____ No _____

   a. <u>How</u> has he affected where the family will live?

            -3 -2 -1 0 +1 +2 +3

       _____

       _____

56. Would you say _____'s handicap has had any effect on the job of the household head?

                                        Yes _____ No _____

   a. <u>How</u> has he affected the job of the household head?

            -3 -2 -1 0 +1 +2 +3

       _____

       _____

57. Would you say _____'s handicap has had any effect on whether the mother will work?

                                        Yes _____ No _____

   a. How has he affected her decision?

            -3 -2 -1 0 +1 +2 +3

       _____

       _____

58. Most people have some problems in bringing up children. What have been your major problems in bringing up a handicapped child?

_____ Social stigma (what friends and neighbors think)

_____ Adjustment of brothers and sisters

_____ Adjustment of parents

_____ Physical demands of caring for child

_____ Time demanded

_____ Discipline problems

_____ Money problems

_____ Knowledge of social services

_____ Lack of services

_____ Other (specify)_____

_____

59. In some families the other children sometimes have a difficult time under-standing or accepting their handicapped brother or sister. How well do you think your other children have accepted or adjusted to _____'s handicap? (If no brothers and sister, skip to 61)

Very well _____ Rather well _____ Not well _____ DNA_____

60. What have been the major difficulties in the brothers' and sisters' adjustment to _____'s handicap? (Probe for anything else)

_____

_____

_____

_____

_____

_____

61. All people have some difficulty learning to get along with other people. As you think about _____ how well do you feel he gets along with

a. Brothers

Very well _____ Rather well _____ Not well _____ DNA_____

b. Sisters

Very well _____ Rather well _____ Not well _____ DNA _____

c. Father

Very well _____ Rather well _____ Not well _____ DNA _____

d. Mother

Very well _____ Rather well _____ Not well _____ DNA _____

e. Grandparents

Very well _____ Rather well _____ Not well _____ DNA _____

f. Other kin

Very well _____ Rather well _____ Not well _____ DNA _____

g. Neighbors

Very well _____ Rather well _____ Not well _____ DNA _____

62. We're trying to find out what can be done to help people with handicaps in Alabama. What would be the greatest help to you?

[Probe for specifics such as: Day-care centers, transportation, special equipment, home child care (or adult care), recreation facilities, companionship].

1. Do you know anyone in this county who has epilepsy; that is, anyone who has seizures, convulsions, fits or falling out spells?

2. Do you know anyone in this county who has cerebral palsy; that is, anyone who is crippled? If so, describe the type of crippling condition. (If description conforms to the image of someone crippled because of brain damage or mal-function, record person as cerebral palsied.)

3. Do you know anyone in this county who is mentally retarded; that is, anyone who is a slow learner or not too bright.

APPENDIX II
FACILITIES SURVEY QUESTIONNAIRE

Name of Facility: _____

Address: _____

Area Served _____

Facility Capacity _____

Phone Number _____

Type of Agency ____ State ____ Local ____ Private ____ Federal

Primary Disability Serviced _____

Number of Full Time Equivalent Staff	Less than B.A.	Bachelor's	Master's	Post Master	Doctorate
General Practitioner, M.D.					
Psychiatrist, M.D.					
Neurologist, M.D.					
Pediatrician, M.D.					
Psychologist					
Teacher					
Social Worker					
Physical Therapist					
Occupational Therapist					
Speech, Hearing Therapist					
Rehab. Counselor					
Nurse					
Aide					
Teacher's Aide					
Administrator					
Clerical					
Fiscal					
Maintenance (incl. janitors)					

Volunteers--No. _____ Avg. hrs. per mo. _____

Source of Support

% Federal Government	
% State Government	
% Local Government	
% Private Agency	
% Client Fees	
% Other Funds (Specify)	
100%	

Number Served

Age	Resi-dents	Day Program	Waiting List

CHECK SERVICES RENDERED	Usually	Sometimes	Never
Evaluation			
Diagnostic			
Treatment			
Day Care			
Training			
Educational			
Sheltered Employment			
Recreation			
Personal Care			
Domiciliary Care			
Special Living Arrangements			
Counseling			
Information and Referral			
Follow Along			
Protective and Other Social and Social-legal			
Transportation			
Others (Specify)			

Briefly describe admission requirements and procedures for each type of service

_____

_____

_____

CASE LOAD

Intellectual Level	Mentally Retarded (1)	Epilepsy Controlled (2)	Epilepsy Non Controlled (3)	Cerebral Palsy (4)	Cerebral Palsy Non Ambulatory (5)	Cerebral Palsy Ambulatory (6)	Cerebral Palsy Non Ambulatory (7)	Cerebral Palsy Ambulatory (8)	Cerebral Palsy Non Ambulatory (9)	Total Col. 1-9 (10)	Orthopedic (11)	Speech (12)	Hearing (13)	Visual (14)	Learning Disabilities (15)	Language Disabilities (16)	Emotionally Disabled (17)	Total Col. 11-17 (18)
		Controlled Epilepsy				Controlled Epilepsy		Non Controlled Epilepsy										
Non-retarded (85-up)																		
Borderline (70-84)																		
Mild (55-69)																		
Moderate (40-54)																		
Severe (25-39)																		
Profound (Less than 25)																		

Check all Diagnostic &
Evaluation Capabilities: _____ Medical _____ Work/Skill _____ Education _____ Other (Specify) _____

_____ Social _____ Psychological _____ Speech & Hearing _____

Describe D & E Process: _____

_____

Please anticipate any changes in your program over the next two (2) years and describe _____

_____

Other information important for our understanding of your operation: _____

_____

_____

_____ Print name of executive

_____ Print name of person filling out form

_____ Title _____ Date

BIBLIOGRAPHY

Adams, Margaret
    1971 "The social evaluation and its significance for mental retardation." Pp. 114–50 in Margaret Adams (ed.), Mental Retardation and Its Social Dimensions. New York: Columbia University Press.

Adelman, Bob
    1972 Down Home. New York: McGraw-Hill.

Adler, Emil
    1961 "Familial cerebral palsy." Cerebral Palsy Review 22 (February): 4–6.

Alabama Department of Mental Health
    1973 1973 State DDSA Plan. Montgomery, Alabama.
    1974 1974 State DDSA Plan. Montgomery, Alabama.
    1975 1975 State DDSA Plan. Montgomery, Alabama.

Alsikafi, Majeed, and Bobby Palk
    1974 "Survey of facilities serving the developmentally disabled in Alabama." Pp. 6–29 in J. Selwyn Hollingsworth (ed.), Report of Phase II of "Survey of the Developmentally Disabled in Alabama: Needs and Resources." Montgomery: Alabama Department of Mental Health.

Alter, Milton, and W. Allen Hauser (eds.)
    1972 The Epidemiology of Epilepsy: A Workshop. Washington, D.C.: U.S. Department of Health, Education, and Welfare, Public Health Service, National Institutes of Health, National Institute of Neurological Diseases and Stroke Monograph No. 14.

Altman, Isidore
    1955 "On the prevalence of cerebral palsy." Cerebral Palsy Review 16:4, 25.

Anderson, C. L.
    1936 "Epilepsy in the State of Michigan." Mental Hygiene 20:441–62.

Bailey, P., F. E. Williams, P. O. Komora, T. W. Salmon, and N. Fenton
    1929 The medical department of the United States Army in World War I, Volume 10 (Neuropsychiatry). Washington, D.C.: U.S. Government Printing Office.

Baldwin, R., E. Davens, and V. G. Harris
    1953 "Epilepsy in public health." American Journal of Public Health 43: 452–59.

Belknap, G., and R. Smuckler
    1956 "Political power relations in a mid-west city." Public Opinion Quarterly 20 (Spring):73–81.

Bird, A. V., H. J. Heinz, and G. Klintworth
    1962 "Convulsive disorders in Bantu mineworkers." Epilepsia 3:175–87.

Blankship, L. V.
    1964 "Community power and decision making: a comparative evaluation of measurement techniques." Social Forces 43 (December):207–16.

Bowley, Agatha A., and Leslie Gardner
    1969 The Young Handicapped Child: Educational Guidance for the Young

Cerebral Palsied, Blind, and Autistic Child. London, England: E. S. Livingstone, Ltd.

Bremer, J.
1951 "A social psychiatric investigation of a small community of Northern Norway." Acta Psychiatrica et Neurologie, Supplement 62.

Brewer, Willis
1964 Alabama: Her History, Resources, War Record, and Public Men. Tuscaloosa, Ala.: Willo Publishing Co.

Brewis, M., D. C. Poskanzer, C. Rolland, and H. Miller
1966 "Neurological disease in an English city." Acta Neurologica Scandinavia 42 (Supplement 24):1–89.

Buckley, Richard E., and William E. Lee, Jr.
1974 "Deinstitutionalization of the developmentally disabled in Alabama." Report submitted to the Alabama Department of Mental Health.

Burks, B. S.
1928 "The relative influence of nature and nurture upon mental development: a comparative study of parent-foster child resemblance and true parent-true child resemblance." Yearbook of the National Study for the Study of Education: 219–316.

Burt, B.
1955 "The evidence for the concept of intelligence." British Journal of Educational Psychology (November):6.

Burt, Cyril
1958 "The inheritance of mental ability." American Psychologist (January): 172–73.

Caveness, W. F., H. Houston Merritt, and G. H. Gallup
1969 "A survey of public attitudes toward epilepsy in 1969 with an indication of trends over the past twenty years." Epilepsia 10:429–40.

Charlton, M. H., and M. D. Yahr
1967 "Long-term follow-up of patients with petit mal." Archives of Neurology 16:595–98.

Chen, K. J., A. Brody, and L. T. Kurland
1968 "Patterns of neurologic diseases on Guam—I: epidemiologic aspects." Archivos Neurologicos 19:573–78.

Churchill, John A.
1970 "On the etiology of cerebral palsy in premature infants." American Academy of Neurology 20:405.

Conley, Ronald
1973 The Economics of Mental Retardation. Baltimore, Md.: Johns Hopkins Press.

Connecticut State Department of Health
1951 The Study of Cerebral Palsy in Connecticut. Hartford, Connecticut.

Cooper, J. E.
1965 "Epilepsy in a longitudinal survey of 5,000 children." British Medical Journal:1020–22.

Crombie, D. L., et al.
1960 "A survey of the epilepsies in general practice: a report by the Research

Committee of the College of General Practitioners." British Medical Journal:416–22.

Cruickshank, William, and George M. Raus (eds.)
1955 Cerebral Palsy: Its Individual and Community Problems (rev. ed.). New York: Syracuse University Press.

Dada, T. O., B. O. Osuntokun, and E. L. Odeku
1969 "Epidemiological aspects of epilepsy in Nigeria: a study of 639 patients." Diseases of the Nervous System 30:807–13.

Dahle, R. A.
1958 "A critique of the ruling elite model." American Political Science Review 52 (June):463–69.

D'Antonio, W., and E. C. Erickson
1962 "The reputational techniques as a measure of community power: an evaluation based on comparative and longitudinal studies." American Sociological Review 26 (June):362–76.

Dingman, H. F., and C. Tarjan
1960 "Mental retardation and the normal distribution curve." American Journal of Mental Deficiency 64:991–94.

Dumas, M., and R. Virieu
1968 "Neurologie au Senegal." Association Medica Lengua Française 4: 112–17.

Edwards, T. I., K. H. McGill, and L. G. Rowntree
1942 Local Board Examinations of Selective Service Registrants in Peacetime. Washington, D.C.: U.S. Government Printing Office.

Epilepsy Foundation of America
n.d. Data Pak: Facts about Epilepsy and the Many Groups Concerned with its Medical and Social Management. Washington, D.C.
1969 Epilepsy: Recognition, Causes, Diagnosis, Treatment: Current Information. New York.
1972a Epilepsy. New York.
1972b Epilepsy: Recognition, Onset, Diagnosis, Therapy. Washington, D.C.

Fein, Rashi
1966 An Economic and Social Profile of the Negro American. Washington, D.C.: Brookings Institution.

Form, W. H., and D. C. Miller
1960 Industry, Labor and Community. New York: Harper & Row, Publishers.

Foskett, J., and R. Hohle
1957 "The measurement of influence in community affairs." Proceedings of the Pacific Sociological Society, Research Studies of the State College of Washington (June):148–54.

Fowle, C.
1968 "Effect of the severely retarded child on his family." American Journal of Mental Deficiency 73:468–73.

Fox, D. M.
1969 "The identification of community leaders by the reputational and decisional methods: three case studies and an empirical analysis of the literature." Sociology and Social Research 54 (October):94–103.

Freeman, L.
  1963 "Locating leaders in local communities: a comparison of some alter-
        native approaches." American Sociological Review 28 (October):791–
        98.
Gamson, W. A.
  1966 "Reputation and resources in community politics." American Journal
        of Sociology 72 (September):121–31.
Geist, Harold
  1962 The Etiology of Idiopathic Epilepsy. New York: Exposition Press.
Goodman, Melvin B., Ernest M. Gruenberg, Joseph J. Downing, and Eugene
        Rogot
  1956 "A prevalence study of mental retardation in a metropolitan area."
        American Journal of Public Health 46:702–07.
Griffith, Lucille
  1968 Alabama: A Documentary History to 1900. University, Ala.: The Uni-
        versity of Alabama Press.
Gruenberg, Ernest
  1955 A Special Census of Suspected Referred Mental Retardation in Onon-
        daga County. Technical Report of the Mental Health Research Unit.
        New York: State Department of Mental Hygiene.
Gudmondsson, Gunnar
  1966 "Epilepsy in Iceland: a clinical and epidemiological investigation." Acta
        Neurologica Scandinavia 43 (Supplement 25):1–124.
Hauser, W. Allen
  1972a "Preface." P. vii in Milton Alter and W. Allen Hauser (eds.), The Epi-
        demiology of Epilepsy: A Workshop. Washington, D.C.: U.S. Depart-
        ment of Health, Education, and Welfare, Public Health Service, Na-
        tional Institutes of Health, National Institute of Neurological Diseases
        and Stroke Monograph No. 14.
  1972b "Sex and socioeconomic status." Pp. 89–93 in Milton Alter and W. Allen
        Hauser (eds.), The Epidemiology of Epilepsy: A Workshop. Washing-
        ton, D.C.: U.S. Department of Health, Education, and Welfare, Public
        Health Service, National Institutes of Health, National Institute of
        Neurological Diseases and Stroke Monograph No. 14.
Hauser, W. Allen, and Leonard T. Kurland
  1972 "Incidence, prevalence, time trends of convulsive disorders in Roches-
        ter, Minnesota: a community survey." Pp. 41–43 in Milton Alter and
        W. Allen Hauser (eds.), The Epidemiology of Epilepsy: A Workshop.
        Washington, D.C.: U.S. Department of Health, Education, and Wel-
        fare, Public Health Service, National Institutes of Health, National
        Institute of Neurological Diseases and Stroke Monograph No. 14.
Heber, Richard
  1954 "A manual on terminology and classification in mental retardation."
        American Journal of Mental Deficiency.
  1961 "A manual on terminology and classification in mental retardation."
        American Journal of Mental Deficiency 64. Monograph Supplement.
  1970 Epidemiology of Mental Retardation. Springfield, Ill.: Charles C
        Thomas.

Henrikson, G. F., and W. H. Krohn
  1969   "The organization of a national system for the medical care of epilep-
          tics." Excerpta Medica, International Congress Series No. 193.
Hollingshead, A. B.
  1949   Elmtown's Youth. New York: Wiley.
Hollingsworth, J. Selwyn (ed.)
  1973   Report of Phase I of "Survey of the Developmentally Disabled in Ala-
          bama: Needs and Resources." Montgomery: Alabama Department of
          Mental Health.
  1974   Report of Phase II of "Survey of the Developmentally Disabled in Ala-
          bama: Needs and Resources." Montgomery: Alabama Department of
          Mental Health.
Holton, Wilfred E., Bernard M. Kramer, and Peter Kong-ming New
  1973   "Locational process: guidelines for locating mental health services."
          Community Mental Health Journal 9:270–79.
Hunter, F.
  1953   Community Power Structure: A Study of Decision Makers. Chapel Hill:
          University of North Carolina Press.
Hunter, F., R. C. Schaffer, and C. G. Sheps
  1956   Community Organization: Action and Inaction. Chapel Hill: Univer-
          sity of North Carolina Press.
Ingram, T. T. S.
  1964   Pediatric Aspects of Cerebral Palsy. Baltimore, Md.: Williams and
          Wilkins.
Jano, Richard
  1970   "Social class and parental evaluation of educable retarded children."
          Education and Training of the Mentally Retarded 5:62–67.
Jastak, J., H. McPhee, and M. Whiteman
  1963   Mental Retardation: Its Nature and Incidence. Newark, Del.: Univer-
          sity of Delaware Press.
Jensen, A. R.
  1969   "How much can we boost IQ and scholastic achievement?" Harvard
          Educational Review 39 (Winter):1–123.
Kaufman, H., and V. Jones
  1954   "The mystery of power." Public Administration Review 14 (March):
          205–12.
Keats, Sidney
  1965   Cerebral Palsy. Springfield, Ill.: Charles C Thomas.
Kennedy, W. A., et al.
  1963   A Normative Sample of Intelligence and Achievement of Negro Ele-
          mentary School Children: The Southeastern United States. Yellow
          Springs, Ohio: Antioch Press.
Klapper, Zeus
  1970   "Developmental psychology." Pp. 1–113 in Joseph Wortis (ed.), Mental
          Retardation: An Annual Review—Volume I. New York: Grune and
          Stratton.
Klapper, Z. S., and H. G. Birch
  1966   "Relation of childhood characteristics to outcome in young adults with

cerebral palsy." Developmental Medicine and Child Neurology 8: 645–56.

Kott, Maurice G.
   1968   "Estimating the number of retarded in New Jersey." Mental Retardation: 28–31.

Krohn, W.
   1961   "A study of epilepsy in northern Norway, its frequency and character." Acta Psychiatrica Scandinavia 36 (Supplement 150):215–25.

Kulkarni, Kamala D.
   1973   Directory of Alabama Resources for the Mentally Retarded. Tuscaloosa, Ala.: The University of Alabama, Mental Retardation Service Program.

Kurland, Leonard T.
   1959   "The incidence and prevalence of convulsive disorders in a small urban community." Epilepsia 1:143–61.
   1973   Tables on prevalence of epilepsy—Rochester, Minnesota, 1953–1967. Preliminary tables. Private correspondence.

Kurtzke, John F.
   1972   "Mortality and morbidity data on epilepsy." Pp. 21–36 in Milton Alter and W. Allen Hauser (eds.), The Epidemiology of Epilepsy: A Workshop. Washington, D.C.: U.S. Department of Health, Education, and Welfare, Public Health Service, National Institutes of Health, National Institute of Neurological Diseases and Stroke Monograph No. 14.

Kurtzke, John F., et al.
   1971   Convulsive disorders, unpublished manuscript by L. T. Kurland, John F. Kurtzke, and I. D. Goldberg, Epidemiology of Neurologic and Sense Organ Diseases (American Public Health Association Monograph), to be published by Cambridge: Harvard University Press.

Lapous, Renia, and Martin Weitzner
   1970   "Epidemiology." Pp. 197–221 in Joseph Wortis (ed.), Mental Retardation: An Annual Review—Volume I. New York: Grune and Stratton.

Leahy, A. M.
   1935   "Nature-nurture and intelligence." Genetic Psychology Monograph (June):241–305.

Leibowitz, U., and M. Alter
   1968   "A survey of epilepsy in Jerusalem, Israel." Epilepsia 9:87–105.

Lemkau, P., C. Tietze, and M. Cooper
   1942   "Mental-hygiene problems in an urban district." Mental Hygiene 26: 624–46.
   1943   "A survey of statistical studies on the prevalence and incidence of mental disorder in a sample population." Public Health Report 58:1909–27.

Lennox, W. G.
   1960   Epilepsy and Related Disorders. Boston: Little, Brown & Co.

Lessell, S., J. M. Torres, and L. T. Kurland
   1962   "Seizure disorders in a Guamanian village." Archivos Neurologicos 7: 53–60.

Lesser, A. J., and E. P. Hunt
   1954   "The Nation's handicapped children." American Journal of Public Health 44:166–70.

Levinson, E. J.
  1962 Retarded children in Maine: a survey and analysis. University of Maine Studies, Second Series, No. 77. Orono, Maine: University of Maine Press.
Levy, L. F., J. I. Forbes, and T. S. Parirenyatwa
  1964 "Epilepsy in Africans." Central African Journal of Medicine 10:241–49.
Lineback, Neal G., and Charles T. Traylor
  1973 Atlas of Alabama. University, Ala.: The University of Alabama Press.
Lione, J. G.
  1961 "Convulsive disorders in a working population." Journal of Occupational Medicine 3:369–73.
Logan, W. P. D., and A. A. Cushion
  1958 Studies on Medical and Population Subjects, No. 14. Morbidity Statistics from General Practice, Volume 1: General. London: Her Majesty's Stationery Office.
McCulloch, T. L.
  1949 "Reformulation of the problem of mental deficiency." American Journal of Mental Deficiency (October):130–36.
Malamud, N.
  1964 "Neuropathology." Pp. 431–49 in H. A. Stevens and R. Heber (eds.), Mental Retardation: A Review of Research. Chicago: University of Chicago Press.
Malzberg, B.
  1932 "The prevalence of epilepsy in the United States with special reference to children and adolescents." Psychiatric Quarterly 6:97–106.
Mental Retardation Services Board of Los Angeles County
  1969 "Estimated number of retarded in Los Angeles County, 1969." Mimeographed.
Mercer, Jane R.
  1973 Labeling the Mentally Retarded: Clinical and Social System Perspectives on Mental Retardation. Berkeley: University of California Press.
Merlis, Jerome K.
  1972 "Epilepsy in different age groups." Pp. 83–86 in Milton Alter and W. Allen Hauser (eds.), The Epidemiology of Epilepsy: A Workshop. Washington, D.C.: U.S. Department of Health, Education, and Welfare, Public Health Service, National Institutes of Health, National Institute of Neurological Diseases and Stroke Monograph No. 14.
Meyers, C. E., E. G. Stitkei, and E. H. Watts
  1966 "Attitudes toward special education and the handicapped in two community groups." American Journal of Mental Deficiency 71:78–84.
Miller, D. C.
  1958 "Industry and community power structures: a comparative study of an American and an English city." American Sociological Review 23 (February):9–15.
Mitchell, Ross G.
  1962 "Mixed types of cerebral palsy." Cerebral Palsy Review 23:3–6, 13–15.
Mullen, F. A., and M. M. Nee
  1949 "Distribution of mental retardation in an urban school population." American Journal of Mental Deficiency 56:291–308.

Mumbauer, Corinne C., and J. O. Miller
  1970 "Socioeconomic background and cognitive functioning in pre-school children." Child Development 41:471–79.
National Health Education Committee, Inc.
  1971a What Are the Facts about Cerebral Palsy? New York.
  1971b What Are the Facts about Epilepsy? New York.
Neilsen, Helle H.
  1971 "Psychological appraisal of children with cerebral palsy: a survey of 128 re-assessed cases." Developmental Medicine and Child Neurology 13 (December):707–20.
New York State Department of Mental Hygiene
  1965 A Special Census of Suspected Referred Mental Retardation, Onondaga County, New York. Syracuse, N.Y.: University Press.
New York State Joint Legislative Committee to Study the Problem of Cerebral Palsy
  1940 A Survey of Cerebral Palsy in Schenectady County, New York. Legislative Document No. 55. Albany, New York.
Olivares, Ladislao
  1964 "El paciente neurológico de consulta externa, estudio comparativo entre el Centro Hospitalaria '20 de noviembre' y el Hospital General." Revista Médica del Instituto de Seguros y Servicios Sociales de los Trabajadores del Estado 1:311–15.
  1972 "Epilepsy in Mexico: a population study." Pp. 53–56 in Milton Alter and W. Allen Hauser (eds.), The Epidemiology of Epilepsy: A Workshop. Washington, D.C.: U.S. Department of Health, Education, and Welfare, Public Health Service, National Institutes of Health, National Institute of Neurological Diseases and Stroke Monograph No. 14.
Oppenheimer, Sonya, et al.
  1965 "Prevalence of mental retardation in a pediatric outpatient clinic population." Pediatrics 36.
Osuntokun, B. O., and E. L. Odeku
  1970 "Epilepsy in Nigerians: study of 522 patients." Tropical Geography Medicine 22:3–19.
Owsley, Frank L.
  1949 Plain Folk of the Old South. Baton Rouge, La.: Louisiana State University Press.
Phelps, W. M.
  1948 "Characteristic psychological variations in cerebral palsy." Nervous Children 7:10.
Pond, D. A., and B. H. Bidwell
  1960 "A survey of epilepsy in fourteen general practices—II: social and psychological aspects." Epilepsia:285–99.
Pond, D. A., B. H. Bidwell, and L. Stein
  1960 "A survey of epilepsy in fourteen general practices—I: demographic and medical data." Psychiatria, Neurologia, Neurochirurgia 63:217–26.
Polsby, N. W.
  1959a "The sociology of community power: a reassessment." Social Forces 37 (March):232–36.

1959b "Three problems in the analysis of community power." American Sociological Review 24 (December):796–803.

Poskanzer, David C.
1972 "House-to-house survey of a community for epilepsy." Pp. 45–46 in Milton Alter and W. Allen Hauser (eds.), The Epidemiology of Epilepsy: A Workshop. Washington, D.C.: U.S. Department of Health, Education, and Welfare, Public Health Service, National Institutes of Health, National Institute of Neurological Diseases and Stroke Monograph No. 14.

Preston, J. D.
1969 "A comparative methodology for identifying community leaders." Rural Sociology 34 (December):556–62.

Pryse-Phillips
1969 Epilepsy. Baltimore, Md.: Williams and Wilkins.

Rachman, I.
1970 "Epilepsy in African hospital practice." Central African Journal of Medicine 16:201–04.

Reed, Dwayne
1972 "The epidemiological approach." Pp. 3–11 in Milton Alter and W. Allen Hauser (eds.), The Epidemiology of Epilepsy: A Workshop. Washington, D.C.: U.S. Department of Health, Education, and Welfare, Public Health Service, National Institutes of Health, National Institute of Neurological Diseases and Stroke Monograph No. 14.

Reed, E. W., and C. Reed
1965 Mental Retardation: A Family Study. Philadelphia: Saunders Co.

Renzaglia, G. A., and A. J. Shafter
1969 "Satellite programs for the retarded in rural areas." In R. C. Scheerenberger (ed.), Mental Retardation. Springfield: Illinois Department of Mental Health.

Ricci, Carol
1970 "Analysis of child-rearing attitudes of mothers of retarded, emotionally disturbed, and normal children." American Journal of Mental Deficiency 74:756–61.

Richardson, W. P., A. C. Higgins, and R. G. Ames
1965 The Handicapped Children of Alamance County, North Carolina: A Medical and Sociological Study. Wilmington, Del.: Nemours Foundation.

Robb, J. Preston
1972 "A review of epidemiological concepts of epilepsy." Pp. 13–18 in Milton Alter and W. Allen Hauser (eds.), The Epidemiology of Epilepsy: A Workshop. Washington, D.C.: U.S. Department of Health, Education, and Welfare, Public Health Service, National Institutes of Health, National Institute of Neurological Diseases and Stroke Monograph No. 14.

Rose, S. W., J. K. Penry, R. E. Markush, L. A. Radloff, and P. L. Putnam
1973 "Epilepsy in children." Epilepsia 13:1–19.

Schlesinger, E. R., Helen C. Chase, and Clark Le Bouef
1954 "Evaluation of mandatory reporting of cerebral palsy." American Journal of Public Health 44:1124–31.

Schrag, Howard L.
   1973 "Program planning for the developmentally disabled: using survey re-
          sults." Mental Retardation (October):8–10.
Schulze, Robert O., and L. U. Blumberg
   1957 "The determination of local power elites." American Journal of Sociol-
          ogy 63 (November):290–96.
Self, Helen H.
   1970 The Relationship Between Parental Acceptance and Adjustment of
          Mentally Retarded Children. Unpublished Ph.D. Dissertation, The
          University of Alabama.
Shadak, M., and H. M. Skeels
   1949 "A final follow-up study of one hundred adopted children." Journal of
          Genetic Psychology:91–114.
Shere, Eugenia, and Robert Kastenbaum
   1966 "Mother-child interactions in cerebral palsy: environmental and psy-
          chosocial obstacles to cognitive development." Genetic Psychology
          Monographs 73:255–335.
Shuey, M.
   1966 The Testing of Negro Intelligence. New York: Social Science Press.
Skeels, H. M.
   1966 Adult Status of Children with Contrasting Early Life Experiences. Chi-
          cago Society for Research in Child Development.
Sollie, C. R.
   1966 "A comparison of reputational techniques for identifying community
          leaders." Rural Sociology 31 (September):301–09.
Speer, G. S.
   1940 "The intelligence of foster children." Journal of Genetic Psychology:
          49–55.
Tarjan, G., S. W. Wright, R. K. Eyman, and C. V. Keeran
   1973 "Natural history of mental retardation: some aspects of epidemiology."
          American Journal of Mental Deficiency 77:369–79.
Taylor, J. L., et al.
   1965 Mental Retardation Prevalence in Oregon. Portland, Oreg.: State
          Board of Health.
Tizard, Jack
   1968 "Social psychiatry and mental subnormality." Pp. 50–64 in Micheal
          Shepherd and D. L. Davis (eds.), Studies in Psychiatry. London, Eng-
          land: Oxford University Press.
Ueki, K., and S. Sato
   1963 "An epidemiologic study of epilepsy in infancy and childhood in
          Niigata city." Psychiat. Neurol. Paed. Jap. 3:3–13.
United Cerebral Palsy Foundation
   1973a Fact Sheet. New York.
   1973b Rule of thumb prevalence rates. Private correspondence.
United States Bureau of the Census
   1971 Census of Population: 1970. Number of Inhabitants, Final Report
          PC(1)-A2: Alabama. Washington, D.C.: U.S. Government Printing
          Office.

1972a Census of Population: 1970. General Population Characteristics. Final Report PC(1)-B2: Alabama. Washington, D.C.: U.S. Government Printing Office.

1972b Census of Population: 1970. General Social and Economic Characteristics. Final Report PC(1)-C2: Alabama. Washington, D.C.: U.S. Government Printing Office.

United States Department of Health, Education, and Welfare
1965 Epilepsy: A Review of Basic and Clinical Research. National Institute of Health Publication 73-415, Washington, D.C.

1968 Health Interview Survey. Washington, D.C.: National Center for Health Statistics.

1971 Cerebral Palsy: Hope through Research. Washington, D.C.: Public Health Service, National Institutes of Health. DHEW Publication No. (NIH) 72-159.

1972 Epilepsy: Hope through Research (rev.). Washington, D.C.: Public Health Service, National Institute of Neurological Diseases and Stroke. DHEW Publication No. (NIH) 73-156.

1974 Vital Statistics of the United States—Mortality. Part A, Vol. II. Washington, D.C.: U.S. Government Printing Office.

University of Alabama, Center for Business and Economic Research
1973 Alabama Business. University, Ala.: Center for Business and Economic Research.

Wajsbort, J., N. Aral, and I. Alfandary
1967 "A study of the epidemiology of chronic epilepsy in Northern Israel." Epilepsia 8:105–16.

Warner, W. L.
1959 The Living and the Dead. New Haven: Yale University Press.

Warner, W. L., and J. O. Low
1947 The Social System of the Modern Factory. New Haven: Yale University Press.

Warner, W. L., and P. S. Lunt
1941 The Social Life of Modern Community. New Haven: Yale University Press.

1942 The Status System of Modern Community. New Haven: Yale University Press.

Warner, W. L., M. Meeker, and K. Eells
1960 Social Class in America. New York: Harper & Row, Publishers.

Warner, W. L., and L. Srole
1945 The Social Systems of American Ethnic Groups. New Haven: Yale University Press.

Weinberg, Warren
1972 "Epilepsy: a study of a school population." Pp. 57–58 in Milton Alter and W. Allen Hauser (eds.), The Epidemiology of Epilepsy: A Workshop. Washington, D.C.: U.S. Department of Health, Education, and Welfare, Public Health Service, National Institutes of Health, National Institute of Neurological Diseases and Stroke Monograph No. 14.

Welfare Council of Metropolitan Chicago and the Chicago Association of Commerce and Industry

1953   Problem of Cerebral Palsy in Chicago. Chicago, Illinois.

Wilson, Warner

1970   "Social psychology and mental retardation." Pp. 229–62 in Norman R. Ellis (ed.), International Review of Research in Mental Retardation: Volume 4. New York: Academic Press.

Wishik, Samuel M.

n.d.   Georgia Study of Handicapped Children: A Report on a Study of Prevalence, Disability, Needs, Resources, and Contributing Factors—Implications for Program Administration and Community Organization.

1956   "Handicapped children in Georgia: a study of prevalence, disability, needs and resources." American Journal of Public Health 46:195–203.

Wolfe, W. G., and L. Leon Reid

1958   A Survey of Cerebral Palsy in Texas. Austin: United Cerebral Palsy of Texas.

Wolfinger, R. W.

1960   "Reputation and reality in the study of community power." American Sociological Review 24 (October):636–44.

WPA Writers Program

1941   Alabama, A Guide to the Deep South. New York: R. R. Smith.

Zielinski, J. J.

1972   "Social prognosis in epilepsy." Epilepsia 13:133–40.

Zigler, Edward F., and Susan Harter

1969   "The socialization of the mentally retarded." Pp. 1065–1102 in David A. Goslin (ed.), Handbook of Socialization Theory and Research. Chicago: Rand McNally.